BRIELLE

and ME

Our Journey with Cytomegalovirus
and Cerebral Palsy

Kerith Stull

Brielle and Me

ISBN 978-0-9912122-0-0

Library of Congres Control Number: 2014930719

Cover photo by Pat Meazell from Preferred Photo

Published by:
Fugue Publishing
Woodstock, GA USA

Dedication

To the precious life God gave me.

Acknowledgements

It takes a village to raise a child. Writing a book is much the same process. I have not been alone in this journey. Many people helped, contributed, and supported me along the way.

First and foremost, I praise and thank God for the life He gave me and for the precious lives that He entrusted to me. I thank Him for preparing me in countless ways and without my conscious knowledge at most times. It is with much gratitude that I received His gifts and pray that I use them to the best of my ability. May this work from my hands, mind, heart, and soul be pleasing to Him.

I thank Brielle whose sweet, simple life is as it is. Although she understands little of what I have written here, this work revolves around her. In her own way, she has made me a better mother, friend, wife, daughter, and member of my community. This child changed me. I wonder sometimes if God created me for her or if He created her for me.

I am grateful to my family, especially for their patience with me during this process. They never complained about the many hours I stole from them to spend writing, researching, or with my writers group.

Special thanks to my best friend and husband, Brian, for going on the entire journey with me. Although this book represents my journey with Brielle, it is truly a reflection of our journey together. Like a simple machine with all the parts moving together for a single purpose, we are as one.

Thank you to my firstborn daughter, Ashley, for her cheerleading and support. I appreciate her honest opinions and suggestions that helped shape the tone of this book. I especially thank her for her straight-forward answers in the chapter dedicated to her voice.

I want to thank my best girlfriend, Manthia Zaccaria, whom I also call Mom. She helped me so many times and in so many ways, I could not possibly list them here. Just… thanks.

Thank you to my best teacher ever. I am proudly able to call him, Dad. Joseph Zaccaria may not realize it, but with everything that he did and still does, his daughter watched him and learned. I am so proud of what he has accomplished in his life, especially since his stroke twenty years ago.

I would like to thank my parents especially for their love and skills raising the daughter that I was. I cannot imagine going through the most difficult times with Brielle without their love and support. Moreover, their constant cheerleading and positive attitude about Brielle's accomplishments kept me going, especially during my darkest days. Thank you for reviewing some of my final drafts. Their input all along the way was invaluable.

Thank you to the best in-laws, Jerry and Connie Stull, I could have ever hoped to have. Although I cannot call them Mom and Dad, they treat me with the love and acceptance of parents. God bless you, Connie. I miss our Wednesday chats, but feel you near me so often.

Thank you to our extended family members, my brother, Jason Zaccaria, and Brian's sister, Tracy Stull. I would also like to remember our grandparents, especially Brian's grandmother, Ruth Stull, for their loving support and worry while they were with us in this life.

Thank you to Anthony Elmore, Karen McGoldrick, and Christina Ranallo who were members of my first writers group, theWriteClub. Special thanks to Christina who encouraged me to put aside my horrible first version of our story cloaked in a poorly written novel. Without her suggestion to start over and write our story as a memoir, I never would have found the courage to dig deep into those hard places, be truly honest and open, and find my authentic voice.

Thank you to Mary Helen Witten and Sue Horner who were members of the Write Club and continued on the journey with me when we formed a new writers group. I am enormously grateful for their dedication to bring out the best writer in me through compassionate suggestions, constructive criticism, and occasionally a cattle prod when necessary. Thank you also to Jason van Gumster, a late arriving member of our new writers group, who brought a fresh pair of eyes and sharp mind to my project when I began re-writes.

Thank you to Pastor Phil Rikard for answering my random texts and emails asking for Bible passages that reflected particular chapter themes. Special thanks for his guidance on my chapter about faith. His expertise was incredibly valuable. However, it is his care and support for me and especially his love and compassion for Brielle that I am constantly grateful for. He is a great teacher – practical and direct – just what I need. His church was the eleventh we visited. Because of him, I knew within moments that Tapestry Community Church would become our home. It is a church home like no other I have ever known.

My test readers were particularly helpful reviewing one of the final drafts of this book. Thank you to Ann Marie Walker, Dani and Greg Pierce, Jan Songer, Kelli Joy, Sarah Kostusiak, and Tracy Wilson for their donation of time, energy, and perspective on this project.

I especially thank the best therapists Brielle had – Martha Cowan, Rhonda Thomas, and Pam Davis – who were teachers first, therapists second, and always supportive friends. Special gratitude to Martha who gave me my earliest and best lessons. Her friendship over the years means the world to me.

Thank you to special friends that truly touched my life in a way that was simple, supportive, and unwavering in openness to my child. Special thanks to Angie Weber, the most casual and accepting of all friends, and Lee Delancey, who keeps me sane by never letting me take life too seriously. Thank you to Bobbi Dykstra for being such an enduring gift in my life. Her friendship and laughter has been truly special and a blessing to me. We are simply kindred spirits.

Thank you to my best cheerleaders – Sarah Kostusiak, Kelli Joy, Pam Evans, and Jan Songer. I appreciate their support and enthusiasm for my project as well as their patience while it took so much time to complete.

Thank you to the members of CMV Mommies on Facebook. Their friendship, although very rarely face-to-face, encourages me and brightens my day. I cannot express what peace and comfort it gives me to finally know that we are not alone.

I thank the many people described on these pages who had an influence on our story and our lives. Even in the less positive situations, they all helped shape our lives and helped bring us to where we are today.

Finally, I am indebted to the many trailblazers who paved the way to create today's world. Without the journeys of the generations of parents of special needs children who went before us, we would not have had the same journey written here. I am grateful for their vision, hard work, and sacrifices that shaped laws and attitudes to form the culture we now raise our daughter in.

Contents

Introduction

I am an ordinary person, someone you might pass in a busy grocery store or overlook in a crowded movie theater. Everyone has a story and bears the scars from life's journey. Let me tell you about the story of my scars and the beauty I found along the way.

There are lessons to learn in this life and I have learned my share. Some of them are things I thought I would never need to know. Life throws everyone a few unexpected curves and we must continue down the path in front of us.

I own this story. It is uniquely mine. I started to write and stepped back in time to when I walked the path alone, before my path joined with my husband's and we helped guide our daughters as they took their first steps on their own journey. I remind myself that I am still on a continuation of that same journey I started before our paths merged.

This is Me

Expectations were high when I was young. I worked hard to fill my life's potential. Looking back, I had simple, self-centered goals that I was just starting to achieve. I had a nice home, a career in marketing, my husband Brian, and our daughter Ashley. Then I became pregnant with our second child Brielle.

With her birth, motherhood and life itself began to unfold differently than I anticipated. Although I did not see it as transformational as it was happening, I grew exponentially and became much more than I ever envisioned for myself. For that, I am grateful.

I do not remember what normal felt like, what life was like before Brielle. Frankly, I do not think normal ever existed. There was simply different.

I know different because our life with Brielle is different. It's not OK, but that's OK. I have learned to want what I have. Without Brielle, where would I be? As difficult as that other life is to remember, I am glad my life now is so connected to Brielle's.

My days are largely devoted to serving Brielle's needs, motivated by the urgency of a future when I will not be with her. I did not choose this life, but being the mother of a special needs child still became part of my identity.

It is difficult to describe myself without basing the description on a relationship with another person. I am a daughter to my parents, sister to my brother, wife to my husband, mother to two daughters, and friend to many people. More than anything, I define myself as the mother of Brielle. Without her, I do not have a compelling story to share.

Excavating the Past

This memoir is not realistic fiction, something that could be true but is not. This is my truth, but not *the* truth. No writer can capture all of the truth. Our story is simply a reflection of my field notes while on my journey through life. Each chapter describes experiences and observations this researcher made while participating in the natural setting of her life.

A major disadvantage of field notes is that an observer, an imperfect recording device, chronicles them. Both objective and subjective data are included and based on the memory, interpretation, and the possible bias of the observer. This is how the notes on my life got complicated.

People collect memories like t-shirts, postcards, or other souvenirs on a trip. Like many mementos, this collection of good times and bad eventually becomes the miscellaneous clutter in a junk drawer. The story of our lives is largely what we choose to remember and proudly put on display. Everything else gets lost in the shuffle of life.

As I wrote this memoir, I browsed through my own junk drawer of memories. I dug down deep, not knowing exactly what I might find. Like reaching into a Christmas stocking or tugging on a fishing line, I had a few surprises as I pulled the memories into view.

Time reveals the past in patterns. Certain moments seemed to be insignificant as they occurred, but in the end, had a substantial impact on our lives. Looking back, I realized that alongside the simple accounts of our days, there were issues of identity, loss, obsession, loneliness, and fear. Although I knew these issues were part of my baggage I hauled along the way, they came into clearer focus as I began to rifle through my memories.

Writing forced me to shine a light on my deepest emotions, the ones I never choose to put on public display. The process gave me transformational healing by allowing me to come to terms with the painful dust-bunnies of motherhood and life I thought I had long since swept under the rug of denial. Through a slow process of emotional purging, I learned to speak with conviction to the other mothers, fathers, teachers, therapists, and others who may read my words and be touched by them.

If I did not write our story on these pages, it would simply fade and become a quiet memory, fragmented among the lives we touched. Instead, I share with others so that they might benefit from our experiences.

My Imperfect Memories

Memory is a fickle thing. Details of our lives are not always organized and carefully put into storage for later recall. Some are lost immediately to the sands of time. We might only remember important events. A special birthday. A wedding. The birth of a child. Even then, there are holes in the data recorded. On the other hand, it is easier to recall the memories of feelings. The excitement of a special vacation. The nervousness of the first day on a job. The grief over the death of a loved one.

Most of our stories written here are based on memories whose accuracy are morphed by time and tainted by the perspective I now have. Thankfully, I had family and friends who were witnesses to our lives and able to fill in certain gaps. My husband, Brian, and I are proud parents who recorded our family history by videotaping often and taking many photographs. My nearly lifelong habit of keeping a diary was invaluable in jogging my memory. I also kept good records including medical reports, therapy notes, and stacks and stacks of school papers. All of these safeguarded relics contributed to my research and helped me pinpoint events, dates, and details when my memory failed.

Some of my research materials were painful to examine. However, reviewing the events of my life, especially those as a mother, was a cathartic process. It was also a valuable experience for my family as they shared their memories, thoughts, and feelings with me. The unifying narrative that emerged from the process brought us closer together.

Life has its emotional hills and valleys. I shed many tears over the last 18 years of our journey with Brielle. Some tears fell for Brielle while others, more selfishly, fell for me. It was difficult to let my authentic emotions seep onto these pages. I could not begin to articulate parts of our painful moments until I was no longer enduring them. As time passed and I brought our story to paper, my feelings became clear and my heart began to heal.

The W's Included Here

Let me be perfectly clear about what is not here. This is not a "how to" book. There are no step-by-step instructions on how to raise a special needs child, build a well-adjusted family, or heal emotionally.

However, between the lines, you may discover how I was able to unearth simple joys from dark shadows, celebrate tiny triumphs in huge shortcomings, and slow down to enjoy life's smallest moments. My goal is for you to reflect on the lessons I learned and find your own path in life. Every family is unique and must deal with life's hurdles in their own way.

I am a single voice, speaking only from my experiences. I certainly do not speak for all families with special needs children. They each have their own story. This is ours, specifically from my perspective.

Who, what, where, when, why, and how. They are all here.

One of my goals in writing this memoir, and in life in general, is to break down barriers, shift the perceptions of others, and create a community of understanding. In these pages, I placed a magnifying glass up to our world so you could examine it and see the big picture as well as the details of a family that may be different from yours. The stories here reveal first-hand accounts of family, school, friends, medical crises, and faith.

Motherhood, from my experience, is not humorous. There may be moments of joy and silliness. However, it is not naturally funny. Motherhood is my life, my job. My accounts here are not often lighthearted. However, even the darkest scenes of worry, frustration, and weariness are speckled with shades of hope, determination, and discovery.

Brielle is not the sum of the pages here. I could not possibly write enough words to truly capture her. My goal was simply to reveal her in the most complete way possible in this limiting medium.

The vignettes at the beginning of each chapter contain Brielle's voice. Those vignettes are her words, nearly verbatim. This is an opportunity for the reader to know her because I believe my daughter is worth knowing.

I tried to write in my authentic voice, one that most accurately reflects the events of our lives and our feelings at those times. Extracting my "then" voice revealed how I behaved, spoke, and felt when the events happened. The woman who lived this story did not have the same voice I have now. My "now" voice is more experienced and reflective because of the benefits of time and perspective.

Some of the stories here are actually several episodes consolidated to help the flow of the tale. In most circumstances, remembering each word spoken was impossible. Therefore, the dialog used reflects the tone of the conversations rather than the precise words. In an effort to maintain full disclosure, certain things will remain private and I chose not to reveal them here at all.

It was difficult to capture and incorporate Brian and Ashley's experiences, but I wove in their perspectives whenever possible. Near the end of this book, I included chapters interviewing them. Their words are theirs exactly. My goal was to give them a voice, an opportunity to directly share their thoughts, feelings, and experiences.

I struggled with the balance of maintaining our privacy and sharing our story. This is not entirely my story to tell. By sharing it here, I am "outing" other people, especially my family, forcing them to come out into public view. Some stories reveal less than flattering descriptions of others. Nonetheless, I wrote this memoir with a sense of respect and compassion.

Each chapter closes with a Biblical verse, God's voice from His book. They reflect the content of the chapter and some were particularly important to me over the years. Once I learned the value of opening its pages, the Bible was a reassuring drumbeat in my life.

The Never Ending Story

There are many books about families with special needs children. Some are a compilation of short essays from multiple writers. Other books tell the beginning of a child's story only because the child is still quite young and the story has not yet unfolded beyond those first years.

As I grew as a mother of a special needs child, these books were a source of great support, a reminder that we were not alone. However, I found myself wanting to know more about the future and fate of those young children. I wondered where the epic chronicles were and if others craved those narratives as well. This memoir has that unique perspective others do not, reflecting on the entire childhood of a special needs person.

With God's grace, Brielle's life has many other chapters left to be written. Although we have a long list of legitimate things to worry about for her future, we have many hopes. In the end, we have no way of knowing the content of those future chapters. One thing I know for sure, God created a wonderful person when he blessed us with Brielle and entrusted the composition of her story to us.

CHAPTER I

Welcome to Our Story

*My name is Brielle. I am 17 years old. I was
sick when I was inside my mom's tummy. The
doctors told my parents I might die. But, I
am OK. I am happy. My mom helps me.*

You may know another family with a special needs child or maybe
your family has a special needs child and you are part of the club.
My husband, Brian, our 19-year-old daughter, Ashley, and I became
members when Brielle was born in 1996. Brielle's disabilities changed
each of us and the path of our lives. I invite you to learn about our
family and our private world of disability.

Maintaining my strong, confident, positive façade is a well-
crafted smokescreen. My head pokes through a carnival cutout of
what I think others might want to see. The smile on my face might
imply happiness, but it merely means there is appreciation for what I
have and what I do not.

Fundamental characteristics describe our lives, mine and Brielle's
in particular. Before I share our story, it is important to understand

the basics so that there is a framework for everything else I am about to share.

Disability

Cytomegalovirus (CMV) affected Brielle when I was pregnant with her. It is a common virus, but can result in damaging effects to an unborn child when the virus is an active infection during pregnancy.

Unlike certain disabilities such as Down Syndrome, there is no typical case of children affected by CMV. However, Brielle's issues are fewer and more manageable than most children visibly affected by CMV.

She does not experience any complicated medical issues (despite having a seizure when she was 11 years old) and rarely gets sick.

MORE ABOUT...
Cytomegalovirus (CMV)[1]

- 50–80% of people are infected with CMV by the time they are 40 years old
- Symptoms include: fever, sore throat, fatigue, and swollen glands (although most healthy people do not experience any symptoms)
- Once infected, a person can be contagious for up to eight years
- The virus spreads through saliva, urine, or other bodily fluids and can be transmitted from a pregnant woman to her fetus during pregnancy
- About 1 in 150 children is born with the congenital CMV infection
- About 1 in 5 children born with the congenital CMV infection will develop permanent problems (such as hearing or vision loss, mental or developmental disabilities, seizures, and death, in rare cases)
- No drug is currently licensed to treat congenital CMV infection
- No vaccine is currently available

However, the CMV caused her moderate cerebral palsy (CP). It affected most of her body, which now exhibits the obvious physical hallmarks of a disability. The CP left her unable to speak. Instead, she communicates through sign language although she has no hearing loss.

Despite her limitations, Brielle manages and conquers life where so little of her body works correctly.

M O R E   A B O U T...
Brielle's Physical Disabilities

Right leg

- Foot permanently turned out like a ballerina's third position
- Walks with a flat-footed limp
- Difficulty going down steps

Right arm and hand

- Cannot lift her arm above her head
- Elbow usually bent at 90 degree angle or less
- Wrist bent down

- Poor fine motor skills (doing things with her fingers)

Mouth

- Cannot control her saliva
- Cannot chew hard foods
- Cannot close mouth when eating
- Cannot drink from a straw or open cup
- Cannot give a kiss
- Cannot speak any words (although she can make noises and uses sign language to communicate)

Knowing

Brielle only knows the body she inhabits. Brielle never asks, "What's wrong with me?" or "Why am I different?" Once in a while, I get a hint that maybe she is now starting to recognize that her body does not work like everyone else's. However, she does not seem to feel bad about it, at least not for long.

Occasionally, I must remind Brielle that she walks differently, cannot talk like other people, or cannot do something others are doing because of her physical limitations. Brielle cried when she turned 16 and I told her she would never learn to drive. I cry when my disabled daughter talks about becoming a mother one day.

Intelligence

People assume Brielle is not smart because she cannot speak. True, Brielle's I.Q. scores are well-below normal with her academic skills well-below those of other teenagers (generally on a fourth grade level). However, Brielle is more than a list of scores and percentiles. Brielle displays a great memory, particularly for directions, and uniquely connects new things to things she already knows.

Navigating technology is one of Brielle's strengths and allows her to be linked to the world other teenagers live in. She is especially adept at navigating the internet to find favorite websites and other activities on the computer. Technology also provides her with a voice through an iPod app when I am not able to interpret her sign language.

It is difficult to describe Brielle's social-emotional skills. At 17 years old, she is happy to cuddle with her doll at bedtime and watch preschool television shows. However, we limit her time with things that are not age appropriate and encourage more age appropriate interests.

In some ways, she is naturally like most teenagers. She likes make-up, fixing her hair, wearing nice clothes, listening to teen idol bands, and watching typical pre-teen television shows.

Beautiful Soul

Brielle sees life with a beautiful simplicity. A constant smile announces the joy pulsing through her heart. Brielle sees the best in other people, always showing kindness and sensitivity. On the other hand, most people see Brielle's problems first and overlook her strengths completely. If they took just one extra moment, they could see Brielle separate from her disabilities.

I believe God puts something extra special in disabled kids like Brielle. Through my eyes, the line between where heaven ends and her earthly form begins is blurred.

Exhaustion

Parenting, by its very nature, is exhausting. Parenting Brielle, in particular, is like having a perpetual early preschooler who needs constant care. Those demands require me to put all of my parenting skills to use just to get through a typical day. How many times have I bathed her, fed her, or wiped her bottom? Considering how many more times I will do those things for her is a more daunting thought.

Add in extra appointments to doctors, therapists, and other specialists, often several each week. Pile on extra stress from learning sign language and becoming knowledgeable in the language of medical jargon and therapeutic techniques. Top all of this with the rigors of homeschooling my child with learning issues without any help or teaching support from others.

The time and energy necessary for Brielle's basic care and development drains me emotionally and physically, leaving me overwhelmed with the inescapable weight of responsibility. I know that I should guard my own physical and mental health, but I cannot often give myself the attention I need. Some days, especially the days when she was little, it is enough just to get through my required duties.

Jealousy

Sometimes, jealousy poisons my thoughts when I see:
- families with healthy children who developed normally, participate in athletics, and experience all of the typical childhood milestones and events

- other special needs families with a child who appears "less disabled" than Brielle
- working mothers with flourishing careers
- single women with no children who live a carefree, spontaneous life

I envy these seemingly easier lives and feel cheated. I am not supposed to feel that way, but I do and it hurts.

Loneliness

There is an innate craving for contact with others, and yet I have few close friendships. Perhaps moving so often made it more difficult to form bonds. My job as mother and homeschool teacher to Brielle certainly creates a more solitary life, leaving me with few opportunities to connect with others. Our lives are so different from most families. I feel like no one around me really understands me and what it takes on a daily basis just to keep up. No matter how well-meaning people try to be, I still feel alone, like an outsider.

Self-doubts

I am not naturally brave and must work hard to muster up my inadequate confidence. I worry that I do not do enough for Brielle and make too many mistakes, falling short of my own expectations. If only I just tried harder, spent more time, and invested more financial resources. I feel guilty about the times I backed down or took the path of least resistance when advocating harder for Brielle could have improved her life.

When people stare at us, shame engulfs me as if I did something wrong. The seemingly heavy eyes of judgment from others stems from the way therapists and doctors judge every one of my parenting skills at each office visit based on my child's progress. Those negative feelings are difficult to escape.

Burdens on Her Big Sister

There are seasons of our lives when so much of our time, energy, and emotions focus on Brielle, sometimes pushing Ashley's needs to the side. Does Ashley feel more pressure to do well in school, activities, and life in general, because Brielle cannot excel at most things? Have we sometimes placed too much responsibility on Ashley? There is guilt that one day, when her father and I are gone, Ashley will be ultimately responsible for her adult sister's care.

Did having a disabled sister change who Ashley would have become, and perhaps not for the better? Ashley tells me not to worry and that she is just fine. Is she? Has she ever been?

Fears for the Future

Will Brielle have a job, friends, and activities she likes? Who will care for her when we are no longer able to do that? Can we save enough money to provide for our daughter's needs after we are gone?

In selfish moments, I worry about our future. Will Brielle always live with us? Will Brian and I ever experience something that resembles a normal retirement? No matter how we much prepare, the future seems like an unusually dark abyss.

Mourning

I mourn the child Brielle could have been, the person I could have been, the sisterly things Ashley could have experienced with a "normal" sister, and the life events Brielle will never have: a driver's license, a first date, prom, college graduation, a wedding, children, and so many other things. How can I go through the healing process of grief when the loss is so great? In an effort of self-preservation, I must work each day to stay ahead of self-pity and its debilitating effects.

> ### M O R E   A B O U T . . .
> # Preventing the Spread of CMV
>
> - wash your hands properly and frequently
> - do not share food, drinks, utensils, or toothbrushes
> - do not put an infant's pacifier in your mouth
> - avoid contact with saliva when kissing a child
> - thoroughly clean toys and all surfaces that come into contact with children's urine or saliva

Anger

Despite disability naturally occurring in all forms of life, no one deserves to be disabled. Life is neither fair nor predictable and we certainly never expected this.

An intruder entered our world during the critical formation of our daughter's life. In one fell swoop, the CMV and cerebral palsy monsters evicted our family from the lives we could have had.

Fate made me the conduit for a vicious virus. I question what I could have done differently. When did I forget to wash my hands? When did I share food with someone who had the virus? I wish I could watch a movie of my pregnancy, hear the music score loudly announce the villain, and know the exact moment CMV targeted us. My anger bubbles up as I imagine killing the beast before it destroys what could have been.

My anger is a tool I need. It empowers me and gives me fortitude to deal with the devastation those monsters left behind. Sometimes, it even fuels my tears.

Blessings

I did not ask for this life, and yet it was given to me anyway. My education and experiences gave me skills to manage the demands of Brielle's disability. My husband is loving, faithful, and a good provider. Ashley is a kind-hearted soul who was and is a joy to be a mother to without any major drama, even through her dreaded teen years. Extended family and my small group of close friends provide support and encouragement.

We experienced situations and met people we would not have otherwise. We acknowledge that Brielle's disabilities could be more difficult to manage for us and for her than they already are. There is a heartfelt, private appreciation of her small successes since they so often overshadow any public accomplishments she might have.

I give so much to Brielle, but am grateful for what she can give back. Love is the oxygen of life and Brielle loves me completely and unconditionally.

Hope

Self-pity and despair are not my constant companions. In spite of everything, I hold on to hope. Hope inspires my dreams for Brielle, which guides my goals and focuses my energies. With optimism and determination, hard work transforms our hopes for Brielle into reality. I delight in the small achievements and push through disappointments.

Hope is my beacon. Optimism sustains me in my darkest hours.

Connections

Mothers and their children connect in special ways. Due to the amount of time Brielle and I spend together, the experiences we share, and the communication bond we share (sign language), our connection is tighter than most mothers experience with their 17-year-old daughters.

Because of Brielle's disabilities and what I am uniquely able to provide for her, we are forever tethered together. My daughter's disabilities became my calling card as it changed the path of both of our lives. We are inextricably interwoven into a complicated yet beautiful tapestry that became *us*.

Complex

Our lives are a paradox of disability and being unaware, isolation and unique connections, jealousy and appreciation, fears and hope, burdens and blessings. It is a complicated concoction of experiences and emotions. We live each day as most other families do while striving for coherence in the additional chaos disability brings.

Here, on these pages, I come out from behind the carnival cutout and drop the façade to give you a glimpse into our lives. This is how we live, who we truly are, and how it all came to be.

For better or worse, this is our story.

> *...Be strong and courageous. Do not be afraid;*
> *do not be discouraged, for the LORD your God*
> *will be with you wherever you go.*
>
> *— JOSHUA 1:9 (NIV)*

CHAPTER 2

Life Before

Feeling a bit nostalgic around our wedding anniversary, I pull out some old photo albums and go back in time as I thumb through the pages. Always eager to look at old photographs, 16-year-old Brielle shuffles over and plops down beside me on the sofa.

"Look," Brielle signs, pointing to a page. "You and Dad. So cute."

Brian and I are clasping hands and leaning in together by a small river in Colorado for our first picture. I hardly remember being that girl. Those teenagers were so naïve and full of expectations 28 years ago. How dramatically their lives have changed since then.

Kids Will Be Kids

Before cytomegalovirus, cerebral palsy, doctors, and therapists filled our lives, there was just Brian and me in simpler times.

We were both fortunate to have carefree lives growing up in stable, loving, middle-class homes in Champaign, Illinois. Our foundational childhood experiences were like most children in the 70's – watching Saturday morning cartoons in our pajamas, playing outside until Mom blew her whistle, staying up late listening to records, and building blanket forts with friends at sleepovers.

Brian's father owned a family jewelry store while his mother worked in an office at the University of Illinois. Brian's younger sister, Tracy, was a tomboy, often joining him in adventures in the neighborhood with friends. Close to all four of his grandparents, Brian made the rounds to cut their grass each week. His grandmothers made him special meals and his grandfathers slipped him a few dollars.

Brian spent his summer weekends at his family's small cabin fishing on the river or swimming at the commons pool. School was not a priority, just something he had to do. When he was not playing baseball or basketball, he was watching sports on television or listening to the games on the radio with his dad. After high school, he studied business administration at Parkland Community College with plans to transfer to a state university a few years later.

My father was a professor at the university and my mother was a homemaker. My brother, Jason, was five years older, so we rarely spent much time together unless forced to on family vacations. We traveled to Florida over Christmas breaks to visit one set of grandparents and to New York to visit the other grandparents and extended family over spring breaks.

My parents pushed me to be an overachiever as a young person, with success at academics as the major focus. Girl Scouts and ballet were childhood interests that fell by the wayside. By middle school, I spent my time practicing the clarinet for concert band and tenor saxophone for jazz band. We spent most weekends and summers at Lake Shelbyville on my family's 26-foot sailboat, where I soaked up sun on the foredeck, read novels, and wrote in my diary.

I was often restless and could not wait for my "real" life to begin, my life as an adult. Marketing and public relations appealed to me, but I also had a heart for teaching. I assumed that with some hard work, a successful career and family would fall into place.

After two summers of classes at the community college, I graduated from high school a year early so that I could move on to the next phase of my life. Taking extra classes over the next few summers, I graduated from the University of Illinois in three and half years, two weeks before my twentieth birthday and just three months before my wedding day.

A Walk Around the Corner

Brian and I went to the same high school with a population of about 1,500 students. His status as a popular, six-foot five-inch jock kept him from even noticing me – a studious, band geek who was several years behind him.

We first met at my church the summer before my last year in high school (I was fifteen and a half; Brian had just turned 19). Brian's best friend attended my church and persuaded him to come on our youth group's trip to Denver. Brian's family did not attend church, but he agreed to go. Assuming it would be a boring trip, I resisted going until a friend of mine badgered me into going on the trip since her parents forced her to go.

I walked through the unfenced backyards of my neighborhood to the first pre-trip meeting at my nearby church one Wednesday evening in the early summer of 1985. He and his best friend leaned on a car procrastinating about going into the church. As I walked around the corner of the church, Brian and I locked eyes on each other. The three of us nervously made small talk, but it was clear from the start that Brian and I made a connection.

Love at first sight? We were believers.

Brian and I began dating within weeks and maintained a relationship relatively free from any teenage dating drama. We were two young people in love going to movies or just walking hand-in-hand around the neighborhood. I sat on the bleachers with Brian's parents to watch him play softball. He took me to my homecoming and prom, and sat with my family during my high school graduation ceremony.

When I began studying psychology at the University of Illinois, Brian transferred there as well so that we could attend college together. Since we were "townies," we each lived with our parents and had non-traditional college experiences commuting to campus each day. We focused on succeeding at college while also working part-time. I worked as a bank teller. Brian worked at a discount store.

We spent what little free time we had together and our relationship gracefully transformed from a couple of naïve teenagers to young adults building their future together. We were inescapably happy, in love, and had big plans.

After graduating from college, Brian's first job was in personnel for the fundraising candy division of Nestlé about an hour away in Bloomington, Illinois. We saw each other on weekends as I finished my degree, continued to work part-time at the bank, and graduated from college nine months later.

Nearly five years after I walked around the corner of my childhood church, Brian and I walked down the aisle in a traditional marriage ceremony at a large Methodist church on our university campus in March of 1990. After a two-week honeymoon cruising the Bahamas and playing tourists in Florida, we settled into our new lives together as a married couple living an hour from our hometown.

Living like Grown-ups

Brian continued to work at Nestlé while I worked on my Master's degree in communication at Illinois State University and taught Introduction to Public Speaking at the same college. Brian golfed with co-workers one night a week. We split pizza and beers with friends most Friday nights. When I was not overwhelmed grading tests, attending study groups, or completing research projects for graduate school, we spent weekends traveling back to Champaign to spend time with our parents.

Although we were busy, we were young newlyweds untethered by many worries. I regularly brought some sort of lunch for us to eat at the park during our busy workweek. It was common for us to sit on the floor of our apartment in the evenings, split a decadent slice of cheese-cake from a nearby expensive steakhouse, and share the events of our day. We worked together to complete household chores, connecting over grocery shopping, folding laundry, and washing the dinner dishes.

As soon as I finished graduate school, Brian got a promotion and transferred within Nestlé to the infant and medical formula manu-facturing facility in Eau Claire, Wisconsin. Our mothers cried when we shared the news that we were moving eight hours away, but we were ready to be more independent and begin a new adventure.

Life was beginning to truly blossom. Married for over three years, we wanted to start a family. Our plan was to try to get pregnant while I was looking for a job in marketing, not knowing which would come first – the job or the baby.

The double blue lines appeared on the pregnancy test the first month we tried. We were elated and excitedly shared our news with family and friends. On their first visit to Wisconsin to see us, we gave each of our fathers a special belated Father's Day gift. The silver plated picture frames were empty except for the note that read, "Your grandchild's picture here by March." It took a few moments for it to register, but the grandmothers could not contain their delight. They jumped to their feet immediately, squealing and hugging us.

It was an incredibly exciting time, but Brian and I were a bit uneasy. I was ready for life after graduate school, but job offers were not flooding in and Brian's modest salary was barely enough to support the expected baby and us. By the time I was four months pregnant, I could not easily hide my condition in front of prospec-tive employers and worried they would not want to hire an obviously pregnant woman. I felt obligated to take the next job offered to me even if it was not directly related to my college degrees. The baby was coming and we needed the extra money.

Working with Worries

The first job offer was as a caseworker for graduating disabled high school students who were looking for employment. I worked with members of the local school system and helped find students volunteer positions or work-study programs to develop simple job skills. I also talked with prospective employers about hiring disabled young people, convincing the companies that two "slow" young men could work together to clean hotel rooms or a young woman with autism could roll silverware for a restaurant.

Although this was not the type of job I went to college for, it felt more natural than I expected it to ever be. I visited their high school classroom regularly and often joined in their activities as they learned cooking or cleaning skills. I drove them to job sites to meet potential employers and then drove them home where I spent a few minutes getting to know their parents. It was not difficult to have favorites and connect to a few of the students in special ways.

I saw what the lives of those young disabled people and their families were like and wondered how I would cope with their circumstances. It was hard to be so close to disabled teenagers and their parents and not have concerns about the potential of a similar plight for our unborn child and us. Constantly reminded of that very real possibility, I never assumed our baby would be healthy and normal.

I had not attended church much since before college and was not particularly religious. However, I wondered if God was using this job experience to prepare me for life with a disabled child. Throughout the pregnancy, I silently worried, never sharing my fears with Brian or anyone else. Years later, Brian confided in me that he worried about the same thing.

And Baby Makes Three

My pregnancy was uneventful. I escaped any morning sickness and only endured the usual swollen feet, restless nights, and tired days. Despite our unspoken fears, Ashley was born healthy on a snowy day in March of 1994. I was induced on her due date and eventually had a C-section following 22 hours of non-productive labor. Our little bald-headed but beautiful daughter was a complete joy. I kept asking myself in disbelief, how could something so precious be given to us?

I went back to work soon after Ashley was born, but became restless wanting to work at something more closely related to my college education. I was delighted to find a job in personnel for a non-profit health care organization, although the details of doing payroll frustrated me. When a new position in their marketing department was created, I promptly applied and transferred to the small but growing department.

We checked Ashley's developmental progress with the baby books, proud as could be when she accomplished some new feat ahead of schedule. As she grew, our toddler's bouncy, light brown curls and crooked grin made us smile while her amusing little phrases and mispronunciation of words made us laugh. We followed our little girl around with our camera and video recorder like paparazzi and she was the star of the show. Our parents made frequent trips up to Wisconsin to spend time with their first grandchild and shower her with toys and clothes.

These early years were incredibly joyful times. We settled into life like it was a comfortable chair. Brian's job was fulfilling and I was finally working in a field I really enjoyed. We lived in a three-bedroom ranch-style home with our loving little family and had a busy social life with friends, neighbors, and visits from our parents. I began to regularly attend a nearby Methodist church once Ashley was born and found a new community of friends there. Although Ashley was still a toddler, we were eager to add another child to our family, as we had always planned.

MORE ABOUT...
Our Timeline*

1985 June: Brian and Kerith meet

1990 March: Brian and Kerith marry

1993 May: Brian and Kerith move to Wisconsin

1994 March: Ashley is born

* For our complete timeline, see Appendix A

Life as Planned

We had plans, most of them fairly ordinary plans about our careers and having a family. We both wanted to advance and make more money. A more modern house with a little more room would have been nice. Although we delighted in little toddler Ashley, we were eager to eventually see her off to kindergarten and watch her in school plays, band, or choir. We hoped she and her little brother or sister would be interested in some sort of organized sports. Remembering our own childhoods, we assumed we would one day need to break up arguments and rough housing between our children. I imagined helping Ashley get dressed for school dances and her wedding day. Brian and I teased each other about the prospects of becoming old and gray-haired while rocking on the front porch as empty nesters and eventually grandparents.

Some of our plans came to fruition. Others we chose to change or drop completely. A few we still have yet to know if they will happen.

Some of our best-laid plans were disrupted in spite of what we did to try to make them happen. Fate had something else lined up for us, something we never planned on that transformed our lives completely and set us on a new path.

"For I know the plans I have for you," declares the LORD, "plans to prosper you and not to harm you, plans to give you hope and a future"

— JEREMIAH 29: 10-12 (NIV)

CHAPTER 3

The Call That Changed Everything

The house phone rings. A few moments later, I hear Brielle's distinctive "step-slide-step-slide" coming down the hardwood floors of the hallway. "Who that?" Brielle signs to me.

My cell phone pings to announce a text. I slide it open and Brielle is snooping over my shoulder trying to read the text.

Brielle is a nosey kid, always hovering over me wanting to know to whom I'm talking.

"They say hi to me," she signs as a statement rather than a question.

"Yes," I lie often. "They said to tell you 'hi'."

Unwanted Spots

Working at the health care organization on a typical day in June of 1995, my phone rang. It is never a good thing when your child's daycare calls in the middle of the day. The caregiver said Ashley might have chicken pox.

MORE ABOUT....
The availability of the vaccine for chicken pox[1,2]

Although the chicken pox (or varicella) vaccine was first available in Japan and Korea in 1988, it was not available in the United States until 1995 (about the time I became pregnant).

Chicken pox? To my knowledge, she had not even been exposed (and this was before the vaccination became available).

I told Ashley's daycare I would come pick her up as soon as possible. One of my co-workers suggested I stop at a drug store to get oatmeal bath to soothe Ashley's itchiness, if she actually did have chicken pox.

I also picked up a pregnancy test.

Eighteen months after Ashley was born, we started trying to have a second child. We hoped to be lucky enough to have the same easy time getting pregnant. We had only been trying a month or so. However, now I was worried about a possible pregnancy.

Neither my brother, Jason, nor I ever had chicken pox as children. How could two kids in the same family go unscathed from such a common childhood disease? I dreaded the spotted, itchy prospect. More concerning, what would chicken pox do to my unborn child if I were pregnant?

When the daycare providers showed me the three little, pale spots on my toddler's pudgy tummy, I almost had to chuckle. Those were chicken pox? The women at the daycare had to be overreacting to some little reaction to soap or laundry detergent or something. Nevertheless, I took my child home.

Ashley happily played the rest of the afternoon, but by the time we bathed her and put to bed that night, there were more spots on her tummy and they were darker. No denying it. Ashley had chicken pox.

Passing the Test

Brian was in bed watching television when I came in to deliver the results of the home pregnancy test later that same evening. I walked in the bedroom, pointed to my stomach, and said, "Bun."

I was pregnant.

Brian and I sat there in bed the rest of the evening a little stunned. Our hearts still held out hope that I would not get chicken pox.

Maybe I was exposed to it enough over the years to build up immunity. Maybe I experienced a mild case of it at some point and did not even realize it. Maybe our tiny unborn child would be OK.

I called my OB/GYN the next morning and talked to the nurse about my fears.

"Your daughter has certainly been contagious for days," the nurse explained. "You've already been exposed. So, if you're going to get it, there's nothing you can do now. Call us back if you show any symptoms."

At that point, I was worried, but not distressed, mostly because the nurse had been so matter-of-fact with me. Surely, if there were cause for alarm, she would have prepared me.

Hundreds of itchy sores covered Ashley within a few days. She played contently at home while I caught up on a few projects to stay busy and keep my mind off my worries.

Our excitement about the baby was subdued with the looming unknown risk to the pregnancy. Although we shared our news about both Ashley's chicken pox and my pregnancy with our parents, we otherwise kept the baby news to ourselves.

Spots Times Two

Two weeks later, Ashley was back at daycare and I was back at work. Only a few days after we settled into our routine, I was at my desk when I noticed a relentless itching on my temple. I looked in the ladies' room mirror and saw five pale spots on my forehead.

I was six weeks pregnant and had chicken pox.

I drove home from work that day in utter distress, my eyes clouded by tears. I knew this day might come. However, since so many days had passed spot-free, I was starting to believe chicken pox would not pop up on my skin.

Although I could have called Brian to share my concerns, I first called my OB/GYN's office to consult with the nurse. She assured me the doctor would call me back as soon as she was available. A few hours later, with a steady, but wary voice, my doctor told me what she knew about the risks of chicken pox to an unborn child.

"Your chance of having a baby with brain damage or limb deformity is perhaps as high as twenty-five percent," she reported. "And there is a real possibility that your child may die at birth. I am sorry to tell you that there is nothing you can do to prevent any harm to your child from chicken pox at this point."

She then gingerly reminded me that since I was in my first trimester, abortion was still an option. I brushed off her last remark, stifled my tears, and ended the call quickly.

Being sick at home only provided time to let my mind race and privacy to let my tears flow. Chicken pox disturbed the harmony of our family and put us on a path of worries.

The Choice

Brian and I thought we knew how we felt about abortion, but we had never faced that choice. We got pregnant twice when we wanted to and never got pregnant when we did not want to.

We wanted this baby, but the prospect of having a severely disabled child or worse, not having a baby that lived, was horrifying. We shared the grim news with family and a few close friends. We did not ask for opinions. Most of them tried to be supportive without indicating their views on the abortion issue.

Conversely, boldly and not atypically, my father told me exactly what he thought. "How could you accept the risks if you have an alternative?" he pleaded with us. I knew he was only thinking about what would be best for me, but it was painful to hear those words from him. After all, he was talking about the fate of his own grandchild growing inside of me.

"Please, Dad," I tried to cut him off. "I know what you're saying, but it isn't that easy." As I began to sob uncontrollably over the phone, he seemed shocked that I was reacting that way instead of handling this dilemma in a more logical manner.

My mother stayed remarkably silent and respectful of our fragile situation. Behind her stoic façade, her heart ached for us. She later told me that she felt guilty for not purposely exposing me and my brother to chicken pox as children, as so many mothers did back then. Beyond her choice years ago, she knew there was no clear right or wrong choice to the dilemma her daughter and son-in-law were facing.

Later that afternoon, I stood in the kitchen of my good friend and neighbor, Jayni, trying not to scratch the new spots on my arm. I was glad everyone in her family had already had chicken pox so that I could be there to share my worries with her.

I gave Jayni my rendition of the phone conversation I had with my parents including my father's direct comment as she fixed a snack for her children. My friend held her breath for a moment, examining the pain on my face.

"I want to share my story with you, not to persuade you one way or another, but to offer you a little hope," she told me as she dried her hands on a kitchen towel. "Eight years ago, when I was pregnant with Chad, the doctors told us there was a chance he had Down Syndrome."

Stepping back to lean on the counter behind me, I simply stared at her, unable to give any other reaction. Even after three years of friendship, Jayni had never shared this with me.

"Of course," she continued, "he was born perfectly healthy. But, I know a little of what you're going through and I am here for you," she said putting her hand on mine.

M O R E   A B O U T . . . .
Our Faith (during the early weeks of the pregnancy)

Religion and faith played only a small role in our lives at this point. Although Brian's parents both grew up attending church, they stopped going when they got married. Church was a foreign place to Brian and even though he came along on that youth trip years before, he still was not sure if he believed God existed.

Although I grew up regularly attending a Lutheran church, I rarely went while I was in college and only started attending a nearby Methodist church while I was pregnant with Ashley. I went out of habit and went through the motions because I thought it was the right thing to do for my young child.

I believed in God and had leaned on Him in tough times in the past. However, at this time of great sorrow, I found little comfort in what little faith I had.

Friends like Jayni offered a shoulder to cry on, but most never knew quite what to say. The few people who knew seemed terribly uncomfortable around us. Brian's parents listened to our worries and offered their support without revealing their opinions. On the other hand, my father's words cut through my heart and continued to reverberate in my head.

After a few days, we realized we might have made a mistake telling anyone at all. We needed to decide without the influence of others since we were the ones who would have to live with the consequences.

One day, we thought the risk was simply too great and contemplated having an abortion. The next day, we reconsidered and decided to take our chances. Another day, we would re-think it all over again. If we made the choice to keep our baby, would he or she be severely disabled or die at birth? What if the baby was perfectly healthy and we aborted it? How could we know? How could we live with ourselves?

We had more questions than answers. Despite the compassion of family and some close friends, we felt quite alone. We were on shaky ground as we struggled with this decision. Each day that passed made it that much more difficult to make a choice, and yet the three-month deadline loomed out there in front of us. We only had a few more weeks to decide.

A New Hope

Several weeks after my outbreak, a genetic counselor from the regional genetic counseling office called me after our OB/GYN consulted her about our case. This specialist had much better news to offer us.

"The information from your doctor was based on older data and on worst-case scenario individual case reports," the genetic counselor told me. "There is typically a three to four percent risk of any newborn having a medically significant birth defect. New, more comprehensive data on chicken pox outbreaks during pregnancy indicates an additional one to three percent risk of birth defects."

"So, that means our risk is a total of four to seven percent?" I asked after doing the simple math.

"Exactly," the genetic counselor continued, "In most cases, the fetus does not even get the virus because it does not cross the placenta."

Although the genetic counselor confirmed there were no treatment options, she told me we should get ultrasounds monthly and detailed ultrasounds at least twice during the pregnancy to provide information about the baby's general development, especially about the limbs.

"However," she said cautiously, "only time will show us if the virus has affected the child's brain."

The genetic counselor mailed us a letter summarizing what we talked about and included a copy of two recent medical studies. I greedily read and reread the reports looking for more clues or something that might offer us an extra sliver of hope. Although I felt enormous relief about the information she gave us, those studies offered no guarantees.

MORE ABOUT....
What doctors now know about the risks if a pregnant woman gets chicken pox[1]

Ten to twenty percent of pregnant women who contract chicken pox develop pneumonia and then consequently have a chance of a maternal death rate as high as forty percent.

If contracted during the first trimester through the nineteenth week, the baby has up to a two percent chance of low birth weight, scarring of the skin, and problems with limbs, brain, and eyes.

Birth defects are quite rare if contracted after the twentieth week of gestation.

If contracted during the final days of pregnancy or first days after birth, the baby can develop chicken pox as well and have a thirty percent chance of death due to pneumonia.

Brian and I never had opposing thoughts about our choice. We each struggled emotionally as we tried to face the decision in a logical way. However, once we discussed our options a handful of times and the conversations continued to go in circles without any resolution, we settled into our own private thoughts for a while.

Hours and days passed by with some anxiety, but we were generally able to keep the most extreme emotions at bay.

With heavy hearts, we made our choice as my first trimester came to a close late that summer. We would keep our baby.

MORE ABOUT....
The Role of the Placenta[3]

The placenta is a pancake-shaped organ that attaches to the inside of the uterus and allows the transfer of nutrients and oxygen to the unborn child and waste elimination from the fetus. However, the biological system of the placenta does not allow the mother and fetus to share blood directly. In addition, the placenta also functions as a filter to provide a barrier to certain microscopic organisms including certain diseases, but it does not protect the child from all harmful substances. The placenta is expelled from the mother's body after the child is delivered.

Testing, Testing, One, Two, Three

Although Brian came to many of my doctor visits when I was pregnant with Ashley, he came to every appointment with this pregnancy. Each visit, the doctor slopped cold gel on my growing belly. We listened carefully for the sound of galloping hoof beats as she ran the probe over my abdomen to find the baby's heartbeat.

To provide additional monitoring of the baby's development, my doctor sent me to the hospital to get ultrasounds each month. We watched in the blurry monitor as the ultrasound technician measured the baby's length, head size, and limb buds. The technician never reported any results. It was difficult to wait for our doctor to provide us with answers.

We wanted our doctor to assure us there was nothing abnormal about the pregnancy or about our baby. Our doctor never uttered the words we desperately wanted to hear, that the baby had gone completely untouched by chicken pox. Nonetheless, she never gave us any reason to assume the worst.

After each encouraging appointment, Brian and I walked out hand-in-hand and tried to breathe a little easier hoping that we were one step closer to having a healthy baby. Those little spots had tainted our pregnancy experience. However, it would be many months before we knew for sure if chicken pox had affected our baby.

We could not allow the worry train to start to go too far down the track. The few close friends and family members who knew about our concerns, never spoke about them. I was glad no one wanted to talk about the worries we still had for our baby. Talking about them with anyone would have made our situation feel worse.

Ashley was about as excited as any toddler could be about the prospect of a new baby sister or brother. We read stories about becoming a big sister, but she had no clue how her world would change. Of course, we did not really know either.

Our curly-headed little girl was growing up so fast, changing almost daily and starting to say the funniest things as her vocabulary quickly expanded. We stayed as busy as possible that fall by filling our free time playing with Ashley, flying kites at the park, showing her how to jump into big piles of crunchy leaves, and going to the local pumpkin patch.

In October, when I was five months pregnant, we traveled about 90 minutes to Marshfield Clinic to get the first of two detailed ultrasounds. Besides the usual full bladder and cool gel they splatted on my rounded belly, they had to use a very uncomfortable internal probe. We squinted to make out the form on the monitor and were so relieved when the technician pointed out our baby's angelic little profile with perfectly formed limbs and digits.

Most prospective parents say they do not care what gender their baby is, as long as it is healthy. We were certainly more focused on having a healthy child than most, but had honestly hoped it was a boy since we already had a girl. With our first pregnancy, we wanted the baby's gender to be a surprise. With this one, we needed as few surprises as possible.

When we asked, the technician told us it was another girl. Our hearts only dipped for a moment since the test results showed a healthy baby. Ashley was going to have a little sister. We were going to give her a best friend for life.

What's in a Name?

We were so worried up until that first detailed ultrasound that we had not even considered any baby names yet. Once we knew our child had all of her proper limbs, we skimmed through the baby name book with a new sense of excitement. We wrote a long list of options for girl names on the back side of Christmas wrapping paper, taped it to the back of our bedroom door, and crossed off one name each day to narrow down our list.

One evening in late October, Brian was leafing through a *Sports Illustrated* magazine as we watched television in bed. "This evening Favre makes a 10 p.m. run to Mariucci's house to give his four-week-old daughter, Brielle, a birth gift," Brian read from an article[4] about Brett Favre, quarterback for the Green Bay Packers. Brian commented on the name, Brielle, and I immediately fell in love with it, refusing to consider the other names on our list after that. She was no longer the mysterious fetus inside me. She was our baby girl and her name was Brielle.

The Gift

Over Thanksgiving week, we drove the long eight hours to our hometown in Illinois to visit our families. It was a typical Thanksgiving with a big turkey dinner, lots of family, and laughing over Ashley's antics. Although it had been a difficult year, we still had a lot to be thankful for.

The days between the holidays were a bit of a blur as we busily did our shopping and prepared to return to Illinois for Christmas. We looked forward to our first year with Ashley old enough to really enjoy the wonders of the holidays and it was a wonderful day indeed.

Ignorance was bliss that holiday season. I have thanked God more than once for that gift of not knowing. We were able to enjoy the holidays with our little girl and finally find some real joy in being pregnant.

There were things we were unaware of as we rang in the new year and took down our Christmas tree. It would only be a matter of weeks before we learned something was wrong with Baby Brielle, something that would change the course of our lives.

> *May the LORD answer you when you are in distress; may the name of the God of Jacob protect you.*
>
> – Psalm 20:1 (NIV)

CHAPTER 4

Bad News in the Doctor's Office

"Where we go?" Brielle signs as she shows me my appointment book.

"You're not supposed to be digging through my purse," I tell my 12-year-old daughter as I take it from her and zip up my purse.

Despite telling her each night what we'll be doing the next day and reviewing our wall calendar together each morning, Brielle still seems fascinated with my appointment book.

"Sorry, Mom," she signs. "Where we go?"

"I told you last night," I say. "We have to go to the chiropractor today and then go to the grocery store."

"Oh," she signs, smacking her hand to her forehead. "I forgot."

Ten minutes later, she is standing in front of our wall calendar carefully examining its details.

Days of Grace

After the holidays, Brian and I felt like we were in the homestretch. Brielle would be born in just over a month. We were finally starting to embrace the joy of the pregnancy.

In preparation for the birth of her little sister, we moved Ashley into a "big girl bed" in the third bedroom. After just two rough nights, she fell asleep without incidence and seemed to feel at home in her new surroundings. She talked about the baby using endearing phrases like, "When Baby Brielle comes..." and "Baby Brielle will be a cute little sister."

I decorated the baby's room with pink decorations. Tiny onesies, sleepers, and diapers filled the dresser drawers. I turned little booties over in my hand, trying to fathom how small our baby girl would be. I stood back to study the room, pleased with my decorating flair. Resting my hand on my growing belly, I anxiously awaited the room's new occupant.

Throughout the pregnancy, I felt good. I had escaped morning sickness in the first trimester once again and simply endured general pregnancy issues, including being tired most of the time. Nothing else could be expected while working full time, chasing a toddler around, and being pregnant over the bitter cold Wisconsin winter.

Like many expectant fathers, Brian whispered sweet things to the little life kicking inside me and kissed my bulging stomach, which was becoming increasingly uncomfortable. I was tired of my limited maternity wardrobe, my feet swelled, and I thought I would never be able to tie my own shoes again. However, Brian saw nothing but pure beauty in me.

In mid-January, with just five weeks left, we went in for yet another monthly ultrasound. As Brian stood by my side and watched the monitor, the ultrasound technician ran the probe over my belly. She took measurements, snapped a few images, and pointed out Brielle's perfect little arms, legs, fingers, and toes.

The technician took her time and seemed very serious about her work. We were not particularly concerned. We had been through this process so many times by this late in the pregnancy. We certainly knew better than to ask any questions. There was little the technician could tell us, even if we asked.

The Unexpected Call

The next day, I received a call from my OB/GYN's nurse. The doctor wanted to see us in her office. My heart dropped violently inside my chest and I tasted that bitter, metallic taste of fear as my mouth went dry and my stomach churned like morning sickness.

Thoughts jumped around my head as I tried to compose myself. I managed to meekly ask the nurse why the doctor wanted to meet with us, bracing myself for bad news. However, the nurse quickly brushed off my questions and told me the doctor would talk to us at the appointment.

Our world changed with a distinct shifting of gears.

Brian and I nervously fidgeted in our seats in the doctor's waiting room the next day. Other women with bulging bellies practically glowed with joy as they thumbed through pregnancy magazines or chatted with their smiling husbands. Tormented with visions of bad news from the doctor, my husband and I did not dare to speak as we held hands over the wooden armrest of the uncomfortable chairs.

Brian and I thought we had already pushed through the worst part of this pregnancy. Brielle's limbs were all there despite the higher risk of deformities because of chicken pox. Her heartbeat was regular and strong. I could feel Brielle moving energetically inside me every day. What now?

The nurse announced my name and motioned for us to follow her. Instead of going to an exam room and taking my vitals, she ushered us into the doctor's office. A thick haze of apprehension distorted time as we sat across the desk waiting for the doctor to enter. Stacks of papers and file folders cluttered the surfaces. Diplomas and awards hung with pride on the pale yellow walls. A whitewashed wooden frame held a wedding picture where a younger, thinner version of our doctor smiled out at us.

The office door opened, startling us from our silence. Our doctor was about to deliver grim news and that was clearly reflected in her solemn expression as she sat down.

"Yesterday's ultrasound showed the baby's head is small," she said, looking at us sympathetically. "We cannot know for sure why or what this means. You'll need to have more tests to help us figure that out."

We asked questions, but the doctor did not have any answers.

Heartbreak did not ease its way in. The pain came at us with force. One day our lives seemed to be finally getting back in order. The next day we were in the grips of painful circumstances that were beyond our control.

When we walked slowly to our car that cold January afternoon, all we knew was the doctor had newfound, serious concerns about our baby and now we did, too. The nightmare was starting all over again. Only this time, the possibility of it resulting in tragedy felt more tangible because whatever was wrong, it had already caused our baby's head to develop abnormally.

Final Exam

Our doctor referred us to a perinatologist (a doctor who cares for women with high risk pregnancies). She also made us an appointment at Marshfield Clinic to have another detailed ultrasound as well as an amniocentesis. Hopefully, those could give us more answers.

On Wednesday, January 17, the internal probe and external wand pushed on my enormous stomach. With a full bladder, the procedure was even more uncomfortable than it had been the first time back in October. Brian held my hand as the ultrasound technician took careful measurements and called in her supervisor to do the same. Except for a few clicks of the ultrasound machine, the room was silent, dark, and cold.

Our hearts reflected that room.

Then they called for the doctor to do the amniocentesis. The ultrasound tech found an empty pocket of fluid and the doctor swabbed that spot on my belly with cold iodine. I squeezed Brian's hand and looked away as the long needle pushed through my taut belly.

MORE ABOUT....
Amniocentesis[6]

- Amniocentesis is a diagnostic procedure usually used during the fourteenth to twentieth weeks of pregnancy, but can be used as early as eleven weeks as well as much later in the pregnancy.
- Genetic testing is the primary reason for this procedure, however other tests can be done on the extracted fluid.
- Ultrasound is used to find a location for the needle to enter the amniotic sac.
- A sample of amniotic fluid (which contains cells shed from the fetus) is collected through the needle.
- Risks of harm are low, however the risk of miscarriage may be as high as 1 in 200.
- Results from the laboratory can take anywhere from a few days to a couple of weeks.

When it was over, the technician unwrapped a Band-Aid with its distinctive plastic smell and placed the small adhesive over the pinprick on my huge abdomen. Without a word, the doctor took the fluid-filled syringe out of the room. I tried to stifle tears as I watched our future and the future of our precious baby go with him. All we could do after that was wait. News of the results would take several days, several very long days.

The Other Shoe Drops

Trying not to jump each time my office phone rang, I submersed myself in the tasks of the day. I cringed as I pressed the "play" button on the answering machine each evening when I arrived home from work. I resumed my breathing only when the friendly voice of a friend or my mother echoed on the tape machine.

I was sitting at my desk one day the week following the procedure at Marshfield Clinic when the perinatologist called with our test results. I put her on hold to take the call in a small private conference room down the hall. Although the room seemed to be oxygen deficient, I took a deep breath. Holding a pencil firmly in my hand, ready to take notes, I lifted the receiver and clicked the line with the blinking light.

Without any initial pleasantries at all, the perinatologist told me that the genetic testing was normal and the baby was definitely a girl. She then explained that tests from the amniotic fluid showed that the baby had cytomegalovirus (CMV).

"Cyto-what? Could you spell that?" I asked, scribbling on the notepad in front of me.

She spelled out the foreign word to me and explained that CMV is an infection that many adults get with symptoms like a cold or the flu, although some may have almost no symptoms at all.

"Have you been sick at all during your pregnancy?" the specialist asked. I searched my memory, now clouded with whirling emotions and racing concerns. I had been sick twice with mild cold symptoms, but again, this was Wisconsin in the winter and my toddler regularly brought home sniffles from daycare.

The perinatologist continued to tell me that if a baby is infected prenatally with this virus, the newborn could have a purple-spotted rash, abnormal blood counts, or liver damage as well as vision or hearing problems.

"Your baby's motor skills and ability to learn could be impaired, perhaps severely." She delivered the bottom line results of the testing with little emotion in her voice. "Her risk for mental retardation is about seventy percent. There is also a forty percent chance your child could die at birth due to liver complications."

Our baby was very sick and I felt as lifeless as I did helpless. Cytomegalovirus silently permeated our family's lives. Until this moment, we never even knew its name.

Shock gave way to dread and anguish in equal parts. I crumpled under the weight of this new information, crying for a long time in that small conference room before collecting myself enough to be aware of my surroundings again. Dreams for our future fluttered away like autumn leaves dropping from tree branches. That one phone call ended the small shred of hope we so desperately wanted to hold on to.

I sometimes recall that January day, turning the events over and over again like a smooth, flat stone in my hand. Remembering the doctor's words, her tone of voice, and my reaction to those words, I replay it in my mind.

As if watching it on home videos, I wish I had the ability to press the "pause" button and rewind the recording to happier times when Brian and I were dating or when Ashley was first born. I want to somehow find a way to save my younger self from the pain she was about to endure. However, there is no other button on the recording device except "play." Life simply keeps moving forward.

That one phone call marked the true start of the rest of our lives and the new course they took. How many calls in a lifetime have such a profound impact?

Sharing the Bad News

As the only one who knew about this bad news, I felt alone. I dreaded telling Brian and wondered if the doctor felt the same way before she called me. I debated when to tell him, at that moment in the small conference room or a little later in the day, by phone or in person.

Wanting to spare him, but knowing I could not protect him from the inevitable pain made me feel helpless.

After wiping my nose, I took a deep breath and dialed Brian's office number. He was quiet as I reported the details of the doctor's call. He then asked me questions I could not answer. How did I get this virus? How soon after she was born would we know how bad things would be for Brielle? What about children we might have in the future? His questions multiplied like cells dividing in a high school biology video. After a few minutes, silence took over, shrouding our phone conversation in fear. The only sound came from our synchronized tears.

After making some excuse to my boss, I collected my things and drove to Ashley's daycare. Our firstborn child never looked so beautiful or more precious than she did that day. She jumped into my arms greeting me with chatter about playing *Duck, Duck, Goose* and making pictures with colored macaroni. The drive home was a blur.

I knew that eventually more calls had to be made to our parents and a few trusted friends.

The news was just a few hours old when I summoned up the courage to pick up the phone. I desperately needed to hear my mother's voice at that moment, to cling to her like I was five years old, afraid to go to my new kindergarten classroom. My fingers felt as heavy as my heart as I slowly dialed the phone and shared the information with my parents. My mother just repeated "Oh God, oh God" over and over again as she heard the awful details in my grief-stricken words.

When my father was getting his PhD in Educational Psychology, he observed patients at a mental institution. The facility had a ward where adults with severe disabilities lived. The stroke he had several years before Ashley was born made him forget to filter certain things. He blurted out in much detail about how they looked and how awful their lives were.

At this emotionally fragile time, I did not need to hear about what he observed in that mental institution in the early 1960's, what could possibly become the life of our child. I realize my father felt a responsibility to inform me, to share his knowledge and experience. However, at the time, it only startled and angered me, magnifying my fears.

Becoming hysterical, I hung up on them, something this daughter had never done before. My courage to make more calls that afternoon was deflated. I lay lifeless on my bed in dread and shock while Ashley played contently in her room. Our cute little girl was completely unaware of the impact of that day's events.

Brian shared the news with his parents that evening. There was a somber silence on the other end of the phone as their son relayed the specialist's information. They peppered him with questions, but, so typical of them, never offered any unsolicited advice or their own opinions. They simply tried to give their unconditional support in a way that did not interfere with what we were going through. However, they were also weary from the rollercoaster ride of emotions the last seven months brought.

The Meeting

A few days later, back at Marshfield Clinic, Brian and I solemnly sat around a small, round table in a sterile conference room with the perinatologist, a neonatologist (a doctor who cares for newborns), and a social worker. They went over the amniocentesis results in more detail and we asked questions we had carefully written out in a notebook.

Chicken pox and CMV were not related. I had been struck by two different viruses during my pregnancy. CMV had caused our baby's head to be small, not chicken pox. From the test results, it appeared our baby was left unscathed by my itchy spots. Just what else CMV had done to our baby, they did not know.

The doctors explained CMV is very common in adults and usually has no side effects. The virus only poses a risk to an unborn child if the mother contracts it for the first time during the pregnancy. Out of all babies born infected with CMV, only a small percentage shows any side effects from the virus. Since our baby already showed side effects (because her head was so small), she was in that small percentage.

They told us that if Brielle survived, it would be months or years before we knew if she had mental retardation or cerebral palsy. She could lose her hearing at any point in her life. Any future children we had would not be at any additional risk for CMV prenatally because I had already been exposed.

There was an experimental anti-virus drug therapy, gancyclovir, which the doctors could prescribe. However, the side effects were so harsh that the medication was quickly ruled out. There was nothing that could be done to repair the damage or undo what had already been done.

Although it is not highly contagious, the virus spreads through close contact with bodily fluids. They told me I might have contracted it by not washing my hands after being in a public place, sharing food with our toddler who could have been exposed to it at daycare (where CMV rates are very high), or simply kissing my husband who could have picked it up at work or somewhere else.

The doctors nor anyone else ever specifically blamed me, but I still felt guilty. I had not taken precautions to keep the virus away from our unborn child. But, how did I know? I had never heard of CMV until a few days before this. I had no time to truly consider my guilt or innocence. There was more information to digest.

They suggested that I probably contracted the virus in the second trimester. One of my two colds must have been CMV. We would never know exactly when or how I contracted it, just that the blow had been delivered.

Near the end of the meeting, the perinatologist showed some humanity and gave her sincere condolences for our situation. In a moment that is firmly tattooed on my brain, she then offered the only alternative we might have.

"I know a place in Colorado that performs abortions up to 32 weeks. Would you like me to contact them and ask if they would do the procedure for you?"

We were stunned by her suggestion. I was 36 weeks along and we knew what abortion at this stage in the pregnancy would mean.

"It doesn't matter if the clinic in Colorado would do it," I spoke for both of us. "Abortion is no longer an option for us."

Our child had a name. She was no longer an "it." We would see this pregnancy through to the end, no matter what it might bring.

> *So do not fear, for I am with you;*
> *do not be dismayed, for I am your God.*
> *I will strengthen you and help you;*
> *I will uphold you with my righteous right hand.*
>
> – ISAIAH 41:10 (NIV)

CHAPTER 5

The Waiting

The whole family is sitting in the living room on an early Saturday morning. Sixteen-year-old Ashley nervously bounces her leg up and down and fidgets with the number two pencils in her hands.

"It will be fine," I reassure my teenager, putting a hand on her knee to stop her jittery leg.

"I know," Ashley says, forcing a weak smile. "I just hate taking tests."

She leans forward to look at the clock for the fourth time in less than 10 minutes. Little does my oldest daughter realize that her nerves won't calm down much until the results of her SAT test arrive in the mail weeks later.

"I'm just going to go," she says, grabbing her purse, calculator, and car keys.

"You'll do great," Brian tries to encourage her as he gives her a high five.

I give my daughter a quick hug, but she's now fidgeting with her keys. I'm not sure she even noticed Brielle giving her a "thumbs up."

After Ashley drives away, the three of us sit back down with our coffee and juice. Her waiting is over while ours is just beginning.

"Look," Brielle says, smiling proudly while awkwardly shaking her leg up and down. "Like big sister."

Under a Heavy Cloud

We lived the next four weeks of our lives in chronic fear, bystanders on the sidelines of what our growing baby was going through. We went to work. We came home. We shared the awful news with friends and family. I watched as my friends reacted with shock and tears. Well-meaning friends who called or stopped by to visit only left us in deeper despair. The sound of the telephone or doorbell became a source of dread. Facing others and their reactions to our despair felt like an added burden.

Brian's boss, Russ, started his career as a biochemist. When Brian told him about our devastating news, Russ offered to help us find out more about cytomegalovirus. Through his access to research publications, he was able to find several summaries about the virus and a handful of articles in medical journals. Clinical descriptions of children like our baby were difficult to digest and we could not get past the practical implications that potentially faced our baby – deafness, blindness, mental retardation, cerebral palsy, death at birth.

One night while painfully thumbing through *What to Expect While You're Expecting* to look up information about vaginal deliveries after C-sections, I stumbled across a small blurb about CMV right there on page 314. To think a warning about this virus was there that whole time.

During each of my pregnancies, I probably read that page more than once. If I had paid more attention to its list of precautions, could I have prevented this? I was supposed to be the gatekeeper, but I failed to protect our baby. Shaking off those guilty feelings, my heart could not let my mind go there for long.

We stayed busy with work, responsibilities at home, and keeping things steady for Ashley. Despite his own weariness from worrying, Brian was especially good at not letting Ashley sense our distress. He chased her around the house, accepted countless cups of pretend tea, and continued to use funny voices when they played with puppets. The only thing I could manage to do to keep things "normal" for our toddler was to read to her. In those stacks of books, I could just read and not have to do any real pretending that things were OK.

MORE ABOUT....
My Faith and the Role of My Church (during the last weeks of the pregnancy)

My faith was in its infancy and brought me little strength at this time. I had several good friends at my church (including my neighbor friend, Jayni) that supported me during the entire pregnancy. Although I served on the preschool board at my church, I did not attend any small groups or Bible study classes to build many other strong relationships there.

The pastor had only been there a few months. Although he presented a compelling sermon each Sunday morning, he seemed quite business-like instead of personable when interacting with him.

He was well aware of our situation and read my prayer requests aloud to the congregation each Sunday. However, I was discouraged when he never called, stopped by, or even spoke personally to me after services about our concerns for our pregnancy. I wondered if my prayer requests were just a source of "news" to him since I felt so neglected.

Because I had other pastors in my past who clearly demonstrated how they cared for members of their congregation, this particular pastor's behavior did not taint my view of church, religion, or my faith. I certainly knew God had not abandoned me.

By playing with Ashley and keeping things normal for her, we could help our family enjoy the small moments of life rather than focus on what was sure to be a difficult road ahead. We decided to tell Ashley the baby might be sick, but the doctors were taking good care of us and we hoped the baby would be OK. At not quite two years old, Ashley did not really understand. We just hoped that in case something did go wrong with the baby, our firstborn child might be a little more prepared. She went on with her carefree little life and that brought us brief moments of joy.

However, sudden gusts of grief and fear swept through me, threatening to implode my composure. I worked especially hard to keep my tears at bay in the office. Distracted and overwhelmed with anxiety in those last weeks, my work began to suffer. I made careless mistakes and was late to meetings. After abruptly cancelling the baby shower my co-workers planned for me, an explanation was in order. Once I told them, I felt their eyes of pity on me and wished the cubicle walls could close in on me to protect me from their sorrowful stares.

Only one close co-worker friend gave me exactly what I needed. Minnette often just quietly hugged me, seemingly out-of-the-blue. Her hugs were powerful and her wordless compassion gave me the resolution to get through my work on many days.

What should have been a time of celebrations and excitement was not that at all. We could not celebrate the impending birth of our second child when there was a forty percent chance we were not coming home with a baby at all.

Baby showers were put on hold. I stopped nesting preparations in the baby's room. The crib mattress was bare, boxes of Ashley's hand-me-downs went unpacked, and the overnight bag for the hospital stayed empty. We even closed the door to the baby's room for a while.

Our continued worries were a heavy cloak we put on each morning when we woke up and tried to scrape off each night before bed. Contemplating the harshest possibilities Brielle might face was difficult. We never spoke in any real terms about our baby's possible death and need for funeral plans. The only special planning we did was to investigate staying at a nearby Ronald McDonald House if our baby was hospitalized for a long time.

During those last weeks of my pregnancy, time moved in slow motion. The same 60 minutes in each hour that existed in the weeks before Ashley's birth seemed so brief and joyful. How unfair that they felt unbearably long and full of worry before Brielle's.

In quiet moments, thoughts of Brielle being sick could not be pushed out of the forefront of our minds. Not knowing what the future held kindled up more fears and worry as the days went by. We grieved for the child we worried we had already lost since the risk of disability and death were so high.

We had gotten through the chicken pox scare and now this. How could two such awful monsters strike our baby?

We were propelled forward into what seemed like an impending horrifying car wreck. Brian and I were on high alert with adrenaline pulsing through our bodies from the fear of our unknown future. We struggled to regain control of our lives, bracing for impact, hoping to avoid tragedy. A sickening feeling made itself at home in our bodies and life seemingly drained out of every one of our pores.

As I sat in bed with Brian in the evenings, trying to concentrate on the television or the open magazine on what was left of my lap, I felt Brielle move inside me and cringed. What had once given us joy and assurance was now a continuous, haunting reminder. Our lives had already drastically changed and our baby's life might not even get a chance to be lived.

Our Impending Delivery Date

We continued our prenatal visits with the perinatologist, who took over my care since this was now classified as a high-risk pregnancy and delivery. We traveled the 90 minutes to her office each of the last few weeks of the pregnancy and discussed our options for delivering our baby. Most women can try to have vaginal delivery, even after having a C-section with a previous birth. However, my doctor did not want to put our baby through labor, especially if she was medically fragile.

I was due on February 17th, but the perinatologist scheduled us to have a C-section on February 13th. Was it a bad omen to deliver her on the thirteenth, even though it was Tuesday not a Friday? A delivery on the thirteenth was better than having a baby on Valentine's Day. My birthday is on Christmas Day, so I knew all too well the perils of sharing a birthday with a holiday. I wanted Brielle to have her own special day. More than anything, I hoped that there would be many birthdays for her to celebrate.

We could have ensured I would avoid labor by delivering our baby even earlier, but our doctor booked a tropical vacation the week before and the thirteenth was the first date she could schedule our delivery. I found her cheerful announcement of the trip irritating. I wished I could have escaped on a tropical vacation. There was no escaping the inevitable for us now.

Our parents arrived from Illinois a few days before the scheduled C-section. We had not seen them since the holidays six weeks before and their presence gave us the familiar support we needed. They were in the hospital waiting room when Ashley was born and would be there for us during this delivery as well.

My mother clutched me in a long embrace the moment she walked through our front door. Nearly crumpling into her arms like a child, my body was weary from the burdens and heartache of the last months, especially the last weeks. She looked past me to Brian, certainly noticing his limp frame, pale face, and dark circles under his eyes. I knew my mother saw the same on my face as well.

The sad expressions of Brian's parents matched their quiet dispositions. Brian naturally followed them to the room where they would be sleeping to help them unpack. Understanding the value of being with your own parents, I let the three of them spend some time together. Instead of the usual joking, laughing, and loud exclamations about the wins and losses of their favorite sports teams, there was just the quiet hum of their solemn conversation.

The day before the scheduled delivery was mostly like any other day. The mothers went through the motions of cooking a big turkey dinner. We quietly ate the tasteless meal as the looming fear sucked the flavor out of our lives entirely. I forced myself to eat that night, transforming it into one last nourishing meal for our unborn baby while she was still safely inside my womb.

Ashley sang every song she knew to her grandparents. She proudly showed them her new room with her big girl bed. They played and laughed with her, attempting to be no different from any other visit. We appreciated their efforts, knowing just how difficult it was.

We tried to make the best of the last threads of joy we could grasp onto that night for little Ashley as she opened early Valentine's Day presents. However, our ragged hearts were heavy and the six of us struggled to keep the conversation going. No one dared to speak of what the next day would bring for our whole family.

As Brian and I lay there in bed the night before Brielle was born, we fought back any remaining tears we had. Six years before, we vowed to be with one another through sickness and health, for better or worse. We huddled in each other's arms as sleep eluded us. The Wisconsin winter nights never felt as cold and lonely as that one did. We were keenly aware that the events of the next day would change our lives forever.

But we are looking forward to the new heavens and new earth he has promised, a world filled with God's righteousness. And so, dear friends, while you are waiting for these things to happen, make every effort to be found living peaceful lives that are pure and blameless in his sight.

– 2 PETER 3: 13-14 (NLT)

CHAPTER 6

Birth Day

Brielle and I are shopping at the mall on a quiet weekday morning. We see a man with his arm around a woman coming towards us. She is pregnant, probably nearly full term, and walking gingerly with her hand pressed against her lower back.

"That lady is going to have a baby soon," I sign in secrecy to Brielle as the couple strolls closer to us.

"Oh, cute," signs Brielle back to me. "I don't have a baby in my tummy." My 14-year-old startles me with her statement.

"No," I sign back as the couple passes us. "Me neither."

Final Preparations

Parents remember their child's birth in great detail. The memories become somewhat like a war story that they share with others for years to come. Our tale of Brielle's birth is a war story indeed.

The day we looked forward to, as well as dreaded, finally arrived. We woke up before the sun the morning of the delivery. I am not sure how, but Brian and I managed to get a few hours of sleep.

Brian and I, along with our parents, moved around the house silently going through our typical morning routines on a day that would be anything but typical. Brian got our sleepy little Ashley ready. One of the grandparents could have stayed home with Ashley, but they all wanted to be at the hospital for us, whether things went well or not. Each of us mustered up a cheerful good-bye for her. I could not help but to think about how her life would change this day as well.

Brian and Ashley were waiting as the doors to her daycare opened. By the time he returned home, we were all ready to go. He loaded our suitcase and the infant car seat into our minivan with hopes that it would carry our new, healthy baby home in just a few days.

Brian, his parents, my parents, and I gathered in the living room, a somber group anticipating the events that were about to unfold. As the six of us stood shoulder to shoulder in a circle holding hands, I led us in a simple prayer for my safety during the delivery and for the health of Brielle. That short, quiet time together calmed and connected us together like soldiers about to do battle.

As we walked out of the house into the cold Wisconsin February air, I wondered if we would be bringing our baby back through those doors or if our child would be part of that forty percent of babies affected prenatally with CMV that died.

The hospital in Marshfield was better prepared to handle our sick baby than our local hospital just a few minutes from our neighborhood in Eau Claire. We drove three separate vehicles to the hospital 90 minutes away. Brian and I held hands straddling the center console, but rode those miles in silence.

As the rising sun streamed light across the road ahead, I looked out the window past my own reflection. Trees and farmhouses dotted that stretch of country roads edged with the remnants of a previous snowfall. Memories of happier days kept rolling by. I began to think about how our lives were going to change this day no matter what happened and knew Brian was thinking the same thing.

Settling In

We went through the regular hospital registration process, signed all the paperwork, and attached a white, hospital identification bracelet around my wrist. By mid-morning, they assigned me a pre-op room with a single bed in it and asked me to change into the usual stylish hospital gown.

Heaving myself onto the hospital bed, nurses moved around the room setting things up while an anesthesiologist asked me a few questions. One nurse stretched an oversized belt around my mammoth waist to monitor our baby's heartbeat while another poked the back of my hand to insert an IV port. Working in perfect coordinated movements, the medical team was a NASCAR pit crew buzzing around me.

Our parents waited just outside the door while Brian leaned against the far wall of the room trying to stay out of the way with his hands shoved deep into the front pockets of his jeans. I could not help but wonder what he was thinking, although I had a pretty good guess.

The perinatologist came into the room, asked her own prepared questions, and recited a long list of risks of having a C-section before asking me to sign yet another form. The nurses enthusiastically gathered around her, complimenting the doctor on her tan as she spoke about her recent tropical vacation. I lay there listening to their merry chatter, annoyed and wondering how anyone could be so cheerful when this dreadful day was unfolding around us. Brian rolled his eyes at the absurdity of the situation and shifted his weight nervously from one foot to the other. I pulled up the thin blanket over my chest. The chill of lingering fears felt as physical as it was emotional.

Moments after the doctor and nurses left and our parents returned to our room, a large bouquet of flowers arrived from my parents' elderly neighbor. Although it was a kind gesture, the premature congratulations card accompanying the fragrant flowers sickened me. We had nothing to celebrate. Sensing my anxiety about the cheerful blossoms, my mother moved the vase to the far side of the small room and simply nodded her head at me with a knowing look.

As I lay there in the hospital bed bracing myself for the 12:30 scheduled delivery of our child, Brian and our parents stood around the edge of my bed. An awkward silence hung thick in the air as I volleyed glances to each of them, trying to ignore the four walls that seemed to be closing in on me.

It was hard to believe that after everything we had gone through over the last eight months – chicken pox, doctors' visits, ultrasounds, the amniocentesis, consultations with specialists, and all of the worrying – Brielle's birth was mere minutes away.

One of life's illusions is the notion that every child is conceived in love, born through pain, and followed by great joy. There had been love. There had been pain. Joy was never guaranteed. Instead, there was the possibility of great tragedy.

We desperately clung to the last bits of hope that seemed to have somehow faded away the night before in our restless sleep or drifted off somewhere on the snowy road to the hospital.

My mother held my hand and looked down at me waiting in the hospital bed. She was a mother looking at her child in emotional pain and about to endure physical pain. She could not help but notice my eyes were dark and lost.

"It will be time soon. You and the baby will be fine," she squeaked out in some sort of optimistic way. "I just know it."

I tried to draw out a smile as her familiar musky perfume enveloped me, but my face was frozen from the dread that gripped my heart.

Each parent told us their good-byes and hugged us tearfully. Brian's mother clung to him, hoping that long embrace would help make the minutes and hours ahead easier. It did. There is nothing like a mother's hug.

With the parents gone, Brian and I were alone for a few minutes before the medical staff took us to the operating room to deliver Brielle. We waited in that pre-op room helpless and silent. What could be said at this point? My husband just held my hand and kissed my forehead. This could have been the time to offer up one last prayer or to talk to our baby still safe inside my tummy. Instead, we savored these last moments alone.

Special Delivery

"Are you two ready to have this baby?" The nurses startled us when they came back to move me onto a rolling gurney. I awkwardly shifted myself over to the narrow gurney with my oversized stomach. This was no easy task with the addition of the bands around my stomach and IV tube coming from my hand.

Brian followed behind as the two nurses rolled the gurney to the operating room. White ceiling tiles and florescent light panels swooshed over my head as we made our way down the hallway. I remember thinking it was like a camera shot I had seen so many times in the movies and on television. What a silly, irrelevant thought at a time like that.

When we arrived at the operating room, a nurse helped me transfer again to the operating table. She sat me up on the solid slab and firmly pulled my head down to hunch over my plump belly so the anesthesiologist could insert a needle between my vertebrae. I was hooked up to more tubes and wires and splayed out like a frog ready to be dissected. Panic rose up inside of me as my arms were strapped down straight out from my shoulders.

Brian, now donning pale, green scrubs as well as a cap and a facemask, crouched down next to my head straddling a small rolling chair. He stroked my hair, looked right into my eyes, and tried to reassure me as tears silently fell from my cheeks. I felt so lucky to have such a supportive husband go through this ordeal with me. He seemed to have a gift for knowing when I needed some encouragement, a hug, a distraction, or even a little space.

Then, it was time to deliver Brielle and I was terrified.

An army of doctors, nurses, and specialists filled that cold, sterile operating room – definitely more people than there were for Ashley's C-section birth. The neonatologist greeted us and told us he would be taking our baby immediately to a nearby room to care for her and that Brian would be told if and when he could follow them.

"So, who's ready to meet their baby today?" a young, bubbly doctor assisting the perinatologist introduced herself to us. "I just finished my cosmetic surgery rotation and I guarantee I can make your scar from this C-section practically invisible," she winked at me.

Like I cared even a little bit about the physical scar from delivering Brielle. What would happen to the emotional scars? Who would help heal those?

Brielle Greets the World

The two female doctors worked quickly and jabbered on about the perinatologist's tropical escape in between calling for medical instruments. Monitors behind my head beeped a rhythmic echo of my heartbeat from the disks taped to my chest while a black cuff around my upper arm automatically took my blood pressure every few minutes.

"You're doing just fine," the anesthesiologist called out lifeless words of encouragement he probably repeated to his patients countless times each day.

From behind the raised sheet that kept us from seeing my innards spread out as they opened my abdomen to pull Brielle from my womb, we heard our baby screaming a beautiful, strong cry. Tears flowed down my face. Brian and I stared at each other and silently reassured one another that hearing her cry was a good thing.

After a few moments to clean her up, a nurse brought Brielle close to my head and let me briefly touch her hand even though my arm was still strapped down to the operating table. Our 7 pound 6 ounce baby was loosely wrapped in a white cloth, still crying but was the most beautiful, perfect looking newborn I had ever seen. She did not have purple spots like the doctors warned us she might have and her perfectly shaped head did not appear particularly small.

The neonatologist took Brielle from the nurse and hustled our baby away to the adjoining room to start examining her. Through a large window in the door, we could see several doctors and nurses crowding around her.

Finally, a nurse came in the operating room and told Brian he could join them. Tears still flowing, I emphatically ordered my husband to stay with our baby, no matter what. He kissed my forehead through his facemask and rushed into the room where little Brielle was the focus of so much attention. And I was left alone.

In the aftermath of the delivery, the room had an eerie silence despite the rhythm of the heart and blood pressure monitors. I surrendered myself to the emotions of the room. The anesthesiologist wiped the tears from my face with a tissue but offered few words of comfort. Laying there for a long time, the young doctor fresh off her cosmetic surgery rotation put me back together and sewed me neatly up.

I tried to see into the room over my right shoulder where our new baby was, but I could not see her with all of the people swarming around. Although I felt scared and vulnerable while at the mercy of the medical personnel in the operating room, hearing Brielle sporadically cry in the next room reassured me. At one point, Brian turned around and gave me the "thumbs up" through the window. Even not knowing exactly what that meant, I breathed a huge sigh of relief from his small gesture. Within a few minutes, they whisked our baby out of that room to some other place with Brian following behind them. Then I was truly alone.

Recovery Room Woes

The doctors finished their work and moved me to the recovery area. A gruff nurse cared for me as I lay there behind a tall, white curtain trying to get the feeling back in my lower body that had been heavily anesthetized. The woman, clad in a polyester white nurses' pantsuit that was at least one size too small for her heavy frame, took my vitals and furiously made notes on my chart attached to a metal clipboard.

"This bracelet matches your baby's, so we know she belongs to you," she explained, attaching a second white identification bracelet to my wrist.

Yes, indeed, the baby belongs to me.

"Can you feel this?" she asked, poking up and down my legs. "Can you wiggle your toes for me?" she asked, lifting the white woven blankets that failed to keep me warm in that cold room.

Other than the nurse's repeated questions, the only sound came from her squeaky, white work shoes and the blood pressure cuff that periodically tightly squeezed my arm. I aimlessly connected the dots of the tiny holes in the ceiling tiles over my head as I twisted the patient identification bands that encircled my wrist. The pain medication made me loopy and any real sense of time was absent.

As the morphed minutes rolled by, thoughts about our baby whirled through my drugged-up mind. Where was she? Was she OK? Did our parents know she had been born and was alive? I thought about Ashley at daycare and how our cheerful, curly-headed, little girl had no idea she was now a big sister.

After I was successfully able to move my toes and ankles in proper circles to the satisfaction of the stoic nurse, two new nurses wheeled me into a private hospital room on the maternity ward. This room would be my home for the next few days as I recovered from the surgery. It was a much more welcoming place than I had been in all day, but I was still alone despite the nurses who bounced in and out of my room recording new vitals on my chart and adjusting extra pillows behind my back.

A Proper Introduction

Finally, Brian came in smiling, still in his scrubs, holding our little girl. She was wrapped tightly in a pink blanket with a knitted hat on her head.

"Mama, meet your little girl," Brian said as he placed Brielle in my arms.

It was a precious moment when I looked down at our baby's sweet face and little body nestled up against mine. Brielle was alive and seemed perfectly healthy.

"She's beautiful," Brian cooed over our new baby. "Just look at her."

I admired my work as I cradled our second-born child close to my aching heart. Her eyes were tightly shut and her bright pink lips puckered as she slept.

"Yes," I took a deep breath and exhaled. "She is absolutely perfect."

We could finally take a moment to relax and enjoy the beautiful moment. Our tears from the tangible sense of dread about the day magically turned into smiles of jubilation.

We did not know yet what our future would bring. There were many questions still left unanswered as Brian and I delighted in our newborn baby. However, we knew that Brielle was alive and did not appear sick or in any life-threatening danger at all. An almost irrational sense of optimism replaced our fears as hope was restored and we could begin celebrating.

February 13th would never again be a day that would go by unnoticed. It was the day we brought our second daughter into this world – alive, crying, and beautiful.

> *Do not be anxious about anything,*
> *but in every situation, by prayer and petition,*
> *with thanksgiving, present your requests to God.*
>
> – Philippians 4:6 (NIV)

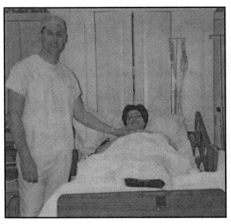 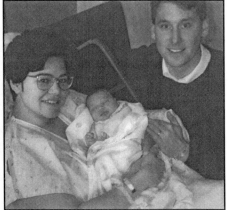

CHAPTER 7

At the Hospital

"Look, Dad," Brielle signs and turns in place with a bit of a wobbly step. "I am doctor like at hospital," she adds.

At eight years old, Brielle already knows a lot about doctors and feels right at home in her doctor's costume for Halloween.

"You look great," Brian tells her as he adjusts the stethoscope around her neck. "I hope you get lots of candy!" he says handing her a trick-or-treat bag with a big pumpkin face on it.

Meet the Grandparents

With cameras at the ready and plenty of fresh film and batteries as backup, our parents were eager to meet their new granddaughter. Brian operated the video camera to record each grandparent holding our sleepy newborn. They took turns rocking our little angel and marveling at how adorably little she was at over a pound and a half smaller than Ashley was at birth.

MORE ABOUT....
The Role of My Church
(during our stay at the hospital)

On the afternoon of the day Brielle was born, the secretary at my church called my hospital room and eagerly asked questions about our new baby and my health. Promising to send the news through the prayer chain, I felt like she was treating our situation as a source of gossip rather than an opportunity for Christian compassion.

My pastor never personally called or took the time to come see us despite our tenuous situation.

"She's so beautiful," my mother kept repeating and Brielle certainly was. Although the doctors had yet to complete more sophisticated tests, she appeared to be perfectly healthy.

My father was still desperately worried about me, even though the worst was over. He focused nearly all of his attention during those first minutes on me, asking me how I was feeling and offering to bring me water or more pillows.

Finally, when the other three grandparents had their turn holding Brielle, he seemed more at ease and eventually took Brielle gingerly in his arms. This was the child he worried might change our lives. Indeed, she had already. Although his primary focus was on me, his own daughter, he now took joy in the birth of his new granddaughter as well. Seeing him hold her like that demonstrated that Brielle had already found a special place in his heart.

Interrupting Family Time

By mid-afternoon, only an hour after Brian brought our newborn to me, a nurse came in with a hospital bassinet to wheel our baby away. The doctors told us before Brielle was delivered that she would need extensive tests to determine how healthy she was and what kind of damage CMV did to her body, particularly to her liver.

Time to play the waiting game once again as the doctors did more testing.

It was difficult to give Brielle up to the nurse. We only had a short time together and she was already being taken away. We tried not to worry as we thought about the testing. We wondered how long they would keep her away, if they would hold her enough when she cried, and, of course, when we would get the results.

Even as we waited, we were eager to share the news of our baby girl with the rest of our family and friends. In 1996, there were neither cell phones for calling and texting nor Internet to email or update social media statuses and blogs. We did it the old-fashioned way. Brian and our parents used the payphone in the hallway and let the news spread through our informal phone tree. Everyone was as relieved and excited as we were.

Our parents left later that afternoon to pick up Ashley from daycare and spend the evening with her at our house. They took the new big sister out for pizza and joyously toasted Brielle's arrival with their water glasses.

Brielle was safely returned to us and Brian quietly rocked her as I dozed. After our emotionally and physically exhausting day, I was happy to have some time to take a catnap. Later, Brian made a trip down to the hospital cafeteria to get some dinner for himself while I had chicken broth and wiggly Jell-O to look forward to.

Unexpected Test Results

The neonatologist came by on his rounds that first evening to share the results of some of Brielle's tests.

"Your child's EKG showed a slightly abnormal heart rhythm," the doctor coolly reported, patting Brielle's head as she lay in my arms.

"What does that mean?" Brian asked him.

> ### MORE ABOUT....
> # EKG (Electrocardiography)[1]
>
> An EKG is a painless test that records the heart's electrical activity through electrodes attached to the skin. It indicates:
>
> - How fast the heart is beating
> - Whether the rhythm of the heartbeat is steady or irregular
> - The strength and timing of electrical signals as they pass through each part of the heart

In usual medical jargon, using way too many technical terms, acronyms, and abbreviations, the neonatologist explained what Brielle's heart was doing. He showed us the extra spikes on her EKG printout. Throughout the long strip of grid paper, tiny spikes were circled in red pen.

Between the pain medication and the effects of the spinal anesthesia clouding my brain, I could not process what the doctor was telling us. My eyes could barely focus on the spikes that looked more like a topographical map of some majestic mountain range rather than an interpretation of our newborn's little beating heart.

I was grateful Brian was there to make sense out of this news. He peppered the doctor with questions. Why didn't we see this on the ultrasounds? Is this serious? Does she need medication for it? Will surgery be necessary?

"It's nothing to be highly concerned about and will probably resolve itself within a few days," the doctor replied, almost too casually. "However, we'd like to keep her in the NICU while she's here to monitor it."

Nothing to be highly concerned about? Had this doctor ever been on this side of the metal clipboard receiving news about something wrong with his newborn's heart?

Once the neonatologist left our room, Brian sat on the edge of my hospital bed in silence just staring at Brielle who lay quietly in my arms. NICU? Neonatal Intensive Care Unit? It was frightening to imagine our baby in an incubator hooked up to monitors just like preemies and frail, sick newborns.

Within a few minutes, a nurse wearing scrubs decorated with clowns appeared at our door with a rolling bassinet to whisk away our baby. With my mind still trying to process the news about Brielle's heart, my motherly protection instincts kicked in and I was reluctant to abruptly hand my baby over to this stranger.

"Could we please have a few more minutes with her?" I pleaded with the nurse.

"The doctor wants her admitted to the NICU immediately," the nurse replied without a smile. "But, I'll give you two minutes," she begrudgingly added with only a hint of kindness.

We kissed the top of Brielle's head, let her briefly grasp our fingers with her tiny hands, and hesitantly placed her in the bassinet for the nurse to wheel down the hall to the NICU. I felt like someone was ripping her out of my body all over again and my eyes began to swell with tears.

Brian started to follow the nurse pushing the bassinet out of the room, but she promptly put up a hand in warning.

"We'll need some time to get her set up," the nurse said firmly. "I'll let you know when you will be allowed to visit your baby."

Allowed to visit? Something was very wrong with that. Suddenly, it was as if our daughter was in prison and we had to obtain visitation rights from the warden, cleverly disguised as a nurse in colorful scrubs.

Neonatal Intensive Care Unit

The nurse finally came back to our room an hour later to tell us that Brielle would be paroled back to our room for regular feedings and that

Brian could spend some time in the NICU visiting her every few hours. He did not waste any time and immediately took off to see Brielle.

As Brian explained to me when he returned to my room, it was quite a process to be admitted back to see our baby. Parents first had to don fresh scrubs including a hat, booties over their shoes, and a facemask. There was a cavernous sink with foot pedals in place of knobs and a poster over the sink that spelled out explicit washing instructions along with detailed diagrams. There was even a large timer on the wall to make sure visitors soaped up for long enough. Finally, a nurse verified the matching hospital identification wristband before the properly dressed and scrubbed parents were allowed into the NICU.

Once a nurse buzzed Brian through the locked doors into the dimly lit room, there was a strict protocol for visitors. Although the large NICU area was cheerfully decorated and at a perfectly warm temperature, it was a cold, sterile place. The nurse escorted Brian past incubators, each draped with a colorful blanket that demanded anonymity for the precious soul inside. He could only guess what the many tubes and wires coming out from under the coverings were for. When machines beeped and buzzed, nurses scurried around and, sometimes, at the piercing sound of demanding alarms, visitors were hastily escorted out of the room.

Brian went to the NICU often and for as long as the nurses let him stay. From a rocking chair next to Brielle's incubator, he listened to her breathe rhythmically like the steady beat of a metronome and watched the bouncing green dot on the EKG monitor draw an endless series of mountain spikes to the beating of her little heart.

For a long time, the monitor was silent. Brian felt encouraged and gave silent coaching to his little girl to "keep it up." Then, a loud single beep on the monitor would break the silence and anger would come over him – anger at the machine, at the situation, and at his helplessness.

MORE ABOUT....
NICU (Neonatal Intensive Care Unit)

Talking with other parents visiting their babies in the NICU was discouraged. Nevertheless, as visitors walked through the encampment of incubators in that large NICU room, the worried, sad, and exhausted faces of mothers and fathers could not be ignored. Over the years, I thought back to those babies and their parents and wondered how they were doing, if they survived their stay at the hospital. I wonder if they ever think of Brielle and us.

My husband came back to my room weary, fighting back the tears he worked so hard to dam up. He had little news to share with me, but I was glad he was back to keep me company, just as I was glad when he left to check on Brielle.

When he was not visiting Brielle in the NICU, Brian ran for take-out food and goodies from vending machines to supplement the bland hospital fare. He continued to feed the hungry payphone in the hallway to give updates to friends and extended family members. The nurses did not allow parents to go back to the NICU during the night. Brian stayed with me in our hospital room sleeping on a pullout sofa with the feet of his six-foot-five frame dangling off the bottom.

Every few hours, a nurse brought Brielle to me for feedings as Brian perched on the edge of my hospital bed. This newborn had no idea what her parents were going through and how reassured they were to simply gaze at her sweet face. Then, right on schedule, the nurse would be back in our room within 30 minutes to bring our baby back to the NICU. Brielle's temporary parole was over.

Mom Recuperates

Once the fog from the anesthesia and pain medication lifted, my head was still swimming with worry as Brielle divided her time between feedings in our room, sleeping in the NICU, and going through a battery of tests elsewhere in the hospital. I was restless and could not concentrate long enough to read a book or page through a magazine. The soap operas and game shows that littered daytime television had no interest to me.

My mother was nearly always in a state of motion. When she was not cleaning up around my hospital room or refilling my water pitcher, she was watering and repositioning the growing number of plants and bouquets of flowers from well-wishers. She brought me warm cloths to wash my face and hands. When she brushed my hair, it brought back reassuring memories from my childhood. I think all of her busy work was my mother's way of contributing, somehow easing the stress and worries within the walls of that hospital room.

My perinatologist checked on me each morning and encouraged me to take things slow. I was eager to get up and moving, but tried to follow the doctor's orders. Wearing a flannel nightgown, warm robe, and fuzzy pink slippers brought from home, I took lackluster laps around the maternity ward halls to build up my strength. The muffled pages over the PA system echoed the hallways while newborns' crying streamed out from individual rooms.

When I got back to my room, I often found a few butterscotch disks on the rolling tray table next to the bed. My father-in-law would wink at me. He knew they were my favorite and always kept a few in his pocket.

Sometimes one or more of the grandparents walked with me to be a shoulder to lean on and to keep me company. They shared stories about how Ashley was doing and gave me drawings she had scribbled at daycare. We were reassured to have our parents with us at the hospital during the day while Ashley kept her routine at daycare and had fun with them in the evenings.

"This is such a special time in your lives," my mother-in-law told me as we shuffled down the hall arm in arm. "These days when your children are so little and depend so completely on you. Treasure these moments."

"How am I going to manage two small kids?" I asked her, imagining life with two children under the age of two.

"You're going to do great. You'll see. These years go by so quickly. One day, they won't be children any more at all."

With that melancholy statement, I realized just how difficult it must be to watch your grown children have their own children. It felt strange to think about Ashley or little Brielle having their own babies. Our parents had probably never imagined Brian or me as a parent when they first brought us home either.

On the afternoon of the third day in the hospital, my doctor finally cleared me to make the trip to see Brielle in the NICU. After the arduous walk down the long hallways to don the full regalia of proper NICU attire and scrub my hands at the cavernous sink with foot pedals, I sat in a rocking chair and watched Brielle in the incubator.

I hated being in that room with that unique, overpowering hospital smell. I hated, even worse, that Brielle had to be in there, but was glad she would never remember these first scenes of her life. The beeps and buzzes from all the babies' monitors made me jumpy. However, the silence in between was even worse. Those sick babies hardly ever cried. Other parents with grim faces hovered over bassinets, their own family's drama unfolding next to ours.

I never went back to the NICU. It was not that I did not want to see Brielle or that the preparation process was too difficult. It was just too painful to see those tented incubators, especially the one holding my baby.

The Final Results Are In

The neonatologist came into my hospital room during his rounds at the end of each day to report the test results. We mentally and emotionally prepared for his daily visits. We never knew what news he might bring, something encouraging or something completely devastating.

Most of what the neonatologist shared with us each afternoon was good news. The tests confirmed what we already knew. CMV was in her system, both in her urine and blood. Her white blood count showed signs that her body was still fighting that infection, but this was expected and not at all alarming. Her liver was functioning properly and initial hearing test results were normal. The full body ultrasound and x-rays showed only normal results.

The only other notable result was from the CT, which showed two very small calcifications on the left side of her brain. The doctor explained that calcifications are places in the brain where there have been inflammations, such as what CMV might cause, where calcium builds up.

"Does that mean she has brain damage?" Brian asked.

The doctor said it was difficult to say what the calcifications might mean and what effect they might have on her.

"Just monitor her for any developmental concerns over the next months and years," the doctor stated nonchalantly. He certainly did not seem alarmed and we were eager to believe him.

MORE ABOUT....
CT Scan (Computed Tomography Scan, also known as a CAT Scan)[1]

It is a noninvasive, painless medical procedure using sophisticated computer and special x-ray equipment to produce a series of images (much like slices of bread) of the inside of the body.

By the evening of the third day in the hospital, Brielle's doctor reported that her heart irregularity had resolved and was no longer a concern. Just as he said it probably would, that issue was now behind us. Although they continued to keep her in the NICU for observation, we breathed a huge sigh of relief and could not wait to be home with our beautiful baby.

Cue the music from "Rocky" as we triumphantly celebrate.

On the morning of the fourth day, the nurse came in to take my vitals and check my incision. She casually asked if I had passed gas yet. Really? On top of exposing my private parts to this complete stranger, I have to report my bodily functions, too? I knew what my answer needed to be in order for the hospital to release me. So, I lied.

"Sure have," I answered enthusiastically.

"Looks like you all will be able to go home this afternoon," she replied. With that, the nurse added notes to my medical chart and we were one step closer to going home.

Our Final Parole

My perinatologist gave the go ahead for me to take a much-needed shower as long as I was careful and Brian waited outside the door in case I needed help. I let the dirt and grunge run down the hospital shower drain along with the worries from the last days, weeks, and months. I truly felt renewed.

After my cautious shower, I begrudgingly put on loose-fitting maternity slacks over the mushy remains of my pregnant belly. I had hoped to be able to leave the hospital wearing something that was not from my well-worn maternity wardrobe, but that was just wishful thinking.

After my last bland lunch of mashed potatoes and flimsy turkey slices, I eagerly packed my few belongings while Brian rolled a cart into the room and gathered the grand assortment of flowers that had arrived from friends during our four-day hospital stay.

When the nurse finally came back with papers for us to sign and final instructions, Brian put Brielle in her oversized snowsuit and strapped her little body into the infant car seat. We could not get out of that hospital with our baby fast enough. We were grateful for the care we received, but we were even more grateful that we were all paroled for good this time.

I gingerly got myself into the backseat of our van to sit next to Brielle for the ride home. Every curve and bump in the road shot pains to my fresh incision, but I did not care. We were going home, all of us.

As we passed dairy cows on the snow-covered Wisconsin farms, I could not help but to think of the somber ride down that same road to the hospital just a few days ago. Our worries still lingered. What would be the lasting impact of CMV on Brielle's body? However, on this ride back home, we were filled with relief, joy, and hope for our new life to begin as a family of four.

> *May He give you the desire of your heart*
> *and make all your plans succeed.*
> *May we shout for joy over your victory*
> *and lift up our banners in the name of our God...*
>
> – Psalm 20:4-5 (NIV)

CHAPTER 8

And Baby Makes Four

When we arrive home, our little white dog greets us at the door. He yaps with ear-piercing terrier barks and jumps aimlessly in excitement.

"We're home, Cooper," Brielle signs to him over and over again until I interpret for her, as if our dog does not already know.

"We're home, Cooper," I finally say aloud for my teenager, as if our dog understands my speech any better than he understands her sign language.

Home Sweet Home

As we crossed the threshold of our house with our newborn baby, thoughts about the last time we were home entered my mind. It seemed so long ago that Brian and I, along with our parents, stood in a circle praying for our unborn child and worried that we might not come home with her at all.

The house felt very different. It was as if the windows had been left open to air it out, pushing out all the worries and bad energy of the previous eight months. In their place, fresh hope swept in and lit up the space.

Our lives were refreshed when Brielle was declared healthy and we walked out of the hospital. The dense fog that clouded our world and hung heavy on our shoulders just days before was lifted. We could finally fully embrace the experience of having a newborn. What a joy to arrive home with Brielle, alive and well, in our arms.

Our parents welcomed us home with hushed voices while Ashley was taking her afternoon nap. The grandmothers decorated the front picture window with balloons, streamers, and a big, colorful sign that read, "It's a girl!" Flowers, cards, and presents delivered to the house lined the window shelf. Once we added those from our hospital stay, the room looked like a crowded hospital gift shop.

We whispered in the living room while Ashley continued to sleep, completely unaware of our homecoming. The proud grandparents took turns holding Brielle and photographs were snapped from all angles like a professional photo shoot.

Sisters

When we heard Ashley moving around in her room, my father was holding Brielle but scrambled to get her into my arms for our first family photograph. My mother-in-law went into Ashley's room to bring her out. With cameras and video recorders in hand, everyone was ready to capture the big moment. When our sleepy little girl finally made her way over to where I was holding Brielle, she seemed only faintly interested in meeting her new baby sister.

"Juice, please," she asked Brian as she rubbed her nose.

Ashley was a typical two-year-old, more interested in her routine than she was in the bundle in Mom's arms. Naps and then juice. That was Ashley's routine. Why would this day be any different?

With sippy cup in hand, she came back over to her little sister with curiosity. Her bouncy, dark blonde curls were a frizzy mess all around her face. I had a fleeting desire to take a few moments to brush through them to make her more presentable for all of the pictures. But, I let that thought go. Who cares about coiffed hair on a two-year-old at a moment like that?

That evening, the pasta dinner with salad the grandmothers made for us was the first meal we all shared together since that tasteless turkey dinner just five nights before. My in-laws bought a "welcome home" cake for us and we opened the gifts and cards well-wishers had left on our doorstep. Several had sent along gifts for Ashley and she was thrilled to have presents to open as well.

Because of their jobs, Brian's parents had to head back to Illinois after we had only been home one day. Since my dad was retired, my parents were able to stay for another week and we were grateful for the help. Caring for a newborn and a two-year-old was more than Brian and I expected. It would take some time to adjust to our new, more complicated parenting duties.

Recovering at Home

To maintain her routine, Ashley continued to go to daycare during part of the day. After being away from his office for nearly a week, Brian went back to work Monday morning, just two days after arriving home from the hospital. I had no intention of rushing back to work any sooner than I had to, but instead planned to take advantage of the full three months of maternity leave available to me.

Nursing every few hours was physically exhausting, but Brielle was a calm newborn those first few weeks otherwise. I continued to recover from the surgery while my parents took over most of the household duties. My mother prepared dinners and took care of Ashley while my father did what he could by emptying the dishwasher, folding laundry, and running the vacuum. The Wisconsin days in February were too cold and icy to be outdoors. So, I made laps around the house, slowly increasing my pace and duration each day.

Two weeks after Brielle was born, when we were finally alone in the house, just Brian and me with our two little girls, we began our life as a family of four.

We played with Ashley and listened to her tell stories about her friends at daycare. We lay Brielle on a blanket on the floor and kissed her ten perfect little fingers and ten perfect little toes. Brian and I talked and laughed together when we were alone late at night. Despite the fatigue of feedings that repeatedly interrupted our sleep, it was so good to feel normal again. We had almost forgotten how that felt.

Ashley was also warming up to Brielle and her new role as the big sister. She did not seem to care if having a little sister meant suddenly halving the attention she received from her mom and dad. It did not take long for her to start being Mommy's little helper by bringing me clean diapers and burp cloths. She made silly faces at her baby sister and pretended to read to her while Brielle was in her bouncy seat. Ashley put her dolls in the baby swing, gave them bottles, and fussed over them just as she watched us do for Brielle. It was precious.

Appreciating Our Circle of Friends

Neighbors and friends came by to see our new baby and showered her with more gifts. Some of them had shared our concerns from the first weeks of my pregnancy when I had chicken pox. For the first time, we could all celebrate the relief of knowing Brielle was healthy and thriving.

"I just felt sick inside thinking about what you and Brian were going through," my neighbor friend, Jayni, told me as she held our baby.

"I prayed and prayed for you, but I just felt so helpless," another neighbor friend, Nancy, chimed in as she rubbed the dark peach fuzz on Brielle's head.

Their comments startled me. For the first time, I realized how oblivious I had been to my friends' pain while trying to cope with my own. Stumbling over my words, I tried to apologize for my self-centeredness.

"Don't be ridiculous," Jayni said, adjusting Brielle in her arms. "It wasn't about us. It was about this child. You were in no state of mind to do anything for us and our worries and we never expected you to."

"Don't give it another thought," Nancy reassured me. "We just tried to be there for you and thought it best not to tell you how truly worried we were."

"Just look at Brielle," Jayni said, holding up our child. "She is a precious gift."

The baby showers that had been put on hold before Brielle was born were back on again. My co-workers hosted a luncheon a few weeks after Brielle was born. From the moment Brielle and I arrived in the office, the women swarmed around us to catch a glimpse of my newborn. My steady friend, Minnette, was the first to hold her. To my surprise, my sophisticated young boss eagerly snatched Brielle from Minnette's arms without a thought for her expensive suit.

I was excited to celebrate my baby's birth with my co-worker friends and also proud to show her off. There was a time just a month before when I felt like a ghost walking through the maze of cubicles at that office. Now my ghostly days were behind me. We packed into the conference room among the food and decorations passing Brielle from one co-worker to another as I opened presents and retold the story of the day she was born and the days that followed.

Brian's co-workers hosted a baby shower for him as well. Brielle and I stopped by at the end of the party so that everyone could meet Brian's newborn. Although men were invited to all of the baby showers given for mothers and fathers-to-be, Brian's male co-workers seemed uneasy in this festive environment. As the large group of women gathered around us, the men perused the long table of food.

Brian's boss, Russ, shyly gave me a knowing look of relief from across the cafeteria. Russ was one of the few people in Brian's world that he opened up to during the pregnancy and truly knew our struggles. When we had a moment alone, I thanked Russ for researching CMV for us and for being such a good support for Brian.

"I'm happy that everything turned out so well," he added as the biochemist's façade cracked a little while giving me a one-armed embrace.

The rest of the men and women at Brian's office baby shower knew very little about our struggles with the pregnancy. Brian rarely opened up to his few friends, and certainly not to his co-workers. For once, I was glad Brian had kept things to himself. Brian's story of being a father desperate with worry was his own. And that story was now history.

When we walked through the grocery store or other public places with Baby Brielle, I beamed with pride at the wide smiles and compliments from strangers. They did not know our story of worry and pain either. I liked being anonymous, just like all the other moms out there with new, perfect babies.

More Celebrations

Ashley's second birthday festivities in early March included her favorite dinner, macaroni and cheese. We sang "Happy Birthday" to her as she blew out candles on the cake I baked for her. She squealed with delight as she opened presents, each more exciting than the last. Ashley reminded us just how fast she was growing up by using her best manners on the phone to thank grandparents and extended family members for their birthday gifts to her.

Brian and I celebrated our sixth wedding anniversary a week later. It was a quiet evening at home playing with our little girls. No frills or special outings. However, it was a sentimental day at a time when we had so much to celebrate.

As we often do on our anniversary, we leafed through our wedding album. Who were those young people? What did they expect out of life? So many marriages might not have endured the troubles we had already gone through. However, those trials made our devotion and appreciation of one another even stronger. I could not imagine going through that previous year without Brian.

When Easter arrived the first weekend in April, we colored eggs with Ashley and watched *Here Comes Peter Cottontail.* On Easter morning, she found a basket filled with little toys and trinkets. She searched for plastic eggs around the house and became more enthusiastic in her hunting when she learned those colorful eggs had candy inside of them. I dressed both girls in frilly dresses to attend Easter church services and cooked a traditional ham dinner that evening. It truly was a season of renewal and joy.

At the end of April, all four of our parents returned to Wisconsin to be with us when Brielle was baptized. It was the first time they visited since the week of Brielle's birth and were eager to commemorate their visit by snapping photographs all weekend long.

Brian and his parents were not religious. However, they were respectful of the traditional Methodist baptismal ceremony and knew how important it was to me. My parents stood with us and were named Brielle's godparents, formally committing to help her grow spiritually as she grew up.

MORE ABOUT....
My Pastor and Brielle's Baptism

The pastor who presided over Brielle's baptism was the same pastor who had disappointed me with the lack of care during my pregnancy and hospital stay. I could have been bitter. Instead, I let it all go. There was simply so much joy in the moment we dedicated our child to God, I could not focus on what he did and did not do.

My mother lovingly sewed the baptismal gown along with a matching coat and bonnet. Ashley wore the same outfit two years before during her baptism and Brielle looked angelic wearing it as well. This handmade ensemble was quickly becoming a family tradition on its way to becoming an heirloom.

Two weeks after Brielle's baptism, it was Mother's Day. We went to our favorite restaurant for a special brunch and I opened a few presents including a handmade card from Ashley. We played together outside on that warm, spring afternoon. It was a glorious day to celebrate being a mother to our two beautiful girls. We were a family who found hope again and looked forward to a bright future.

Back to the Rest of Our Lives

As my three-month maternity leave was coming to a close, I felt the anxiousness of both sadness and excitement. I loved being at home with Brielle and really enjoyed the extra time I had with Ashley. On the other hand, I enjoyed my job and was eager to get back to my marketing career.

Those months at home gave me time to reflect on the pregnancy and the child it produced. Only after recollecting it all did I realize just how much I held inside of me. I let so many negative emotions overpower all other thoughts during the pregnancy. I did not notice the difference until there was a reprieve from the heavy weight of those worries. For the first time in months, I finally felt like I could breathe again.

Dark circles under my eyes and premature worry lines that made their home between my brows were finally gone. In their place, the mirror revealed something remarkable, a smile.

I believed that in the years to come, the dark days of being pregnant with Brielle would eventually fade. Only the joyful memories of those first months at home would rise to the surface. Those happier times would be the stories we told.

I dreamed about the future, especially about Brielle's first day of kindergarten, her high school graduation, and Brian dancing with her on her wedding day. While toasting the joyous occasions of her life, I imagined that we would tell the story of a time when we worried so much about her very survival. No one would believe us seeing how perfect she will be on those days of great celebration.

Although we had so much to be thankful for and hopeful about, worry and fear were stubborn bedfellows. I became accustomed to their lingering shadows on the walls around me, taunting me that something still could be wrong with my child. Despite all of the happiness in our lives, small wisps of worry and fear persisted in some dark, dusty corner of my mind.

What would the future bring? Would those shadowy feelings eventually fade away? Or would they take a solid form and prove to be right? I had no crystal ball. Only time would reveal the answer.

However many years anyone may live,
let them enjoy them all. But let them remember
the days of darkness, for there will be many...
— Ecclesiastes 11: 8 (NIV)

CHAPTER 9

Troubling Times

"I sick, too," Brielle signs to me moments after I sneeze three times in a row. She imitates the motion of a sneeze and covers her mouth with her forearm. "Good catch," she signs.

"You're not sick," I tell her.

"Yes, very sick," she signs.

I give her a skeptical look and turn away. Brielle is quite the dramatic actress, always on the hunt for a little sympathy.

Joyful Times, Stressful Times

Through the joyful times and celebrations in the first few months after Brielle was born, we had concerns about her health and well-being. Some concerns were haunting whispers echoing our fears and worries from the pregnancy. Other concerns about Brielle became more tangible. A few issues became so overwhelming that they tainted much of our daily lives. Although we tried to focus on the good moments, it was not always possible.

Even from her first days in the hospital, Brielle had difficulty latching on while breastfeeding. She might suck for a few minutes, at best, and then break her seal. She would then begin to cry, as if something was wrong or she lost patience with the activity.

A lactation nurse came by my hospital room to counsel me on feeding positions. Making a few adjustments seemed to help. If nothing else, it made me feel like I was doing something to improve the situation.

Once my breast milk came in, I could hear Brielle swallowing and felt better knowing she was getting some nutrition. However, she continued to break her seal and I ended up with a lap full of milk. It was frustrating to know she was not getting the hang of it and all I was getting was wet pants.

This was not the same experience I had breastfeeding Ashley and I knew something was wrong. Neither my mother nor my mother-in-law ever breastfed their children, so they had no advice to share. The baby books I read did not give any suggestions about what to do if a mom got soaked during feedings. Brielle's pediatrician gave me no useful advice either. I tried the different positions the lactation nurse in the hospital suggested, but things did not improve.

Despite the feeding issues, Brielle slowly but steadily gained weight and I simply placed a towel under her to keep my lap dry. I was managing the nursing problems, but something inside nagged at me. This was not breastfeeding at its best and I wondered why.

Earplugs and Extreme Patience Required

When Brielle was about two weeks old, she started crying inconsolably for hours at a time. We suspected what it was and our pediatrician eventually confirmed it. Colic.

We knew about dreadful colic. As an infant, Ashley had a mild case lasting for about an hour each evening. It was heartbreaking to watch, but it was tolerable and, thankfully, over within a few weeks.

Once Brielle's colic episodes began, her crying escalated to unrelenting wailing. At its worst, she cried during almost all of her waking hours for days at a time. We tried all sorts of positions as well as rocking, pacing, and even trips in the car. Nothing eased her discomfort and crying.

Ashley covered her ears during the day and miraculously slept like a rock through Brielle's crying at night. Brian and I, on the other hand, lost sleep and became increasingly frustrated, desperate for relief.

When I called the pediatrician's office to explain Brielle's symptoms, the nurse told us our baby would grow out of it within a few months.

MORE ABOUT....
Colic[5]

- Is a fairly common condition in which an otherwise healthy baby cries inconsolably, frequently and for extended periods without any apparent reason.
- Affects up to 25 percent of babies.
- Usually starts a few weeks after birth and often improves by the age of three months.
- Has no known causes, although excessive gas in the digestive system is one prominent theory.
- Has no formal tests, but is diagnosed based on caregiver reports about the frequency, duration, and symptoms presented during crying episodes.
- Can be treated with several homeopathic and over-the-counter medications as well as infant formula brands that can ease colic symptoms. (However, these were not available to us in 1996.)

"There's really nothing that can be done," the nurse explained. "Don't worry. Just do the best you can and it will pass."

Seriously? The nurse's words sounded as ridiculous as a fire-fighter telling us that despite the smoke detector going off, there is no fire and to just wait for it to turn off when the battery dies out in three months.

We were not good at being patient and letting it pass as simply as the nurse suggested. As parents, we wanted to do something, anything, to make our baby happy. We continued trying different comforting strategies, but in the end, the nurse was right. Brian and I limped through the motions of parenting, working, and maintaining the household as best as we could. Our only goal was surviving what we assumed would be a short period.

Over the course of a few weeks, Brian and I became increasingly frustrated that our efforts to soothe Brielle's crying were so unsuc-cessful. We lost sleep as well as our confidence as parents.

Brielle's constant crying became a source of anger, marital ten-sion, and despair. When her little sister cried, Ashley simply ignored her, often choosing to play in her room alone. There were other occa-sions where Ashley seemed to get grumpy as well. Our whole family craved peace and longed for happier times together.

Congestion, Worse Than a Traffic Jam

At about a month old, Brielle developed congestion and coughing that persisted despite taking several different over-the-counter med-ications for infants. There were times when she coughed so hard that she threw up. Our baby was sick, unhappy, and exhausted, much like her parents.

Our concerns for Brielle's health grew more intense when the con-gestion and coughing continued for months with no real relief even after completing several rounds of antibiotics. No matter what med-ication her pediatrician prescribed, Brielle just seemed to get worse.

At one point, her pediatrician tested her for whooping cough. As I helped the nurse hold Brielle still, the doctor placed metal sticks that resembled sparkler rods up Brielle's nose to rest for a few minutes on the back of her nasal passage where it met the back of her throat. She cried through the entire process and it was agonizing to watch.

The test results for whooping cough were negative, but Brielle's symptoms were unrelenting. We kept a vaporizer in her room and our ears on the baby monitor at night listening for any gagging or excessive coughing. Brielle developed several ear infections and bounced from one antibiotic to another. Despite the best efforts of her doctor, our baby could not get any relief and neither could we.

Forced Weaning

Between Brielle's feeding issues and congestion, breastfeeding became increasingly problematic. Because she did not latch on properly, suck eagerly, or empty my breasts while feeding, my milk production began to slow down. Attempts to use a breast pump to stimulate my milk were not successful. I increased my water intake, made sure I was eating well, and avoided caffeine products. Nothing seemed to help me produce more milk.

Wondering if Brielle's feeding issues might improve if we tried to bottle-feed her, we tried several different types of bottles and nipples. Our kitchen counter began to look like a test lab for *Good Housekeeping*. None of the bottles or nipples made anything better. Despite our efforts, her feeding issues and my need to use a towel to keep my lap dry did not change. Once my breast milk dried up when Brielle was six weeks old, we had to rely entirely on formula and bottles.

Bottle-feeding Brielle was not the same as breastfeeding. Although it gave Brian an opportunity to feed her, I was saddened to lose our exclusive mother-child bonding activity. Breast milk was best for Brielle and yet I could not give her something that should be so simple and easy to provide. It was out of my control, but I felt like a failure.

Our concerns and frustrations with Brielle's health grew each day. Brielle's cough, congestion, colic, and feeding issues were not improving. She continued to cry until at least the late night news started and awoke three or four times at night for feedings, making restful sleep impossible.

Caring for Brielle drained us. The only thing that gave us any encouragement to press on were the celebrations – Ashley's birthday, Easter, Brielle's baptism, and Mother's Day. However, over time, we became increasingly weary.

Breaking Point

When Brielle was about three months old, I left both girls with Brian one evening to attend a preschool board meeting at my church. When I arrived home a few hours later, I found Brielle behind her closed bedroom door, alone, exhausted, and crying stridently in her crib. Ashley slept soundly in her own room next door, oblivious to Brielle's loud cries. Despite Brielle's bawling, I could hear the volume on the television turned up loudly through the tightly shut door of our bedroom.

Brian crossed his arms firmly against his chest when I opened the door. The television remote lay on the bed next to him, broken into several pieces.

Brian's look of anger told the tale. I could easily imagine what happened at home in my absence. Brielle's endless, colicky crying was like rubbing salt into an already infected wound, painful to the core. It was only a matter of time before one of us reached our wit's end.

Seeing my husband so agitated was worrisome because it was so atypical. I often teasingly called him "Mr. Even Steven" because of his mild-mannered disposition. However, every person has his or her breaking point and my husband clearly hit his the evening I was gone.

I tried to manage Brian's frustration by helping him avoid the stress of Brielle's colic until her symptoms eventually subsided.

Without any real conversation with Brian about it, I took over almost all of Brielle's care and, when necessary, Brian took over Ashley's.

This sent us into a division over parenting duties in our household. Although relinquishing parts of our parenting responsibilities would cause complications later, dividing to conquer was necessary at a time when Brielle's colic was so horrible and Brian's patience was worn so thin.

MORE ABOUT....
My Faith During the Most Frustrating Times

Although I continued to attend church and serve on my church's preschool board, I merely went through the motions of being a Christian. I did not yet have a strong faith or a personal relationship with God, therefore, praying did not even occur to me.

Based on necessity, I used several strategies to cope with Brielle's endless crying. Going through the mental checklist parents use to try to comfort their child, I fed, burped, and checked her diaper. Finally, when repositioning and rocking did not soothe her wailing and I started to feel my blood pressure rise, I simply gave up and put Brielle in her crib, often closing the door behind me.

I breathed in. I breathed out. Finding my calm within, I surrendered to the helplessness and continued with my day as if I were deaf to Brielle's cries. My heart yearned for a positive mothering experience and I felt conflicted. Although I bonded with and loved Brielle very much, my exhaustion, frustration, and helplessness made it difficult to enjoy my time with her.

Our division of duties had many consequences. Sometimes I had to prompt Ashley to go to Brian for help with things when I was too busy with Brielle's care. There were times when her disappointed face at my refusal to play with her broke my heart. Watching Brian have special moments with Ashley that I was left out of was painful. I knew I could not do it all for both girls at this difficult time when Brielle was so needy. If only we could get through Brielle's colic, I assumed Brian and I would restructure our parenting and life would be better for all of us.

Routine is Comforting

During my maternity leave, Ashley attended daycare in the mornings most days to maintain her routine and keep her spot in her class-room. It also gave her a break from Brielle's colic cries. I picked up my toddler from daycare after lunch and tried to keep her awake until we arrived home. The girls took their afternoon naps and I had a little time to get housework done. We played together in the afternoon as Brielle's colic started to rev up in full force for the evening. When Brian came home from work, we all ate dinner together. He spent the evening playing with Ashley as I went through my routine trying to calm Brielle's escalating crying. Baths, bedtime stories, and off to bed we would all eventually go, only to be awakened through the night for Brielle's feedings. That had been our routine for three months.

However, it was time for me to get back to my job. Although I enjoyed being able to spend time with both of my girls (at least when Brielle was not crying), my plan was always to go back to work. The fatigue of caring for Brielle, especially at the height of her colic, was overwhelming. I worried about someone else having enough patience to endure the roughest moments, but I had great confidence in the daycare providers since they cared for Ashley so well.

The day I scheduled to go back to work arrived shortly after Mother's Day. Early that morning, I tugged on my old work clothes that had somehow shrunk since I last wore them. There was a tall pile of rejected garments on the floor by the time I found something that actually fit. I swiftly fed both girls their breakfast, dressed them, and loaded them into their car seats.

"Excited?" Brian asked me, holding his tie back as he leaned in the van to give each girl a kiss good-bye.

"I suppose," I replied, tossing two diaper bags in the passenger seat next to my purse. At the office I would not need to wipe anyone's nose, cut up anyone's food, or endure endless, inconsolable crying. I was thirsty for the adult companionship that work brought me.

"It will be fine," Brian said, brushing my short hair behind my ear. "Let's keep it simple tonight and order pizza."

"Sounds like a plan," I said, relieved to have one less thing to worry about in my day.

Driving the familiar road to take both girls to daycare, I found myself a little nervous. Three months away from the office was a long time. I wondered how much work piled up on my desk in my absence.

Ashley eagerly walked into her room at daycare as if it was any other day. A young woman in the infant room greeted me warmly and took Brielle from my arms. I hung my daughter's pink diaper bag on the wall hook below a freshly printed label with her name on it. I gave the young woman a few brief instructions as another helper took the bottles of formula and put them in a mini-fridge across the room.

And that was that. I walked out empty-handed, left with a strange feeling of peace mixed with longing.

Without the sounds of Ashley's chatter about her day or the sing-song voices from the van's cassette player chanting familiar children's tunes, I flipped on the radio to listen to the news. Even boring election talk about Clinton and Dole helped to drown out the silence that felt so unusual and uncomfortable.

As I pulled up to my office across town, I parked in a spot close to the door, a benefit of arriving early. I made my way to my cubicle and greeted several other early bird co-workers. It was nice to see familiar faces and they welcomed me back with smiles and hugs. Plopping my purse down on top of my desk, I was startled to find the flat surface nearly empty.

I placed a picture of Brielle on my desk next to the picture of Brian and Ashley taken the previous Christmas when I was still pregnant. I stashed my purse in an empty bottom drawer and took a deep breath, preparing to face my first day back at work. I then heard the familiar click-clack of my boss' high heels before I heard her voice.

"Oh, you're here already," she said enthusiastically. My stylish young boss greeted me with a hug, shifting a stack of files and papers in her arms. "I don't want to overwhelm you before you've even had a chance to get settled back in, but I've got plenty of work for you to do." With that, she dropped that stack of paperwork on the formerly empty space on my desk.

"Terrific," I replied sarcastically while mindlessly thumbing through the papers each tagged with instructions on yellow sticky notes scrawled with my boss' handwriting.

"It's not as bad as it looks. I'm just glad you're back," she smiled at me. "So, how are things with your baby?"

It was difficult to know how to answer that question. I could tell her about Brielle's feeding problems, her congestion and coughing, and her endless colicky crying. Or I could keep my mouth shut.

"Everything is fine," I said, mustering up positive thoughts and pasting a smile on my face. No matter how close we were, it was inappropriate to share our family's problems with my boss.

However, I did not talk about our troubles with many friends at all. What was the point? I realized other people wanted to show their compassion and interest by asking about Brielle. However, three months after her birth, when the life and death crisis and the initial fears of being severely disabled were over, people assumed everything was fine with her. Even when they asked general questions like, "Is she a good baby?" I did not know how to reply.

Friends could not do anything to help, not really. Whenever I talked with anyone about our troubles, even when it was with family, I only felt worse. Speaking of all of it at once made me realize just how awful things were and made those burdens feel heavy on my shoulders.

Instead, I guarded my thoughts and feelings closely, uttering no more than a few general comments about our "fussy baby" when pressed by friends. Some mothers might react differently, telling every awful detail of life to anyone who would listen. They might find comfort in the unsolicited advice and platitudes that would surely follow. They might even ask for physical help, someone to endure the colicky crying for an hour or two while they enjoy a dinner out with their husbands.

That was just not me.

My fierce independence and need to show I was strong and capable prompted me to keep it all in. I did not even talk with Brian about it. I locked it in a safe place, deep down inside of me, where no one would learn the truth. Years later, I would call that place "The Box." By shoving all of my feelings in "The Box," I did not have to face them. I could continue with some semblance of happiness, even if it was only a façade.

I discovered that my best coping strategy for dealing with Brielle's issues was to keep a routine for the things I could control. I might have succumbed to the vicious undercurrent of frustration and exhaustion if it were not for the routines I embraced. My repetitive schedule became my solace, something predictable I could depend on.

Brian worked long hours and pitched in when he could. Before Brielle was born, we split the household duties. While on maternity leave, I took over everything except lawn care. Somehow, the domestic duties were never divvied up again and I was fine with that. Being physically busy kept my mind off my troubles.

Although Brielle's coughing and congestion went on for months and her feeding issues continued for many years, one major struggle with Brielle thankfully ended early that first summer. Almost magically, Brielle's colic subsided when she was about three and half months old.

It ended without any warning, but over the course of three months, it had taken its toll on all of us. Her colic had worn us out physically, mentally, and emotionally with each other and with her. Finally, we got a reprieve from that stress and slowly began to heal.

There was still a long road ahead of us as the other issues persisted and new ones surfaced. However, for a short time, we found solace in the new peace in our household once Brielle was finally content.

> *"Peace I leave with you; my peace I give you.*
> *I do not give to you as the world gives.*
> *Do not let your hearts be troubled and do not*
> *be afraid."*
>
> – JOHN 14: 27 (NIV)

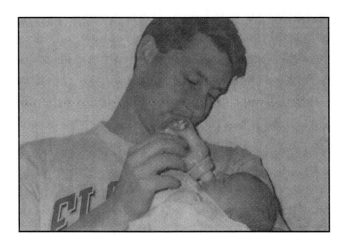

CHAPTER 10

The Elephant in the Room

My pre-teen daughters dig into their stockings on Christmas morning with the same excitement they had when they were little. Ashley helps Brielle pull something out that is wedged in the bottom of her stocking. Brielle squeals in delight as she discovers a new pair of slippers with her favorite cartoon characters on them. Ashley helps her little sister put them on. Brielle jumps to her feet, shuffles across the room, and throws her arms around me.

"Thank you, Mom," she signs excitedly.

"They're from Santa, remember?" I tell my 10-year-old daughter hoping to keep the magic going for just another Christmas or two.

"No," she signs back. "From you. No Santa. You Santa."

I stare at Ashley accusingly.

"I wouldn't say anything to her," my older daughter puts her hands up, claiming innocence.

Nobody told Brielle about Santa's identity. She just knew. Some things are like that.

A Picture is Worth a Thousand Words

On Good Friday of Ashley's first Easter season, I propped up our firstborn one-month-old dressed in a cute outfit on our bed pillows nestled in between a row of stuffed bunnies. Two years later on Good Friday when Brielle was just under two months old, I put our second-born child in the same white romper with pink trim that Ashley wore. Replicating the photograph with Ashley, even consulting the previous photograph for accuracy, I set up Brielle between the same cuddly stuffed animals on our bed.

I soon realized that I was having trouble getting Brielle to hold her head up and stay upright in the same way Ashley had been able to do. Brielle kept sliding down from the pillows, sagging over onto one of the bunnies next to her, or pushing back to slip in between the pillows. Although Ashley slouched over in her picture, she had been a month younger and this was different.

When the pictures were developed (*This was 1996 and there were no digital cameras or camera phones.*) and came back from the drug store the next week, I tried to dismiss the differences between what should have been nearly identical pictures. I rationalized that I should not expect much physically from my two-month-old and that variations between children, even siblings, are natural. However, in my heart, I knew something was not right about Brielle.

Despite the clean bill of health when we left the hospital, CT results showed a small amount of brain damage with those two small calcifications on Brielle's brain and she was still at risk for having developmental problems. The difference in those two Easter photographs continued to nag at me.

Was Brielle already showing signs of delays? I tried to make sense of it all and stay calm, but I began to watch our baby's development even more carefully than before.

Cause for Concern in Black and White

During a time when Brielle's feeding issues, congestion, coughing, and colic were all at their height, frustration and exhaustion magnified my concerns about our daughter's development. Evidence of her development was like a cricket taunting me with bright chirping until I was frantically on the hunt for the source of the racket.

Desperate to compare Brielle's abilities to other babies her age, I wanted to prove to myself that our baby was developing like any other child. Part of me wished I kept a more detailed baby book for Ashley to be able to compare Brielle's developmental milestones to hers. Part of me was relieved I had not. Even as a baby, Ashley was ahead of her peers. Comparing our two children would not necessarily be a fair assessment.

I consulted my copy of *What to Expect the First Year*, a popular parenting book that gave age ranges for when infants should be doing certain things. The edges of the cover were worn and many pages were dog-eared with passages highlighted from reading it while Ashley was little and more recently in Brielle's first months.

With each failure to achieve some small developmental milestone, I clung to the plausible deniability of her differences. I tried to justify that my second-born was not *that* much older than what the book said she should be. I rationalized that maybe her health issues were also compromising her development. However, after so many months of worrying about our baby's health, anxiety was a difficult habit to break, especially with mounting evidence of cause for concern.

My mind was on high alert, unnaturally preoccupied with dreadful scenarios about our child's unknown future. I pressed on alone in that barren landscape of disappointment and worry. Irrationally thinking that if I spoke my suspicions aloud they would be more likely to be true, I did not express my concerns to Brian or anyone else. Not speaking of them also allowed me to keep from truly facing the probability that Brielle had developmental problems.

Mothers Just Know

When Brielle did not start rolling over at four months old, I tried to encourage her by putting her favorite rattles to her side. She turned her head to look at them, but could not roll over to reach them. I helped her roll over part of the way, but she could not finish the turn. Maternal intuition told me something was wrong.

As my anxiety ratcheted up, Brian seemed oblivious to the delays in our daughter's developmental progress in the midst of her other health concerns. I wondered if he truly did not see it or if, like me, he did not want to talk about it until he was sure. I finally broke my silence and talked with Brian about my concerns.

"Is she supposed to be rolling over this early? Did Ashley?" Brian asked.

"The book says she should be," I replied.

"The book?"

"The baby book," I said, picking up my well-read copy of *What to Expect the First Year* from the nightstand flipping to Chapter 8. "See?"

Brian skimmed the highlighted section. "Maybe you should talk to her doctor about it. She is supposed to see the neonatologist again soon, right?"

"Yes," I said. "I'll ask him."

Back to the Neonatologist

A few days later, at Brielle's regularly scheduled follow-up appointment with the neonatologist at Marshfield Clinic, the doctor checked our baby carefully. Listening to her coughs, he diagnosed her with bronchitis and prescribed yet another antibiotic.

MORE ABOUT....
Brielle's Coughing and Congestion Issues Eventually Solved

In the early fall, when Brielle was about six months old, our aging cat died. Soon after, Brielle's congestion and coughing quickly subsided and she was healthy once again.

We later suspected that she must have been allergic to our cat. Neither her pediatrician nor her neonatologist ever asked about a cat in the house or suggested her symptoms could be due to allergies. Although it had been a six-month battle of illness, her symptoms never returned outside of an occasional cold.

In addition, he assaulted me with a battery of questions about Brielle's eating, sleeping patterns, and the contents of her diaper. I was pleased to report to him that our baby's colic had finally resolved a few weeks before. However, when he asked if she was rolling over yet, my concerns just spewed out one after another.

"She should be rolling over by now," he commented calmly, "or at least she should be trying to. Let's get this checked out."

He asked his nurse to schedule an assessment with the High Risk Follow-Up Coordinator at the first available appointment. The doctor's swift move to have our baby's development tested ignited my apprehension in a flash of adrenaline. My thoughts clanged around in my head and I wished Brian were with me to ask the questions I knew should be asking. Despite my lack of questioning, there would be answers when the testing was completed.

"How's her hearing? Does she turn to you when you talk to her or shake a rattle?" the doctor asked, addressing one more issue commonly connected with CMV.

"She seems to hear just fine," I replied, snapping out of my haze.

Since Brielle's ears were clear from infection, the doctor wrote up orders to have her tested that afternoon to confirm her hearing was still intact.

Testing Begins Again

A nurse directed us to a different part of the clinic where an audiologist tested Brielle's hearing using a BAER Study, Brainstem Auditory Evoked Response Study. Brielle cooperated perfectly by falling asleep at just the right time for the technician to complete the painless test. Although it took a week to get the results, our baby's hearing was normal. Relief, at least for a while.

She could still lose her hearing at any point in her life, but we felt comforted knowing she made it this far without CMV taking away her hearing.

MORE ABOUT....
The BAER Hearing Test (Brainstem Auditory Evoked Response Study)[1]

A Brainstem Auditory Evoked Response Study (BAER) also known as Auditory Brainstem Response (ABR) is a test to measure how the brain responds to sound. Electrodes are placed on the scalp and on the earlobe while headphones emit clicks or tones. Young infants and children are sometimes given medication or sedation to keep them still.

Two weeks later, Brian and I took the day off from work to return with Brielle to Marshfield Clinic for more ominous testing with the High Risk Follow-Up Coordinator. The woman greeted Brielle with a big smile placing her finger in our daughter's grasp. We were thankful Brielle was in a good mood – no colicky crying any more.

"This won't hurt a bit," the evaluator reassured Brielle. Of course, we realized the comment was clearly for our benefit. "I'm just going to play with you for about an hour while your mom and dad watch us."

The woman took Brielle from my arms and walked us to a small, quiet room. Brian and I watched this stranger dangle toys, roll a pencil across the table, and present a mirror to our baby. It looked like play to us, just as she said it would be. We wondered how these playtime games could be assessing Brielle's developmental skills. The woman made a few notes on a clipboard, but did not comment on what she was doing until the end of the session.

After filling out some charts and rifling through some papers on her desk across the small room, the evaluator sat down with us to present the results of the assessment. From the serious look on the woman's face, I knew it would be bad news before she even spoke. The lump in my throat felt like I had swallowed an apple whole.

"Your baby does not seem to be meeting certain developmental milestones as she should," the woman began with a weak smile pointing to numbers on a chart labeled with Brielle's name.

The numbers made no sense to us and might as well have been Chinese characters. Not since her Apgar scores of eight and nine in the first moments after her birth had our baby's health and abilities been boiled down to numbers. Brielle was more than just numbers and this stranger irritated me by trying to sum up my child like that.

M O R E   A B O U T . . . .
Apgar Test[1]

Apgar tests assess the baby's health (including breathing, heart rate, muscle tone, irritability, and skin color) at one and five minutes after birth. Scores range from zero to ten. A normal range is seven to nine.

"What exactly does that mean?" I asked, wondering how this woman could force such a smile as she told us our child was not developing normally.

Putting the chart with numbers aside, she explained what things infants of Brielle's age should be able to do. She then presented a long list of simple skills our child was not doing.

- Not picking up toys.
- Not reaching for dangled toys.
- Not chewing on her fists.
- Not adequately controlling her head.
- Not pushing up on her arms when on her stomach.
- Not rolling over.

Her words harshly fell out on to the table in front of us like marbles on a metal tray, painfully piercing our ears. My heart sank deeper and deeper as the evaluator reported each item to us. It was one thing to worry if something was wrong with our child. It was another to hear every disappointing detail from a stranger.

"Some of her skills are borderline," the woman said as she continued reporting her findings from the assessment. "That means that although your baby has not mastered them, she is not significantly behind yet."

Yet. A small, but significant word.

Brian and I exchanged a heartbreaking look with one another. We each searched for some hope in the other's eyes. Brielle started to fuss and squirm. I rearranged her in my arms, put her over my shoulder, and wrapped a blanket over her. I felt the need to shield her from this stranger's harsh report and, for the moment, that pink blanket would have to suffice.

"I recommend that we retest your baby in six months to be sure." With that, the woman closed the file folder in front of her, clearly marking the end of her report and dismissing us.

"Is there something else we could be doing to help Brielle?" I asked, not budging from the hard chair across the table from the woman.

"Well, you could have her start a therapy program or just wait six months to retest her as I suggested. Whichever you want to do," the stranger stated flatly while fidgeting with the tab on the file folder imprinted with our child's name.

"Why would we wait when we know she already has delays?" Brian asked.

"Well, it's very early and we would know more after retesting her in six months," the stranger repeated herself without answering my husband's question.

Brian searched my eyes again. "I don't think there's any question," he boldly committed for both of us. "She should start with the therapy program right away."

As the woman explained the intake process for the Early Intervention program, we struggled to catch the fast pitch of information she was throwing at us. She went on to rattle off descriptions of the role of the service coordinator and therapists using unfamiliar acronyms and jargon as she delivered her well-rehearsed speech.

Clearly, this woman had given this spiel many times in her role as an evaluator. But, did she think about those words and how parents receive them?

"The occupational therapist can help her with her hands." The woman paused and then tentatively continued as she looked directly at us. "I should mention, your baby seems to strongly favor her left hand."

"Does that mean Brielle is left-handed?" Brian asked.

"No, not exactly," she said pausing again for a brief moment. "I suspect there may be something wrong with her right hand."

Disbelief. Brian and I had not noticed any difference in how Brielle used her hands. It was her ability to hold up her head and roll over that concerned us, not her right hand. Already overwhelmed by the testing and seriousness of the meeting, we decided the woman was wrong and dismissed that part of her report. We had taken in enough information that afternoon and were eager to leave.

We drove home in the same eerie silence that haunted us the day we sat around the conference room table as the doctors told us about CMV a month before Brielle was born. Still trying to digest what the evaluator reported, neither of us wanted to speak of the day's events.

It was the loudest silence I ever heard.

Looking back at Brielle asleep in her car seat, I reminded myself that this was the same baby I held just hours before, before the evaluator diagnosed Brielle with developmental delays. Nothing had changed except the label this stranger put on our child. However, those previous feelings of dread about our baby's future came back like an unwelcomed visitor.

Denial

I called my parents that evening to tell them about the testing process and the results. When I told them what the woman said about Brielle's hands, they could not believe it either.

"No," my mother said almost defiantly. "That can't be right. I didn't see that at all when I was there less than two months ago."

I desperately wanted to agree with my mother's assessment, but wanted to confirm it either way. Without telling anyone, I privately put Brielle through my own tests. I dangled toys and put her on her stomach as the High Risk Follow-up Coordinator had done. I still could not see the difference in her hands.

It would be many months before we recognized this blow from fate. Even now, when I look at photographs and home videos of Brielle as a young baby, I cannot see the difference between her two hands.

Over the next few months, as the physical therapist, speech therapist, and occupational therapist began to work with Brielle, we realized just how far behind our child was. Our circumstances forced us to move forward on the path laid in front of us. Reality slowly sank in, caught up with our denial, and pushed us to a new place.

Our heartache was a canyon, deep and wide. Hidden in the dense fog of our grief, there was a vast gorge between who we hoped and thought Brielle was and who she actually was.

Despite our hopes for a "normal" child, CMV left its mark on Brielle. Our child was developmentally delayed and we were about to embark on an entirely different parenting journey.

> *Trust in the LORD with all your heart; Do not*
> *depend on your own understanding.*
> *Seek His will in all you do,*
> *And He will show you which path to take.*
>
> – PROVERBS 3: 5-6 (NLT)

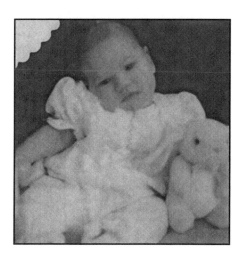

CHAPTER 11

Start Your Engines

Brian navigates our SUV on small roads in our town until we are about to enter the highway on our way to visit Ashley at her college in Orlando.

"Faster, Daddy," Brielle signs from the back seat as I interpret for her.

"I can't go any faster than the person driving in front of me," he says, accelerating on the on-ramp.

Brielle might not know much about driving, but she is eager to get to our destination.

"Ok, Dad," Brielle signs. "Go faster, but be careful."

"You got it, Sweetie," he replies, smiling at her in the rearview mirror. "I'll do that."

The Interrogation

So, you think the thunderous, bone-rattling reverberations of a stock car revving up at the start of a race are loud and overwhelming? Imagine what it must be like for the driver.

Brielle's development was the racecar and we were the drivers gripping the steering wheel, white-knuckled and worried about careening into the wall. The Early Intervention team swarmed in on Brielle's life and ours like a pit crew. They had plenty of skill and enthusiasm, but they overwhelmed us.

Just a few days after the High Risk Follow-up Coordinator evaluated Brielle and delivered the grim news, the service coordinator called me to schedule a home visit to start the Early Intervention (EI) process.

"We'll do the intake process while I'm there," the pleasant woman explained. "I'll have some paperwork for you to fill out and ask you a few questions about your daughter."

We scheduled her visit for the next week on a day when I could leave work early to pick up the girls from daycare and be home for the meeting. The service coordinator arrived promptly at our home as scheduled. A large, leather messenger bag crossed the front of her navy blue, collared shirt emblazoned with a white nametag above the logo of the EI company.

After a few pleasantries, we settled in at the kitchen table with Brielle on my lap while Ashley watched a children's video in the next room. The woman proceeded to take out a stack of paperwork and put it in front of me.

"Just fill these out the best that you can," she said handing me a pen. "Some of the questions are for parents with kids that are a little older than your child, so just disregard them."

I put Brielle in a bouncy seat on the floor where she contently wiggled and batted a little at the toys dangling above her head. As I filled out the usual paperwork one might complete at the first visit to a doctor's office, the service coordinator took out another large stack of papers and started firing questions at me in rapid succession.

MORE ABOUT....
Early Intervention Services (EI)[1]

Early Intervention is a federally mandated system of coordinated services that helps disabled or developmentally delayed children up to three years old or until they improve and no longer qualify.

Depending on the child's needs, in addition to service coordination, on-going Early Intervention might include family training, counseling, occupational therapy, physical therapy, speech therapy, hearing/vision loss services, health/nursing care, nutrition counseling, social work, assistive technology devices, and transportation.

State and federal monies pay for the initial evaluation and service coordination. State policies vary regarding the cost to families for on-going services. Service providers may ask the family to access private insurance or Medicaid (only with written permission) or charge fees using a sliding scale based on family income. In any case, services cannot be denied based on a family's inability to pay.

She asked questions about:
- Our home life including who lived in our household
- Our native language
- Our educational background
- How much contact we had with extended family members
- Who was part of our support system in the community
- Any symptoms or complications I had during the pregnancy
- The results of testing I had done during the pregnancy
- The delivery
- Brielle's birth weight and Apgar scores
- The results of testing done at birth
- What brought us to seek out Early Intervention Services

That last one prompted me to hand over a copy of the report the High Risk Follow-Up Coordinator from Marshfield Clinic sent us. As the service coordinator looked over the report, I could not help but to think about the Good Friday picture that initially prompted my concerns. That is what truly started this whole process. How many photographs make such a difference?

My attention continued to bounce back and forth from the woman's rapid-fire questions to the forms in front of me. Check the appropriate box. Initial there. Sign here. With that, we were officially thrown into Wisconsin's Early Intervention program.

"All of the information we collected today, along with the evaluations of the therapists, will help us write the IFSP," the woman explained.

"I-F-what?" I asked looking up from the paperwork on the table in front of us.

"The Individual Family Service Plan, or IFSP, is the plan we will write and then use to coordinate services for your child," the woman said. "I'll explain more when we get to that process next week."

MORE ABOUT....
The Individual Family Service Plan (IFSP)[1]

Before Early Intervention services start, the parents and all providers who work with the child and family develop an Individual Family Service Plan (IFSP). The IFSP describes the child's current level of development, the family's strengths and needs, the specific services to be provided to the child and the family, and a plan to transition the child to public school.

The family assessment, evaluation of the child, and the IFSP must be completed within 45 days of the initial referral, reviewed every six months, and updated at least once a year.

The woman collected the forms from me and put them in a file folder clearly labeled with Brielle's name. She told me about the EI program, painting a picture of a streamlined intake and evaluation process, and described the team of therapists that would be helping Brielle.

Despite her best efforts to help orient me, I understood little more about Early Intervention than when this stranger arrived at my home and resigned myself to follow her lead and wait for the next step, the evaluations.

A few days later, three therapists dressed in colorful scrubs came to our house to evaluate Brielle. They each took turns putting my daughter through activities as the others scribbled notes on forms and discussed Brielle as if I were invisible. Every few minutes, they jabbed me with questions. Once I answered, the therapists returned to their work without much regard for my presence.

They barked out numbers and descriptions to one another. I did not understand much of it. Everything they talked about and did with Brielle was foreign to me. I felt like a displaced expat, a foreigner in a strange land. The team did little to make me feel comfortable in this new territory. All I wanted was to protect my child from these invaders, but I knew they were there to help her.

By the time they left, I was emotionally exhausted by what felt like a hit-and-run accident. Brielle was asleep on a blanket on the floor.

"What just happened?" I asked my sleeping child as I collapsed in a nearby chair.

The therapists were probably trying to be efficient. However, to the mom looking on as three women encircled my child poking, prodding, and testing her, the experience felt more like a mauling than the "streamlined intake and evaluation process" the service coordinator described.

"Geez," Brian exclaimed after hearing about it all later that evening. "So, did they do anything to actually help her?"

"Nothing that I could tell."

Despite the experience, we pressed on and followed the process.

Therapy Begins

"Of course you can leave work a little early," my boss replied after I told her the therapists were coming to our house to work with Brielle.

"I don't have much vacation time left after my maternity leave."

"We'll do what we can to give you a little flexibility," she said encouraging me.

Grateful she was supportive of my family's needs, I started coming in early and working through lunches. I built up precious minutes I needed for the therapy sessions that took place two or three afternoons a week. Leaving work early, I raced to daycare and then home to beat the therapists.

Over the next few weeks, we slowly gave over part of our child's learning to strangers dressed in brightly colored scrubs who wore nametags with acronyms after their names. PT. OT. SLP. They arrived with large tote bags full of rattles, balls, mirrors, and other toys and swooped in on our lives.

The therapists presented a united front of knowledge and confidence. They acted as if they knew best how to help Brielle reach her milestones like sitting up, crawling, and walking. The words in the therapists' evaluation reports subtly suggested we needed to learn how to help Brielle, as if we were clueless about parenting. Somehow, we had managed to help Ashley meet her milestones without any effort at all. Our past parenting successes did not matter. Brielle struggled and we needed their help.

Their expertise did not equate to being connected to our child. Even if those women knew how to help a child developmentally progress better than we did, I could never believe that they truly knew my child. They knew her body as a group of muscles. I knew my Brielle.

Specialists

The physical therapist (PT) worked with Brielle's gross motor skills – how she used the large muscles in her legs, arms, stomach, and back. According to the evaluations, Brielle's gross motor skills were most definitely delayed. We knew the tests were right. Her inability to roll over had concerned me enough to speak with the doctor and start this whole sequence of events.

The PT worked with Brielle on the floor or bounced and rolled our baby on a huge ball. The woman used toys to motivate Brielle to move the way she wanted her to. These activities were supposed to help Brielle gain better neck and abdominal control so that she could learn how to hold her head steady, roll over, and eventually sit up, as other children her age were already doing.

The occupational therapist (OT) worked on Brielle's fine motor skills – how she used her hands. Although the OT's evaluation report stated Brielle's fine motor skills were also significantly delayed, it did not confirm any specific issues with Brielle's right hand.

The OT offered toys of different sizes and shapes for my child to grasp. The woman sometimes put toys just out of Brielle's reach to make her work for them as the PT did. The OT put Brielle on her tummy and tickled or pushed her belly to make her push up on her hands.

Sometimes the OT would massage her hands, arms, and shoulders. After hunching over a computer at work all week and carrying around Brielle all weekend, I wished I could have had that massage. No massage for me.

The speech therapist, also referred to as a speech language pathologist (SLP), worked with Brielle's oral motor skills – how she used her lips, cheeks, tongue, and jaw for drinking and eventually for eating and talking. Brielle had some delays in this area as well. I had always been concerned about Brielle's ability to suck and swallow properly. She was also slow to get through a bottle and lost milk from her mouth before she could swallow it.

Sometimes the SLP would feed Brielle and suggest different ways to hold our baby or the bottle. She also tried to get Brielle to imitate sounds and facial expressions. The therapist often poked around Brielle's mouth using this funny looking stick with a round, pink sponge on the end of it or a different round stick with little, firm bumps on the end of it. It was difficult to understand how poking Brielle's mouth with those alien tools would help her suck and swallow better, let alone eventually talk.

Throughout the therapists' time with Brielle, I watched and learned, but also wondered why it did not look more like work.

"How could their play be helping Brielle any more than our time with her?" I asked Brian one evening after explaining what the therapists had done earlier that afternoon.

"I'm not sure it does," he replied. "But, they are trained and have the expertise. We should trust them and see where this all goes."

Easy for him to say. He was not there during the appointments, did not have to listen to the therapists' comments that described Brielle as a collection of muscles that did not work properly, and did not have to answer their inquiries that seemed to subtly question my mothering abilities. At least Brielle smiled, giggled, and rarely showed any signs of pain or frustration during their sessions.

In the midst of strangers invading our world, Ashley watched Brielle's therapy with curiosity. I told her that the therapists were helping Brielle learn how to roll over and drink her bottle better. That simple explanation seemed to satisfy our curly-headed, little girl who was not even three years old yet.

Ashley sometimes asked to join in the therapy sessions that certainly looked like playtime with her little sister. The therapists were generally kind, allowing Ashley to play with a toy they were not using at that moment. I often encouraged my toddler to play off to the side or popped in a children's video to distract her. Over time, the therapists' toys and activities bored Ashley and she was content to play on her own.

As we provided additional care and playtime to facilitate Brielle's developmental needs, Brian and I also made an effort to give Ashley undivided attention each day. We drank bottomless cups of pretend tea, put together a continuous cycle of simple puzzles, and read an endless amount of books. During the last days of summer, Ashley ran around our backyard after the huge ball Brian kicked to her over and over again. Without any fanfare or concerns, Ashley continued to thrive and be happy, clearly unaware of the changes in our family.

Parental Supervision Not Required

Caring for a toddler and a baby, working full-time, completing household duties plus Brielle's therapy sessions began to take its toll on me. I tumbled into bed early each evening only to awaken several times during the night for Brielle's feedings and then early each morning to get the girls ready and head off to work. With several therapy appointments each week, it became more and more difficult for me to leave work. Brian could not easily leave work either.

"The therapists could do their work with your daughter at her daycare if that would be easier for you," the service coordinator offered after a few busy weeks of appointments.

It might be easier for me. However, I would not be able to watch and learn from them. Unfortunately, my work schedule was only so flexible and I eventually conceded. Although I loved my job, I began to wonder if being there for Brielle and her therapy would be more valuable to the family.

Having our children in daycare where strangers took care of them was difficult. Having the therapists provide care for Brielle alone seemed even worse.

I felt guilty for not being there and jealous that the therapists were doing something for my baby that I could not. Forced to simply read their reports and hear about it secondhand from the daycare workers, I felt completely out of the loop with this less than ideal system.

The therapists sent one page of hand written notes on how long they were with Brielle and what they did with her. Reading and understanding their reports was like decrypting some sort of code. Deciphering their handwriting was just the first obstacle to overcome. The therapists also used foreign words like hip adduction, ATNR, palmer grasp, bilateral activities, reciprocal movement, tongue thrust, and jaw stability. It took more than a few nights poring over the short reports with a dictionary nearby to learn this new language, the therapists' language.

What an odd juxtaposition. Experienced, loving parents in need of a dictionary to figure out how to best care for their sweet baby.

At the bottom of each report, we had a homework assignment. The therapists instructed us to do things like "brush her tongue and the inside of her cheeks with a soft toothbrush" or "put her on her tummy on the floor more often." We were eager to do something, anything to help our daughter. However, we assumed it might be more serious work, something that involved more time, sweat, research, or doctors. Nevertheless, we complied and sent notes back to them in Brielle's diaper bag or left messages for them on their answering machines at work.

My organizational skills kicked in. I saved each report sent home in Brielle's diaper bag and filed them in a three-ring notebook. When one report repeated something in another, we could flip through the binder and compare them. Keeping the reports organized made me feel like I was participating in the process more than I actually was, more in control by doing this one small task. However, I was not in control at all.

The therapists continued to feel like an invasion into our family whether they worked with Brielle in our home or at daycare. The way Brielle received therapy without us being there felt intrinsically wrong. But, what could we do?

I desperately needed someone who had been through this process to walk beside me and explain it all to me, mother-to-mother. None of my friends were going through what we were. Our mothers did not have any experience with this. My mind sometimes wandered to the only mothers I knew who might understand and be able to offer some advice, the mothers of the disabled high schoolers I once helped find jobs. If only I had a different relationship with them and knew the families well enough to reach out to them.

Cause for More Concerns

With each therapist's visit, we learned Brielle was falling further behind other infants her age. They made it clear in their reports what the gaps were in Brielle's abilities.

They occasionally mentioned other children in their care whose bodies behaved similarly to Brielle's. Portrayals of toddlers and young children who required leg braces, wheelchairs, medications, proce-dures, and surgeries were meant to help us understand what Brielle's body was doing and what others experienced. However, their de-scriptions simply previewed greater losses yet to come.

In addition to gross motor, fine motor, and oral motor delays, the therapists also began to suggest delays in other developmental areas as well. While we desperately wanted to apply the brakes, their reports forced us to accelerate into the curves ahead as they added additional techniques to their therapy routine and our homework.

Cognitive skills are how people interact with the environment using thinking and problem solving skills. It seemed odd to us that Brielle's thinking skills could be tested at her age, but the therapists reported a delay here, too. She did not play with toys much, but they could not say whether this was due to her cognitive skills or her fine motor skills. Either way, it was hard to know what was going on in that little head of hers.

Adaptive skills are the activities of daily living such as eating, toileting, and dressing. Although at four to six months old, Brielle was too young to be able to do any of these things, the therapists suggested she showed delays. Brielle was not very interested in holding a bottle herself and was very resistant to eating any solid foods.

Social-emotional skills include how people interact with others, have a concept of self, and have coping skills. Brielle had a great smile and was always ready to play with others. The therapists reported that this was an area of real strength for her. It was the only strength they reported.

Coping Strategies in Our New "Normal"

Reading reports from the therapists about all of the things Brielle could not do quickly became discouraging. The gap between what the other children could do and what Brielle could not do was getting bigger every day.

When we saw other infants in public, we could usually dismiss the variations. We learned to justify every small difference with little ones we saw at the grocery store or at the park. Surely, those other children were a few months older than Brielle. Surely, Brielle would soon be doing those things, too.

When I picked Brielle up at her daycare, I made a conscious decision not to look at the other infants in her room. Seeing the other children reminded me of how different my child was from them. There was no justifying the hard evidence. Those infants were all within a month or two of her age. Brielle should be able to do everything the other kids were doing. However, our child could not.

Keeping a predictable routine continued to help keep me sane, but it was all an illusion of control. I assumed we were still traveling along the planned trajectory to fix Brielle and have a perfect family. However, despite our best efforts and the work of the therapists, we saw few results in those first months.

Months before, Brian and I had divided our parenting duties to cope with Brielle's colic. While we still worked as a team at some things, I found myself feeling more and more alone as we faced the new routine with Brielle. My guilt from not being with her during therapy propelled me to become more focused on her needs in the evenings. Brian felt compelled to give more attention to Ashley further pushing the division. Each daughter needed us, both of us. And yet, we continued our separation of parenting duties.

I wondered how this could be our new normal. Had I crash-landed into someone else's life?

Close friends and family asked how things were going. I guarded my feelings carefully, but still hoped someone might see through my façade and realize how much we had to endure. As my exhaustion escalated, life started to go into a tailspin. A spectacular crash into the wall in the far turn of the speedway was beginning to seem inevitable.

My emotions were running so high that I could not stop myself from giving in to them. If I was going to cry, I had to make it a good, cleansing cry, and then be done with it. Escaping to the solitude of our basement guestroom, I cried all the tears I could get out before either Brian realized what an emotional wreck I was or one of the girls demanded my attention. Washing my face and pasting on the best smile I could muster, I merged back into the high-speed race called "my life" and went back to its routine.

This routine was turning into our own brand of chaos and was about to become more complicated.

Just two months after Brielle started therapy with the Early Intervention team, Brian got a call from a recruiter about a new job. We were about to plot a new course as life shifted for all of us.

> *...Forgetting what is behind and straining toward what is ahead, I press on toward the goal to win the prize for which God has called me heavenward in Christ Jesus.*
>
> — PHILIPPIANS 3:13-14 (NIV)

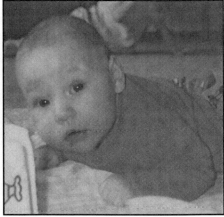

CHAPTER 12

Decisions, Decisions

"How about a ham sandwich?" I ask Brielle at lunchtime while staring into the open refrigerator.

"Or?" Brielle signs back.

"Or what?" I ask her. "You tell me. What else would you want?"

My 16-year-old looks in the kitchen pantry and simply shrugs her shoulders.

"Would you like a ham sandwich or some mac and cheese?" I ask, knowing my child needs a choice to feel in control.

"Ham sandwich," she signs back. "And chocolate milk."

Opportunity Calls

"There is a job available about 100 miles west of Chicago that might be perfect for me," Brian announced as we debriefed our day over dinner.

The fork in my right hand stopped midway to my mouth as I looked up at him. Brian's expression was calm as he casually poked at the meal on his plate. My mind worked in slow motion as I tried to digest my husband's words. Where was this coming from? A move was not on my radar. I wondered why it was on his.

"I didn't know you were looking for a new job," I replied, still trying to process his declaration. Six-month-old Brielle sat half-slumped over in a high chair next to me. I leaned over to pick up a ring of colorful, plastic keys she dropped on the floor, but kept my eyes on Brian.

His mood this August evening was hard to interpret, even after six years of marriage. My husband diverted his eyes from mine, instead looking intently at his vegetables, as if he could find some profound meaning in that forest of broccoli. No eye contact. Experience told me this was the start of something big.

The Life We Had

It was a difficult time to consider moving away from Eau Claire, Wisconsin, where we had made our home for the last four years. Most of our friends, neighbors, co-workers, and people at church knew us before Ashley was born. They supported us throughout the pregnancy, delivery, and first months with Brielle. Moving away would mean leaving them behind, starting a life where no one knew us.

Although Brielle's pediatrician and neonatologist struggled to keep her cough and congestion at bay, they took good care of her and I liked them. If we moved, we would need to find new doctors for her. Would they know enough about CMV and be able to care for her if she had other complications from the virus such as hearing loss or seizures?

Despite feeling no personal connection to Brielle's therapists, they were just getting to know her. Therapists in a new place would need to start all over again. Would we have to go through another detailed intake process and additional evaluations?

Brielle was in a great daycare that accepted children of all abilities and where the therapists could work with her. Ashley was thriving in the same daycare and had friends she talked about all of the time. Could we find a similar daycare experience for both girls?

And what about my job? The health care organization continued to expand and our department was developing a new marketing campaign. Although I was not directly involved with the production of the new television commercials, I was responsible for all of the print advertising and wrote the rough drafts for the radio commercial scripts. My boss was mentoring me to take on more responsibilities. She assured me that she would continue to expand my job, which would soon lead to a change in title and pay.

"Jobs like this don't come around all of the time." Brian pleaded his case and described the human resource manager job at the corporate office of a big, international company. "It would be a good career move."

"I'm not against it," I reassured my husband. "It's a lot to take in and think about."

"It's just a phone interview. Nothing may come of it."

Just a phone interview. Right.

The Interview and Offer

In the next few days, Brian had several phone interviews and then visited the company for face-to-face interviews. When he returned home, he was excited and hopeful about his chances to get this new job.

With a little time to process the potential move, I started to picture how different our lives could be and found myself intrigued by the possibilities. Although we had many supportive friends, there were people in Eau Claire who knew our whole story and felt sorry for us more than anything else. I could feel that every time they looked at us. Their silent pity made me uncomfortable. Moving might not change everything, but we could be anonymous for a while. The thought of being unknown had its appeal.

If we moved to that northern Illinois town, we would be just three and a half hours away from our hometown where our parents still lived. It would be nice to be able to see them more frequently. We could be together for every holiday and even over a few long weekends. Maybe they could stay with the girls occasionally so Brian and I could get away, maybe around our anniversary each March. We often talked about getting away, but had not done that since before the girls were born.

We liked our house in Wisconsin. However, it would be nice to look for something new, maybe something with a porch or a formal dining room. House hunting was the fun part. Moving was the pain. Unpacking boxes. Setting up house. Finding new places to shop, new doctors, and a new church. Making new friends.

The recruiter called early one evening with the company's job offer, which included a significant pay increase. The wheels of change were in full motion. The potential to move had swiftly gone from discussing a job prospect to our new reality, *if* we decided Brian should take the offer. We were moving into uncharted territory and still unsure.

The new company offered to pay the expenses for us to visit their town over a long weekend before we made our final decision. Instead of asking our parents to come up to Wisconsin, I arranged for several friends to take turns caring for the girls over the three days we would be gone. Feeling a bit like traitors shuffling off to a different state, Brian and I took a day off from work without giving even the slightest hint about his new job offer.

We were leaning towards Brian taking the job and hoping this weekend would give us the confidence to move forward.

Checking Out the New Community

Brian and I drove the five hours to what might soon become our new home. Could this place ever be home like Eau Claire was? Although Freeport, Illinois had a population of only about 25,000 people, I could see value in this small town and in making a fresh start. I cannot say it was idealistic, but it had its charm.

The day we arrived, Brian had a few meetings with upper management at the new company including a tour of the offices downtown. While Brian was gone, I explored the city center, only a few blocks from the hotel. Although I walked past the office, I did not to even go in the lobby. Instead, I kept walking and found the library, a few antique stores, and a quaint ice cream shop.

It was so relaxing just to be by myself. Other than the trips to and from daycare, it had been months since I was alone. It gave me time to think.

I let the possibilities of moving to this small town rattle around in my head. I began to think about my guilt of working full time, being away from my girls during the day, and particularly not being there for Brielle when she received therapy.

I never seriously considered quitting my job before this move came up. Certainly, there were times I envied stay-at-home moms and the freedom they had. Now, Brian's pay increase could almost cover my income, especially without the costs of daycare. I dared to imagine how different our lives could be and actually felt pangs of excitement.

I would not have to rise before the sun to get the girls up and ready for daycare before scurrying off to work. Ashley and I could have all the tea parties she wanted and read every book in her collection cover to cover. I would have time to keep the house more tidy and have dinner waiting on the table when Brian came home from work.

How much faster could Brielle progress if I could be there to learn from the therapists and have more time to follow their suggestions consistently? Could I finally feel less stressed? I knew stay-at-home moms had their struggles, but it had to be better than what we were going through.

The next morning, a local realtor took us on a tour around the area. She talked about the businesses, retail stores, and schools in the community and showed us a few houses. It was not a real house-buying search, but simply an opportunity to get an idea of what our budget could buy.

Brian's prospective boss and his wife took us out to dinner on our last evening in town. I felt confident wearing one of my best dresses even though the added pregnancy pounds had not slipped off yet. The man and his wife talked with us about all of the wonderful aspects of the company and their small town. They were trying to woo us (not so subtly), but we were already beginning to envision ourselves in this town.

I could imagine how excited Ashley would be feeding the ducks at the pond, riding on the merry-go-round, and playing on the huge wooden play structure at the city's biggest park. We might all go to the band shell at that same park on Sunday evenings for a summer concert. Perhaps I could meet Brian at the park with a picnic lunch like we did years before when we were first married.

It had only been four years ago when our mothers cried at our announcement that we were moving so far away to Eau Claire. I pictured their tears of joy when we announced a move that would bring us more than halfway closer to them. No more celebrating holidays like Easter, Mother's Day, and the Fourth of July without them.

The thought of moving had originally brought up many concerns. Now, I was beginning to see how it could be the start of a better life for our family.

Decision Time

We spent most of the drive back to Eau Claire discussing the job, the move, and what it would mean for our family. We weighed each aspect of moving to this small town in Illinois versus staying in the large, college town in Wisconsin. We sentimentally discussed how much of our lives had been lived there and lamented about the potential moving process. The loss of friends, my job at the health care organization, the girls' daycare, and the doctors and therapists working with Brielle dominated most of our conversation. Going back to square one was a daunting possibility.

However, we acknowledged the benefits of being closer to family. This new job could greatly benefit Brian's career and open up more opportunities for his future. He was the primary breadwinner for our family and his career had to be a priority.

Our conversation naturally led us to reassess our general life plans. When we married, we had specific goals we assumed we would achieve. Fast-forward six years. We now knew better than to make any firm plans. Our experiences with Brielle certainly taught us that lesson. However, we still had goals and plans for our lives and this was an opportunity to tweak them.

By the time we picked up the girls at our friends' house, with some lingering nostalgic feelings, we made a clear decision. After living in Eau Claire, Wisconsin, where both our children were born, including experiencing all of the joy and heartache we went through with Brielle, we were moving to Freeport, Illinois.

Another Big Decision

As we started preparing for the move, my mind worked overtime considering the changes ahead, especially about my future. I knew that what I needed to do and wanted to do were the same thing.

"I think I should stay at home and not work after the move," I suggested one quiet evening. "I could focus my attention on the girls, especially on Brielle's needs and therapy schedule."

"Are you sure you'd want to do that?" Brian asked incredulously.

"I know this may seem like a snap decision, but I've given it a lot of thought," I replied with firm resolve. "Besides, with your new salary and not having to pay for daycare, we might not be too far behind where we are now."

"If you think your income can replace you, then you haven't seen the big picture and your value to our family," Brian said.

Smiling at my husband I replied, "I have seen the big picture. That's why I want to do this, for our family and especially for our girls."

"I just want you to be sure about this. I know how much you like your job. You might regret a decision to not work."

"It's not a permanent decision. I could change my mind and start looking for a job at any time."

Despite what I said, I realized leaving the working world might very well become a permanent life change. My plan had always been to work, even after we started a family. I went to college and graduate school. I had some lingering thoughts that leaving my career behind might be throwing that all away.

I was exhausted and overwhelmed working, maintaining a household, and trying to take care of both of our children, especially Brielle and her need for additional care and therapy. This was my chance to have a different life without at least one of my usual stressors.

It could also make a difference in my relationship with Ashley. With more time and energy, I could connect with her in new ways. There might still be a need for Brian and me to keep our parenting duties divided with the girls. However, I hoped to establish something different and better with Ashley than what we already had.

Leaving my job was an investment in our family. This could be an opportunity to put my all into making a better life for us. Once we made the decision for me not to work, I had few regrets and was rarely jealous that Brian was able to continue his career path.

So, we threw our master plan right out the window and bravely plotted a new course. Our lives in the new town would be very different. With nervousness and exhilaration, we stepped out into the unknown future in this new place that would soon become home indeed.

> *Commit to the Lord whatever you do, and He will establish your plans.*
>
> — PROVERBS 16:3 (NIV)

CHAPTER 13

New Beginnings

Ten young children gather at our neighbor's house just before the holidays. They jump up and down with excitement when Santa arrives to hear their Christmas lists while their mothers enthusiastically snap pictures. My 16-year-old Brielle doesn't still believe, but I know a good photo op and am happy to get together with my friends.

Somehow, Brielle is standing closest to the chair where Santa will be sitting. The other kids congregate behind her in a semi-organized line.

"You go," Brielle signs for me to tell each small child. "Tell Santa you good this year."

Brielle gives them a "high five" and a "thumbs up" as each little one comes back to sit on the floor and watch their neighborhood friends sit on Santa's lap.

When I ask Brielle why she is letting all the other children go first, she signs to me, "I nice. They little. Little kids go first."

The Hunt for Home Sweet Home

A few weeks after the job offer, after friends and family knew we were moving, and a "for sale" sign was in the front yard of our Wisconsin home, we traveled back to Freeport with the girls to go house hunting.

Our wish list was short. Three bedrooms. Two baths. We definitely wanted to stay well within our means, so we did not have unrealistic dreams about finding a particularly large house. Although we saw dozens of houses, we could not a find a house we wanted to make our home.

As a last ditch effort, our realtor suggested something a bit unconventional. Her neighbors had been talking about moving for a while, but did not yet have their house on the market. She called them and they agreed to show us their house. The house was similar to ours in Eau Claire and we liked it better than anything else we had seen. We made an offer and they accepted it. Since the current owners were not prepared to move, they asked for a closing date 90 days out. Brian would be starting his new job in about a month. Therefore, we were stuck without a house for two months.

When we moved to Freeport, Illinois in October of 1996, Ashley was two and half years old, Brielle was six months old, Brian was starting a new job, and I was anxious to start my new role as a stay-at-home mother.

Part of me was excited about the adventure. I freed myself of the guilt I had being a working mother. I could be with my children all of the time.

On the other hand, I was now going to be with my children... all of the time.

I did not have a job to stimulate my mind and give me a sense of independence. I had no friends. No babysitters. No church community. Moreover, it would be two months before we had a house.

Temporary Accommodations

Brian's company found a furnished apartment for us. We were told it was in a good location and fully stocked with the basics we would need.

"I guess we'll be getting a little exercise while we live here," I commented, shifting Brielle to my other hip as we climbed up the stairs to our third-floor apartment on our first day in Freeport.

"I guess so," Brian remarked. "I'm sorry it's just a two-bedroom apartment. The company said there wasn't anything else furnished available to rent for us."

"I know," I said, trying to stay positive. "We'll make it work. It's only for eight weeks."

What little enthusiasm I had drained out of me as we unlocked the door and crossed the threshold of our new living quarters. Worse than being small, it was old, dirty, and resembled a college apartment. No wonder since the apartment was about two minutes from the town's small community college.

Then it hit us. The smell. Was it mold? Stale beer? B.O.? What was that? I was not sure I really wanted to know.

I resisted the urge to protest. There was no use. If this was the only furnished apartment the company could find for us, we did not have another choice. On top of that, the company was picking up the tab. By the looks of it, they were not spending much on us.

"Eight weeks," Brian muttered under his breath as we walked through the small accommodations.

Brian brought up the few boxes we packed to bring to the apartment. The movers loaded everything else onto the moving truck and put it all into storage. After unpacking our clothes and setting up the girls' room, I started a movie for Ashley and plopped down on the torn vinyl pad of one of the rickety metal chairs. I began to write a list for the grocery store: milk, bread, cereal, air fresheners, cleaning supplies.

I surveyed our temporary home from the kitchen table.

Ashley sat on the threadbare, plaid sofa with her legs pulled up to her chin. Our little curly-headed kid looked pitiful as she clutched her baby doll, Rosie, in unfamiliar surroundings. Brielle threw a rattle from her baby walker onto the stained, multi-shaded brown, shag carpet. I cringed.

As I looked around at our surroundings, I realized no amount of soapy water or bleach could get this place up to the cleanliness I wanted for my children. My first apartment late in college was equivalent to this one. At that time, I was just basking in the joy of freedom. Things like broken, worn out, or dirty furnishings did not really matter. Eight years later with two small children, the condition of our surroundings were now important.

Brian stood at the kitchen sink rewashing the mismatched kitchen-ware items. When he looked up from his work, his face was gloomy and worried, with good reason. Despite the faint smile I tried to firmly plant across my face, he saw the disgust and sorrow that welled up inside me.

Eight weeks. We had to make this work. This was our new life now.

Welcome home, Stull family.

Powerful Words

Two days after we moved into the small apartment, we met with a mortgage broker to prepare for the closing on our new house. Bobbi was professional, helpful, and bubbling with friendliness. As my girls played on the floor behind us, I noticed a picture behind her desk. The adorable, little blonde boy in the framed photograph wore an oversized men's suit complete with a tie and fedora hat. When I complimented Bobbi on the cute picture, her face dropped its smile and she stared blankly across her desk at me.

"My son...," she hesitated with a catch in her throat. "Michael has Fragile X," she cautiously offered, glancing at Brielle. "My son is disabled, too."

Disabled, too? Was this woman calling Brielle disabled? What made her think Brielle was disabled? Was it the way our eight-month-old never rolled over or sat up on her own? Was it her awkward hands?

Then I began to wonder if other strangers recognized my daughter's issues and labeled her as disabled as well. My heart ached at that thought.

Hearing this stranger call Brielle disabled shook me to the core. Her words were powerful. I did not know how to react. I never considered Brielle disabled. No doctor or therapist ever referred to our child using that word. I simply thought of her as a baby who was getting some extra help.

Disabled. What did that even mean? Wounded veterans might be disabled. The greeter at the discount store who uses a wheelchair is disabled. Our elderly neighbor with arthritic hands that could no longer open jars or turn doorknobs with ease might even be disabled. However, unlike these others, our daughter was getting help and doing a little better. Could someone really call Brielle disabled?

Brian instinctively reached out for my hand. My eyes welled up as I looked from Bobbi to the picture of her son who looked so perfect, so cute in what was probably his father's suit and hat. Bobbi seemed so at ease using that word to refer to her son. Maybe since Michael was a little older than Ashley, she had enough time to come to terms with it.

MORE ABOUT....
Fragile X Syndrome[1]

Fragile X Syndrome (FXS) is the most common cause of inherited mental impairment ranging from mild learning disabilities to more severe cognitive disabilities. Delays in speech and language development as well as certain physical and behavioral characteristics such as anxiety, hyperactivity, and avoiding eye contact are common. FXS is also the most common known cause of autism or autism spectrum disorders.

After a few dabs of tissues, we settled into a more relaxed conversation. Brian and I bonded with Bobbi over mortgage applications and our kids who needed special help. She also talked to us a little about the Early Intervention program available in town.

"You're just going to love Martha," Bobbi said with glee. "Martha is an occupational therapist and she's just wonderful. She's done amazing things for Michael. Martha is different from the other therapists. They are all great, but she's...," Bobbi searched for the right word, "...different. You'll see."

After signing our mortgage application papers, Bobbi and I talked about getting together to have breakfast. She encouraged me to call her when we settled into our new house and I knew she meant it. After being in this new town just a few days, I made my first friend. More than just a new friend, she was someone who was going through some of the same things we were going through. In some ways, she was already a few steps ahead of us in the process.

As much as my emotions were initially in shock over hearing Bobbi call my child disabled, I could not quite wrap my head around the words. Brian was a bit stunned as well and made no effort to discuss what she said about Brielle. I was glad he did not want to talk about it. I was not ready to admit to myself or anyone else that Brielle's problems now qualified her as a member in that group. With so much already on my mind with the move, I shoved thoughts about equating Brielle and disabled to the bottom of my list of things to think about.

Early Intervention – Round Two

After setting up the apartment as best as I could, my first order of business was getting Brielle started in the local Early Intervention (EI) program. I had called the local service coordinator two weeks before we even moved to Illinois. During our brief conversation, the woman asked basic questions about Brielle and our family and then scheduled our first appointment for a day shortly after we arrived in Illinois.

I was nervous as the day of our first meeting approached. Although I had been through the EI intake process in Wisconsin, I was not sure what to expect. So much of Brielle's therapy happened while I was not with her. I was determined to reap the benefits of being a full-time mom by becoming an integral part of the therapy process.

Our neatly organized binder of reports and therapy notes was ready to show the new therapists when they arrived at our apartment just four days after we moved to Illinois. This time, I was ready for the invasion and the interrogation.

Upon hearing a firm knock on our door that fall morning, I braced myself before greeting the five women standing there. Their appearance startled me a bit. They wore comfortable clothes. No neatly embroidered uniforms. No brightly colored scrubs. No name tags. However, like the therapists in Wisconsin, each woman had a bag of toys, a big ball, or a file folder in her hands.

As they crossed the threshold of our apartment, each smiling woman gave me her name and title, and warmly shook my hand with her free hand. One of them introduced herself as Martha, the occupational therapist. I was eager to find out what Bobbi meant when she said Martha was different from the others.

I invited the group of women into our temporary living quarters. Although it was now as clean as I could make it, it was still what it was: a shabby, cramped apartment. As I welcomed them in, I quickly explained our living arrangements, although I was sure they had seen worse.

"I'm sorry we don't have enough chairs for all of us to sit at the table," I said, motioning towards the trio of chairs surrounding the little table.

"Oh, we don't need to sit at the table," the physical therapist said, dismissing my concerns as she focused her attention on Brielle who was in her baby walker in the living room.

"We're here to play with Brielle and we play best on the floor," Martha said with genuine enthusiasm. "Do you mind if we get started?"

It was nice to be asked permission for a change before the therapists mauled my child.

The therapists dropped what they had in their arms and plopped down on the floor. Within moments, they had Brielle lying on a blanket and were cooing at her, shaking rattles, and playing with her with an ease I had rarely seen even in other mothers. Dawn, the nurse, sat on our lumpy sofa and took out a clipboard from her shoulder bag. The service coordinator took a seat at the table and asked me to join her.

Not an Invasion, No Interrogation Necessary

"My name is Sharon and I'm going to be your family's service co-ordinator. I'm here to make sure everything goes smoothly and you get all of the services and assistance from the community that you need," the woman said with a generous smile. "If you ever have any questions or problems with any services or just want to talk, I'm here for your family. I mean that."

Really? Someone was there to help and advocate for us? That was not the experience we had in Wisconsin. We had to do everything on our own. If we had questions, we had to look it up in a dictionary. If we had issues with services, we exchanged notes with the therapists in Brielle's diaper bag. If Sharon was truly telling us how things would actually be, this would be quite different indeed.

"And who might this be?" Sharon smiled at Ashley who was being uncharacteristically shy and hiding behind me.

"This is Ashley," I said, attempting to encourage my two-and-a-half-year-old to be sociable.

"You know what I have?" the woman coyly asked Ashley as she dramatically dug through her bag. "I have a special coloring book for you and a brand new box of crayons," she said, offering Ashley these camouflaged trinkets of bribery while winking at me. What a clever ruse.

My toddler hesitated a moment and looked at me, obviously questioning if it was OK to take these gifts from this stranger. Soon my little girl was kneeling on the third empty kitchen chair and entertaining herself as she colored happily and silently in her new coloring book with her new thick crayons.

Sharon asked Ashley a few questions about what sorts of games she liked to play and if she was excited about moving into a new house. Ashley responded to her questions and seemed happy to receive a little bit of attention as the three other women fawned over her baby sister on the living room floor.

The compassion Sharon showed Ashley and the positive playfulness the therapists seemed to be showing Brielle made me feel comfortable with these strangers in their first few minutes with us. Maybe I could take a deep breath and let my guard down a little.

"So, Kerith," the service coordinator asked, turning her attention to me. "Tell me about your family and why you think Brielle might need a little extra help."

I shared our whole story. The pregnancy. Chicken pox. The worrying. CMV. The days at the hospital after she was born. Not rolling over. The picture I tried to take on Good Friday. The testing. Getting therapy in Wisconsin. The move. I found myself spilling my guts while the other four strangers played with my baby and my toddler busily colored a picture of a puppy at the table next to me, thankfully oblivious to my raw emotions. Sharon dug in her purse, pulled out a tissue for me, and took one for herself.

The other women were silent as I told our story. When I finished, Martha looked up from Brielle. With real compassion, she asked, "And how have you and your husband been coping?"

I was not sure how to respond. No one ever asked me that. I had not been looking for sympathy as I shared our story. My emotions from all of the changes must have just caught up with me. I suddenly felt embarrassed by my outburst of tears as I felt everyone's eyes on me.

The truth was we were kind of a mess even though we were getting through each day. However, our emotionally fragile condition was too painful to truly consider and definitely too uncomfortable to report these women.

Trying to restrain my emotions and gather my thoughts quickly, I said something about how we were learning to cope with each day. I figured that was probably what they wanted to hear and it was not too far from the truth. Despite how welcoming these women were, they were still strangers. I did not freely reveal my innermost feelings with close friends or family, let alone these newcomers.

Meet Your New Teachers

As the three therapists continued to evaluate Brielle with the nurse taking notes, Sharon told me about the Early Intervention program and what to expect in the first few months. She slowly explained the intake process, motioned briefly to the stack of paperwork between us, and then let each of the women on the floor explain her role in the EI process.

Martha, the occupational therapist, pointed out different parts of Brielle's hands that she was examining as she dangled toys in front of her and then positioned her on her stomach.

Pam, the physical therapist, explained how she was evaluating Brielle's legs, back, stomach, and overall body strength and coordination as she moved Brielle in a playful way from one position to another.

Arlene, the speech therapist, jiggled Brielle's cheeks between her hands and made different basic sounds trying to encourage Brielle to repeat them as she explained how she was evaluating Brielle's oral motor skills.

Each woman used words I had read in the notes we received when the therapists in Wisconsin worked with Brielle at the daycare. However, each time one of the therapists used a technical term, she immediately defined it in clear terms without sounding condescending or making me feel stupid.

As they talked, the women often demonstrated how a muscle should work and how Brielle's muscles responded. They even briefly showed me a few therapy techniques they would be using with her in the months to come. Seeing everything in person and the therapists' use of "plain English" made it all come into clearer focus. Like switching on a light, their approach shifted my entire understanding of Brielle. I understood what parts of her body did not work quite right. I understood why their therapy looked like play. I finally got it.

MORE ABOUT....
The Differences Between the Two EI Experiences

Obviously, there are individual differences between therapists. Moreover, we only experienced two months with the EI team in Wisconsin while we spent the rest of Brielle's birth-to-three program with the therapists in Illinois. However, that cannot explain the two very different approaches the teams used.

The Wisconsin EI team used an approach that mirrored a medical model (down to the clothes they wore). They primarily focused on the medical diagnosis of Brielle's physical issues and the steps to improve or correct those issues.

The Illinois EI team used a more contemporary, family-centered model focusing on integrating families into the process, teaching basic therapy techniques, and providing well-rounded support to all members of the family by addressing family values and needs.

As Ashley continued to be content coloring at the table and Brielle happy with the therapists playing with her on the floor, Sharon leafed through the paperwork between us and gently peppered me with questions as she filled in the blanks.

Without even a word, Dawn, the nurse, put down her clipboard, switched places with Sharon and asked me a few questions about Brielle's diet and health history. I told her about Brielle's coughing fits and about her recent issues with constipation. She gave me a few suggestions to help ease her cough, but I assured her that Brielle's cough had been better in recent weeks.

Martha told me that infant massage might be able to help Brielle's constipation. She told me she regularly taught classes and when her next class began.

"Maybe Ashley could bring a doll to practice on when she comes along," Martha suggested while subtly letting me know that my toddler was welcome to tag along.

Although these five women were at our apartment for about two hours, the time went quickly and I watched with curiosity as they moved around Brielle like a well-orchestrated waltz.

As Sharon asked me a few final questions and scheduled our first appointments, the therapists invited Ashley to come down on the floor with them while Dawn held Brielle. Martha teasingly ran her fingers though Ashley's curly locks. My toddler giggled, but shook her little finger at the woman for her to stop as the other women laughed at Ashley's scolding. Pam encouraged Ashley to sit in her lap by offering to read her a book Arlene had taken out of her bag.

I was a bit dumbfounded by the attention they gave my toddler when they did not even have to acknowledge her. They were here for Brielle, not Ashley. However, their kindness to all of us was so very clear. These women were just as wonderful as Bobbi had suggested.

Sharon left some forms for me to fill out at my convenience and promised to have the therapists' initial report and her forms copied to give to me within a week. The therapists packed up their bags and thanked me for having them in our home before leaving. Although I felt uncomfortable at the suggestion that the apartment was our home, I felt at ease with these women and knew that they could help Brielle.

After they left and I got the girls down for their afternoon naps, I offered up a silent prayer, something I did not often do at the time. *Thank you, God, for bringing me those women.*

Perhaps my positive feelings about the new EI experience were because I was more accepting of Brielle's delays. Maybe it was because I had been through the process before and it was not such a shock to answer all of the questions and allow strangers to handle my baby.

No matter, I could not wait to tell Brian about our experience with the new EI team when he arrived at the apartment from his new job later that evening. It had been a good day. Maybe this place would feel like home sooner than I expected.

> *Therefore, as God's chosen people, holy and dearly loved, clothe yourselves with compassion, kindness, humility, gentleness, and patience.*
>
> – COLOSSIANS 3:12 (NIV)

CHAPTER 14

Enduring Change

"This is your new room," I tell Brielle as we walk around our new home in Atlanta for the first time. This is the fifth house she has lived in during her 12 years of life. Despite her new surroundings, she just rolls with the changes.

"Love it," she signs, twirling around the empty space. "Want pink."

"You want your room to be pink?" I ask.

"Yes, pink," she signs and then rubs one of the pale yellow walls.

"Well," I pause, trying to imagine the room painted pink. "Let's just see what your room looks like once we get your things all moved in. You might like the yellow."

"Pink best," she signs. "Like old room."

Finding a Familiar Routine
Despite Heaps of Change

Brian's new job was a huge boost to his career. Being only a few hours from our parents was good for all of us. I felt confident that it was going to be better for the girls if I stayed at home. I assumed finding new doctors and therapists would take only a few phone calls. Exploring a new community would be fun. These are the things I told myself before the move.

With Brian working long days at his new job, the girls and I were on our own to find a routine for ourselves. Already feeling at ease with the new EI team, I learned new things at each of their weekly visits and enjoyed having a little adult conversation for the hour they were with us. Tuesday mornings were story time at the library and a local church hosted a playgroup on Thursday mornings. Since these were the only organized activities available, it took some creativity to find things to help fill the gaps in our days.

A few local fun spots like the old-fashioned ice cream parlor downtown and the McDonald's playscape became places of refuge. When the Midwest fall weather permitted, our favorite retreat was the park. I collected quarters for rides on the merry-go-round and bought two loaves of bread each week, one for us and one for the ducks at the pond. Days spent at the park were our happiest.

We joined Martha's weekly infant massage class when it started in mid-October. Ashley brought her doll, Rosie, and imitated the moms massaging their children. Massaging Brielle at least once or twice a day, we could tell a difference with her constipation, just as Martha said we would.

Our weekly trip to the grocery store was usually a fun excursion until we had to make our way back up to the apartment. Leaving everything else locked up in our van, I swung a sturdy bag over my shoulder filled with only the perishables and guided Ashley up the steps while carrying Brielle in my arms. Brian brought up the remaining groceries when he arrived at our apartment later in the evening.

The apartment's basement laundry room left me in a similar predicament. With Baby Brielle on top of the dirty clothes in the laundry basket, I coached Ashley to stutter step each tread of the stairs (going down one step, meeting her feet together, then going to the next step). When it came time to switch laundry from the washing machine to the dryer, I dragged the two girls down with me and fed the hungry machines with quarters. When the laundry was finished, Brielle rode on top of the stack of warm, clean clothes.

Despite our outings, the rest of our existence was dull. I had little creative or natural ability to keep boredom at bay for the girls once we entered the confining walls of the apartment. I read to them, colored with them, and talked to them. I was not typically the type of mother who sat on the floor to play with my children, but I forced myself to do that, too. Kids' television shows were often on just to keep Ashley entertained since she had so few toys. She did not need me to constantly entertain her, but I felt guilty and a little jealous when the television became her favorite entertainment.

On the weekends, our whole family did what we could to stay away from the apartment. We visited a fall festival, went to a playground, flew a kite, or drove over to Rockford to walk around the mall. I welcomed the respite from our small apartment.

Although Brian was not interested in church, I still took both girls somewhere each Sunday morning. However, none of the churches felt right, largely because I did not feel right in our new surroundings. It all felt so unfamiliar, even mothering the girls.

New and Different Does Not Equal Better

In the first week, there was so much to get set up, including Early Intervention for Brielle, that I had little time to enjoy full-time mothering. The girls and I had some fun days staying busy through the second week discovering new things in the community. By the third week, we had our routine and the dreariness of our surroundings set in.

Ashley began repeatedly asking for toys, movies, and books that were packed away in a storage unit. Brielle seemed bored with the few positions I let her be in. I eventually caved and put her on a blanket on the floor despite my worries that the blanket would not be enough protection from the dirty shag carpet. I missed familiar things, especially knowing how to fill my time and our daughters'.

Being a full-time mother was supposed to help me get closer to the girls. Instead, I simply went through the motions of being a mother, aiming my attention at the demands of the day.

Breakfast. An excursion. Lunch. Nap. Play. Dinner. Bath. Bedtime. Next day, repeat.

I assumed peace and contentment would eventually settle in, but I gradually became more agitated by the constant demands of my little girls and the lack of adult companionship. I tried to dig deep, but could not find my footing.

The rigors of being a stay-at-home mom were more difficult than I anticipated and exhausted me in unexpected ways. My cravings for caffeine spiked and my body ached from the physical demands of the activities with the children and the sprints up and down the apartment's stairs with Brielle on my hip.

"You sound tired, Honey," my mother tentatively suggested on the phone one afternoon in late October.

"I am, Mom," I said with some fragment of honesty. How could I explain that level of tired?

"Is there anything I can do? I could come and help out for a while."

"Mom, I don't need help. I can do this," I reacted defensively.

"Are you sure? Maybe just for a few days?"

"Mom, we're fine." I refused to be completely honest or accept her offer to help because I did not want to fully admit just how much I was struggling.

With that, she let it go. So did I.

Father Knows Frustration, Too

Brielle's need for feedings in the middle of the night kept Ashley from getting any decent sleep, often leading to a cranky toddler the next day. The only option was to sandwich Brielle's crib next to our bed. Her close proximity then disrupted our sleep even more than usual, often making a cranky mom and dad the next day. Having a baby in our bedroom did not help the intimacy in our marriage either.

In the evenings and on the weekends, Brian and I continued the separation of parental duties we started months before when Brielle's colic overwhelmed Brian. Even in the small apartment, that coping mechanism only served to distance me from both Ashley and Brian. Our once cohesive family moved into shaky territory.

"What if you and the girls went to live with your parents for a while?" Brian suggested.

"I'm not going to break up our family," I snapped.

"I'm not asking for a divorce here," Brian retorted. "I'm only proposing that you live with them until our house is ready."

"No," I said emphatically. "My mother offered to come here for a while, but there's no room for her. Going there or having her here isn't going to fix things. It would only postpone the inevitable. I've got to figure out how to manage things on my own."

"Then figure things out," Brian stated with a resolve I rarely saw. "At this rate, you are going to burn yourself out."

"I know," I said flatly. "I just never expected it to be this hard."

"It will be better when we get into the house," my husband encouraged me as he put his arm around me.

"I hope so," I whispered back, trying to control my quivering voice.

The next evening Brian brought me flowers. My husband's thoughtful gesture softened my mood that evening, but the next day's routine only gave way to dampened spirits once again. Crying often, my morale was at a tipping point.

Fatigue and frustration with our living situation was hard to ignore. I knew my husband was also getting frustrated with me. I snapped at him often. I ignored his attempts to lighten the mood. His inquires about our day were often met with my complaints. My dismal attitude added to the guilt he felt every morning when he left the apartment to go to the new job he really liked. He then faced the burdens of our family's circumstances every evening when he came back.

Mom Finally Breaks Down

Foolishly, I thought attempting to potty train our two and half year old was a good idea. However, at this chaotic time, it just sparked Ashley's stubborn streak. Potty training left her wet and irritable. It left me angry and with more laundry to do. When all of my training tactics were unsuccessful, I deserted anything beyond a half-hearted effort.

There was one particularly long day at the end of October with the girls. Although there had not been any specific trigger that day, Brielle's fussiness was at an all-time high (at least since her colic ended) and I had countless frustrations potty training Ashley. That evening, Brian came home to an exasperated wife.

"Here," I said, thrusting Brielle at him the moment he entered the apartment. "I can't deal with her and I'm not talking to the other one."

"The other one" was Ashley. Our precious daughter had been reduced to being called "the other one" by her mother. Brian looked at me as if I were an alien. I felt like an alien. How could a mother be so impatient with her toddler that she refused to talk to the child?

I stormed out in frustration without another word. Guilt also overwhelmed me as I escaped and descended the stairs to our van in tears. I had become grumpy, short-tempered, and quick to complain. Moreover, I had never cracked and walked out like that.

Driving around aimlessly for a while, still crying as my mind wandered, our vehicle ended up at the ice cream parlor just before it closed. A pint of French vanilla would be my peace offering, but I could also pretend it was my excuse for leaving in the first place.

I corralled my feelings of self-pity and shame about committing what felt like mommy malpractice, put on a weak smile, and walked through the apartment door about two hours after I left. Ashley was still awake and overjoyed to receive a sweet treat from the mother who had lost nearly all control earlier that day. Brielle looked tired and ready for bed, but perked up when she saw me. Diverting my gaze from Brian, I tried to act normal as I took small bites of the melting ice cream.

Brian and I did not talk about what happened that day. We acted as if my alien behavior never happened and I was relieved to put it behind us. I could never let myself unravel like that again. Never.

Instead, I packed up my emotions like Russian nesting dolls, dug a grave, and buried them as deep as possible. Any time a negative thought or those feelings of self-pity started to rise to the surface, I found a household task or child that needed tending to, distracting myself from the dark abyss of emotions I could so easily stumble into. I put one foot in front of the other and longed for the day just weeks away when we would move into our new house.

More Than Just a Cough

We had been living in the apartment about a month when Brian's office organized a trip to Chicago to watch a Bulls preseason basketball game. The teenage daughter of one of Brian's coworkers came over to babysit the girls. We were eager to see Michael Jordan play, but a bit apprehensive about being out-of-touch and 90 minutes away. (This was 1996 and there were no cell phones.)

When we returned late that evening, Brielle was awake and coughing. Since we were accustomed to her coughing fits, we did not think much about it. We gave her some over-the-counter medicine, but by morning, a high fever accompanied her soupy cough. She was so sick and lethargic that we decided to take her to the emergency room.

"I don't feel comfortable treating your daughter," the female emergency room doctor announced when we told her about Brielle's CMV. "I'm trying to get pregnant and I don't want to take the risk of contracting CMV."

Brielle would continue to be contagious through her bodily fluids for several years, but so were many other children and adults who showed no symptoms at all. We did not have much time or emotional energy to consider the doctor's unreasonable response or provide her with a lesson about the contagious nature of CMV. As stunned and frustrated as we were, we just wanted our child to be treated as quickly as possible.

Another doctor examined Brielle instead. Whatever the cause of her illness, x-rays revealed it developed into pneumonia and she was immediately admitted.

The nurses posted a bright red sign outside Brielle's hospital room door. It read, "Use Universal Precautions. Highly contagious." It was not there for her pneumonia. It was for her CMV. I knew it was for the safety of the hospital staff, but it made me feel like my daughter was some sort of leper and it angered me. I was probably just as contagious at this point as she was. No one required me to wear a sign around my neck with those same words of caution.

With Brielle in the hospital, we had our hands full. My parents came up, stayed overnight, and then took Ashley home with them to Champaign. The grandparents took turns taking care of our toddler while Brian and I stayed with Brielle at the local hospital.

Brielle spent four days in the hospital, receiving breathing treatments every few hours. Brian and I sat like bookends on each side of her hospital crib, sleeping in her room overnight. The scene was reminiscent of the first days after Brielle was born. Watching our child's every breath. Feeding the payphone with coins to update our family. Eating lackluster cafeteria food and snacks from the vending machines.

On the third day, Brielle was finally alert enough to give me a weak smile. In that moment, I felt such relief knowing she had turned the corner and was getting better. I could not help but to send up a quick little prayer of thanks.

The doctors released her from the hospital on Halloween. I took a few days to ensure she was truly healthy again and then traveled to our hometown to bring Ashley back to Freeport. Thankful that Brielle was well and we were all back together again, our surroundings at the apartment mattered less than it had before.

Perfect Timing for Wise Counsel

"Are you OK?" Martha asked at the end of her session about two weeks after Brielle was home from the hospital. "You don't seem yourself today."

"I thought this stay-at-home mom thing would be easier. I just have to do better."

"Don't be so hard on yourself," she said sympathetically. "You've been through a lot of changes. This would be hard on anyone. It's OK not to be supermom."

"I don't always need to be supermom. I'd settle for just being a good mom," I said and then told her about the evening I made my abrupt trip to the ice cream parlor.

"It's OK to need a break. It's natural to get emotional sometimes, too. Let go once in a while. It's not healthy to keep your feelings wound up so tightly."

Despite not knowing me for very long, Martha had a knack of seeing past my façade and her words resonated with me. During the last few weeks in the apartment, I tried to relax a little and not expect perfection from myself. It certainly did not happen overnight, but my better mood spilled over onto everyone else in the family.

Home, At Last

We went through the motions of our remaining days in the apartment as best as we could. We were physically challenged and mentally drained, but we had gotten through it. When the house was finally ours just a week before Thanksgiving, it felt as if things were falling into place and we would finally get a real chance to make this place home.

Removing our possessions from their boxes, I revived them one by one and found a place for them in our new house. Discovering each precious item was better than opening presents on Christmas morning. Ashley hugged her long lost toys each time she was reunited with her treasures. Brian unloaded items and broke down boxes as we negotiated where the best place for each item might be. We carefully studied blank walls before he drove in a nail to make a home for pictures, clocks, or other items for the wall.

With each emptied box and nesting activity, I felt more at peace. After all, a house is more than just a way of protecting a family from nature's elements. This house in Freeport was slowly becoming our home. We had all learned what a powerful word "home" truly was.

Despite our more peaceful existence, our most basic problems lingered. The gap between what Brielle could do and what she should be doing continued to get bigger every day. We still did not have many friends and had not found a church home. Although we had found a babysitter, Brian and I had not been out as a couple in many weeks and were not feeling particularly connected. Moreover, I was still recovering from nearly drowning in a sea of self-pity.

These were not the ideal circumstances to be in at the brink of the holiday season. However, the joy and promise of good times over the upcoming holidays helped renew a spark of optimism for how things could be. That sliver of hope spurred on my determination to make things better for all of us in the months to come. It truly felt like the worst of it was behind us as this new chapter in our lives was just starting to unfold.

...And let us run with perseverance the race marked out for us, fixing our eyes on Jesus, the pioneer and perfecter of faith. For the joy set before Him He endured the cross, scorning its shame, and sat down at the right hand of the throne of God. Consider him who endured such opposition from sinners, so that you will not grow weary and lose heart.

— HEBREWS 12: 1-3 (NIV)

CHAPTER 15

The Education of Mom

Before reading a bedtime story to the girls, Brian has homework to do with two-year-old Brielle. He starts to grab her ankles and she already squeals with delight. He hangs her 22-pound body upside down and starts swinging her side to side.

"Tick, tock. Tick, tock," Brian says rhythmically as he swings her back and forth like a pendulum. "And... KABOOM," he says dramatically as he plops her down on the bed.

"More, more," Brielle signs hardly able to catch her breath from laughing so hard.

Brielle's physical therapist told us that our little one needed these sorts of activities since she didn't move like other children and get it naturally through play activity. I look on in horror. Brian is doing something for Brielle I can't bring myself to do and it bonds them in a special way.

"OK," Brian says, smiling down at our daughter. "Here we go again." He swoops her up by her ankles and repeats what she thinks is just a game.

Learning to Accept Our Child

When Brielle's first birthday arrived in February, we had a lot to celebrate. We traveled to Champaign and had a huge family party for both girls since their birthdays were so close together. Looking at our healthy little girl, it was difficult to believe the doctors had told us there was a forty percent chance Brielle would die at birth.

CMV plundered Brielle's body and left its mark, but it did not take the best of her spirit. However, as the anniversary of her birth passed, the delays in her physical abilities were clear. Although she started to roll over from her tummy to her back at eight months old, there were still so many skills that eluded her. Most children were agile crawlers and starting to take their first steps by their first birthday. Brielle was nowhere near reaching those milestones. She could not even sit up independently yet.

For me, considering Brielle's milestones became difficult. *What to Expect the First Year* was a painful reference book and was relegated to the back corner of the closet. Not able to face her baby book with all of its blanks where achievements should be documented, I set it aside as well and started a journal instead. We were writing our own story now.

The worries of the pregnancy, our first experiences with Early Intervention in Wisconsin, and our initial living situation in Freeport had a huge impact on me mentally, emotionally, and physically. By Brielle's first birthday, life had softened for all of us. Although still a bit brittle, I was never bitter. I could have been angry about Brielle's delays, but that feeling just never occurred to me.

I learned that Brielle was Brielle. She was unique in many ways. She might never fit onto the pages of a baby book or doctor's charts, but she was precious and had found a place in my heart and life I never knew existed.

Learning to Be an Active Participant in Brielle's Development

Fear and fatigue no longer overwhelmed and immobilized me. After spending nearly two years of my life as a worrier, I was becoming a warrior. I saw the challenge put before us and decided to tackle it head on. Instead of mourning the loss of the child Brielle could have been, I transformed myself into the mom she needed. Helping Brielle became my own brand of spiritual morphine, easing the remnants of pain left behind.

Brielle needed intensive therapy to reach missing milestones. Physical therapy. Occupational therapy. Speech therapy. And me. She especially needed me.

The vast valley between the mother I was and the mother I would need to become for Brielle's sake was slowly becoming apparent. Traditional mothering was not going to be enough to help our child get to where she needed to be. I needed to work just as hard as Brielle did during her therapy sessions.

When I was a child, my father teased me that my brain was a muscle and I had to exercise it to keep it healthy and strong. With Brielle, I needed to exercise it with a new approach to parenting. Along the way, I had many encouraging self-talks to get me through the long and sometimes difficult mental workouts.

As the mother of a disabled child, I had to learn incredible patience and to stay calm even when difficult news added to the image of Brielle. Although I had not been the sort of mother that got down on the floor to play or set up messy activities just for the fun of it, I learned to do that, too. I learned medical jargon, the therapists' lingo, and how to advocate for Brielle to ensure her needs were met. In addition to providing basic care and instilling basic moral principles, I also learned to become a teacher and amateur therapist.

I became an extra set of hands during the therapists' home visits. As the PT sat Brielle on a big ball tilting her one way and then another,

I dangled toys up high for Brielle to reach for. With Brielle sitting on a low bench, I supported her hips to make her balance as the OT helped Brielle stack up cups hand over hand. Holding Brielle in my arms, the speech therapist positioned the bottle of milk at just the right angle for my child. As the therapists' helper, I watched, listened, asked questions, and learned.

The therapists taught Brielle and me side-by-side. Although I learned a few things through our experiences in Wisconsin, my real education started with the Early Intervention Brielle received in Illinois.

The therapists showed me how her cerebral palsy manifested itself. They pointed out how awkwardly Brielle's little hands moved, how tight her hamstrings were, how soft her stomach muscles were, and the unusual sounds she made. The therapists' lingo and their acronyms slowly became part of my vocabulary. What had been a mystery to me when Brielle was getting therapy in Wisconsin was slowly becoming second nature as I integrated their techniques into our own time playing together. She was still my Brielle, but now I could see her in a new way.

Learning to Be Fulfilled By My New Career

After not working for months, I was not missing it much. Frankly, there was not enough time or energy to miss it. My marketing career was over, but my parenting career was in overdrive and there was much to learn. Each day and each therapy session was a new project.

Making Brielle better became my new goal and full-time job. Although there were no expectations of any miracles to cure her muscles that did not work right, I worked hard to help her do her best in this race called "life." At the time, I did not realize the race was a marathon, not a sprint. There would be many long days, much hard work, and many therapy appointments with many therapists over the years.

I was the one enduring strand in Brielle's life of therapy. Brian was there for her at home, playing with her and Ashley in the evenings. However, with work and his schedule that, in later years, included traveling, he rarely came to any therapy sessions. He never even met most of the therapists.

I often videotaped parts of Brielle's therapy sessions to show Brian. Brielle made such small progress that the sessions often looked similar for weeks or months at a time. I eventually only videotaped novel techniques or major accomplishments and, over time, we discussed the details of each session less and less.

MORE ABOUT....
Videotaping Brielle's Therapy

It became its own journal of Brielle's progress. Years later, Brielle still loves to watch those old home videos. She squeals with joy when she sees Martha helping her as a baby and claps for baby Brielle for working so hard.

Brian was not a disinterested father, to say the least. We were still connected parents, making decisions together as they arose. Just as couples divide household duties like cooking dinner, doing laundry, or mowing the lawn, we divided therapy duties for Brielle. I was naturally the better-equipped parent since I was there for the sessions, had a better understanding of techniques, and had more time to devote to implementing them at home since I was with her all day.

I fully embraced my job as the lead parent for Brielle. Frankly, I did not mind it a bit. I did not have a job, volunteer work, many friends, or hobbies to fill my days. Despite the sometimes exhausting routine of her care, it gave me purpose at a time I desperately needed it.

I was beginning to see my life from a new perspective. I could see how certain life experiences seemed to perfectly align with what

I needed to parent Brielle. I had not wasted my time and effort in college and graduate school. That education helped me learn faster. Working with disabled high school students was not an eerily timed job. It helped me see what the other end of the road might look like for Brielle and for us. Even the most painful times in the pregnancy and first months seemed somehow necessary. I needed those experiences to get me to where I was.

Learning to Follow My Instincts

In the beginning, we viewed Brielle's doctors and therapists as being not only more knowledgeable but also as better decision makers for our daughter's care. They had treated so many children like Brielle, we assumed and trusted that they were following some sort of clear and tested formula to make our daughter better. Over time, we learned that although those professionals had knowledge and experience, they did not know Brielle like we did and they were not the ones that had to implement the treatment plan and live with the ramifications each day.

Eventually, I defied a professional's opinion for the first time. Arlene, the speech therapist, used a variety of tools to help Brielle with her oral motor development and decrease her oral sensitivity. She sang a happy tune while poking around Brielle's mouth with a toothette (a pink sponge at the end of a lollipop stick), a Nuk (a handle with rounded plastic spikes on the end), or sometimes her gloved hand. Brielle spent most of that part of her speech therapy sessions crying as if those tools were torture devices. Although it was painful to watch this process, I initially deferred to Arlene's techniques and ignored my motherly instincts to protect my child from her prodding.

Meal times were becoming battles and crying sessions whenever we tried to feed her baby food from a spoon. Her pediatrician had little advice to offer and deferred to our speech therapist. Arlene counseled us to continue to give Brielle formula from a bottle, but also to be persistent in our attempts to spoon feed Brielle. Our child refused any food from a spoon. It was as if she saw it as one more way to torture her mouth.

One look at our thin 14-month-old told me I needed to find a way to get more food into her. Knowing our concerns about how Brielle could get enough calories and nutrition, my father made a suggestion.

"I don't know if they still make them," he told me over the phone one day. "But, we used these bottles with big holes in the top to feed you kids when we went camping. I think it started with an 'I'."

"I think he's talking about an Infafeeder," my mother chimed in on speakerphone. "At the time, it was just an easier way to get baby food into you when we were on the road. But, maybe your father is right and it would help Brielle."

Searching the baby aisles of every store, I finally found one. This bottle-shaped device allowed Brielle to suck pureed food. I thought it was a huge success for my little one to be able to finally eat some solid foods. Arlene was not supportive of my find. She argued that using the Infafeeder would interfere with our daughter's suck pattern and only exasperate the spoon-feeding issue. Although I was mindful of Arlene's protests, our thin child needed more nourishment, no matter how we got it in her.

This was the first of many times we made a choice in Brielle's care which did not follow a professional's advice.

We refused a surgical procedure on Brielle's right hand when the potential for improvement was relatively small. We disregarded the orthodontist's suggestion for oral surgery and a mouth full of appliances in favor of a less invasive approach to straighten her teeth. Rather than making Brielle wear a leg brace and knee immobilizer while sleeping every night, doing it every few nights just had to be enough.

Even with simple therapy tasks at home, I was not always compliant. Sometimes, a therapist's homework was too difficult or time consuming. Other times, their suggestions would have disrupted our routine too much for me to feel comfortable integrating it. Stricken with vanity, I sometimes worried about what people out in public might think if I did what the therapists asked of me. Occasionally, laziness due to exhaustion was the culprit. As my knowledge and confidence grew, I learned to pick and choose what to do. I often chose what had the biggest payoff.

The Greatest Lesson I Ever Learned

Martha was pivotal in Brielle's life and in my education as well. As she moved Brielle's body this way and that, she casually kept discussions going about completely irrelevant things like the weather, local news, or her daughters. As teachable moments arose, she gracefully shifted the conversation back to the task at hand.

She was particularly talented at teaching me in a way that sunk in. Martha explained things simply and defined any jargon or acronyms she used, even if it took several times for me to remember. She also demonstrated what she was explaining by pointing things out on Brielle's body, mine, or even on Ashley's from time to time. With that, Martha could more clearly explain what things we could do to get Brielle's muscles to work better. Just as important as what Martha taught me to do, she also taught me valuable lessons about what *not* to do.

"Don't help her so much," Martha counseled me one day during a therapy session at our house. "Let her fail. Let her fall down sometimes, too."

"Fall?" I questioned with alarm. Brielle was less than two years old and still not walking. "How can I let her fall down? She might get hurt."

"Well, don't let her get hurt," she reassured me. "Just let it surprise her. She'll learn as much from failure as she will from success. But,

174

she won't learn anything except how to manipulate you if you always save her and do everything for her."

Her words stung. Was I really doing too much for Brielle? Was I letting this small child manipulate me?

"How many times did Ashley fall when she was learning to walk?" Martha asked.

I looked at my curly-headed preschooler who was happily playing with some toys off to the side.

"Probably hundreds," I replied, thinking of Ashley when she was our little nearly bald toddler falling time and time again on her diapered bottom before learning to walk and eventually run.

"Ashley learned from falling, from her failures. Give Brielle that experience, too. She may be trapped in her little body that doesn't work right, but underneath that, she is really no different from other children. She has to learn to do for herself just as much as she possibly can."

My initial instincts were to make things easy for Brielle. However, I learned to let my child fail, fall down, and precariously maneuver objects without jumping to her rescue. Brielle learned from her failures, just like other kids, while her mom learned to let go a little, just like other moms.

My primary parenting principle is "Empower them." That principle has guided me through many easy parenting situations as well as ones that were more difficult. However, before empowering them, I had to loosen my reigns on them. Before letting them go a little, I had to impart them with my wisdom. Before passing along my knowledge, I had to learn for myself.

Learning is a gift and even an uncomfortable blessing when pain is my teacher. The early years of Brielle's therapy were the greatest lessons for me. Those lessons helped Brielle become more independent and let me eventually get back to enjoying a little more of a life of my own.

I instruct you in the way of wisdom and lead you along straight paths.
When you walk, your steps will not be hampered; when you run, you will not stumble.
Hold on to instruction, do not let it go; guard it well, for it is your life.

– PROVERBS 4: 11-13 (NIV)

CHAPTER 16

Calling All Therapists

Brielle and I stand on the corner waiting for the school bus to take her to her 7th grade class.

She points to the sky and signs, "Why that?"

I look up at the clear blue sky splattered with only a few, sparse clouds.

"Why that?" she asks again.

I then realize she is asking about the vapor trail a jet left behind. My tear-filled eyes stare at her. I take a deep breath as I smile and put my arm around her. My 13-year-old daughter had just asked me a "why" question for the very first time ever.

After working so hard on her language abilities, I did not realize how long we waited to hear "why" from her until she spoke it. What a typical parent might see as a stepping-stone on their child's road of developmental progress, I saw as a game changer.

"That's a trail from a jet airplane," I sign back to her as I also speak. "It's like the smoke from an airplane."

She stares up at the streak in the sky processing my answer. "Oh. Cool."

Therapists at Work

My days were busy mothering our girls. We continued our routine of going to playgroup, library time, the playscape at McDonalds, and the park to feed the ducks or ride the merry-go-round. I got better about designing activities to entertain and involve the girls. Although I still preferred to read, put together puzzles, or color with the girls, we also played with PlayDoh, baked cookies, dug in the sandbox, dressed-up in wacky costumes, and had elaborate games of pretend. The most important part of our days was Brielle's therapy time.

Brielle received weekly home visits from the intervention specialist, Sharon, who was also our service coordinator. Her sessions helped bridge the gap between the therapists' technical sessions and something more practical by using some of our own toys and showing us how to easily integrate their strategies into our daily lives.

Sharon was also there to help us connect with any other services we might have needed such as nursing, vision therapy, or counseling. Although we never used many of the other services, it was comforting to know they were available to us. Her biggest job was to coordinate all of the therapists' visits. And each therapist claimed time with Brielle.

Martha came to our house twice a month. Sometimes she brought different spoons for us to try, each with a unique handle or curve to its bowl, or different writing tools, each with a unique shape or grip with which to write. Martha spent the rest of the session doing activities that stretched and strengthened Brielle's shoulders, arms, and hands as well as improved her fine motor skills overall.

Pam was the only pediatric physical therapist in several area counties. Therefore, she only came to work with Brielle every six weeks. With Brielle's huge delays in gross motor skills, we packed as much as we could into those precious visits. Pam started every visit by showing me how to gently but firmly stretch out Brielle's muscles, especially her shoulders and hamstrings. She helped strengthen

Brielle's core muscles by bouncing her on a big ball, rolling her over a cylindrical bolster, or kneeling her in front of a short bench, all while reaching for toys. She also helped me figure out positioning issues with Brielle's high chair and bath chair.

Arlene came to our house about twice a month. I tried to time Brielle's feedings so that Arlene could watch and make suggestions. We tried numerous bottles, each with a different shaped nipple, to figure out which one might best help Brielle close her lips when drinking. Although Brielle liked playing with spoons, she resisted eating from a spoon and was often agitated by the texture of the food or the spoon itself. Even after we started feeding her with the Infafeeder my father suggested, we kept trying to spoon feed her but only made minimal progress for many months.

By the time Brielle was a year old, our calendar was speckled with one or two therapy appointments each week. We soon realized that the few, intermittent hours of therapy from the team of Early Intervention specialists were not enough for Brielle to progress as we had hoped. Therefore, I arranged for private therapy sessions as soon as the therapists had openings in their schedules.

Brielle's weekly private therapy sessions with Arlene were almost exactly the same as they were during her home visits through the Early Intervention program. There was still poking and prodding in Brielle's mouth. Arlene also tried to encourage Brielle to repeat sounds and mimic facial expressions. It made me very uncomfortable watching Brielle's unhappy reactions to Arlene's techniques, but she was making a little progress.

When a patient of Martha's moved away, we snatched up both of that child's weekly sessions. It was tough getting to her office by 7:30 two mornings a week with both kids in tow, but it was worth it. Martha made the most of each session and worked Brielle hard, but she was compassionate and fun, too.

Need Therapists, Will Travel

Martha took a full body approach to helping Brielle by incorporating gross motor activities as well. However, Brielle needed more intensive physical therapy. Pam did not offer private sessions and the nearest pediatric physical therapist was an hour-drive away in Rockford. Since this was our only option, I made the commitment to do it and we started the weekly trek to Rockford just before Brielle's first birthday.

Although she was not as personable as Pam, Holly worked in a large pediatric therapy clinic and that had its benefits for Brielle. Holly tried different equipment and pieces of technology with Brielle that the other therapists in the small town of Freeport did not have available.

MORE ABOUT....
Ashley During Brielle's Therapy Sessions

Ashley was just a toddler when Brielle started therapy. She often played on the other side of the room with the many fascinating toys. The therapists also tried to include her as much as they could by asking her to fetch toys or hold things high in the air as they worked Brielle's body.

Despite Ashley's happy cooperation, I often worried about the balance between attending to each of our girls. When Ashley turned three, we enrolled her in a preschool that also offered daycare. She spent a few mornings a week there including all day on Fridays when Brielle eventually had back-to-back private therapy in Rockford.

When Brielle was about two years old, the clinic in Rockford started a new aquatherapy program. Therapists worked together and traded off kids in the pool. PTs encouraged the kids to kick. OTs prompted the kids to use their arms or slap the surface of the water to improve their arm strength. Speech therapists modeled holding their breath and blowing bubbles at the water's surface.

Most days, I was right there in the water with Brielle as that extra pair of hands. I was not a fan of the water, but I endured it. It was an ordeal to get me and my toddler who could not yet stand or walk independently into our swimsuits, then dried and changed into street clothes again in the cold, harsh ladies' locker room of the swimming facility. However, Brielle loved the water and showed significant progress.

On several occasions, the therapy clinic scheduled special events. We once met at a farm to try hippotherapy, which is therapy using a horse. Sitting on a horse forced Brielle to balance her body. The gentle rocking motion of the horse's gate mimicked the feeling of walking she should have known by that age. This unique approach helped Brielle and was a lot of fun. However, it was difficult to get insurance to pay for such techniques and sessions could be quite expensive.

Annually, the clinic invited a company from Chicago to bring in special children's equipment from their warehouse. There were all sorts of walkers, standers, wheelchairs, swings, bath chairs, toilet covers, and adjustable hospital beds. There were also smaller pieces of special equipment like cups, bowls, utensils, scissors, sock pulls, buttonhooks, and toys. Although I leafed through the catalogs displaying these things, it was wonderful to see them in person and give Brielle a chance to try each of them.

The clinic once hosted a technology fair. There were electronic switches to activate mechanical toys, touch screens to navigate around the computer (completely novel technology for the late 1990's), and a variety of communication devices. It was overwhelming to see so much in one place. However, events like these demonstrated the additional value of receiving therapy at this large clinic.

The clinic in Rockford also offered other speech therapy options as Arlene and I continued to have differing ideas on several issues. The use of the Infafeeder and her approach to desensitizing Brielle's mouth were the major areas of disagreement but there were a few others. Arlene and I just never "clicked" and given Brielle's reaction to their sessions, it seemed they did not either. After months of therapy that yielded seemingly little progress, we quit speech therapy with Arlene and added it to our Friday routine in Rockford.

Amy, the speech therapist at the clinic, used new techniques and technology in her therapy sessions with Brielle. She also had a knack for incorporating the "torture devices" (the toothette, Nuk, or gloved hands) into play. Brielle never cried during the sessions and made slow, but steady progress with her. In addition, Amy and I never had any significant differing ideas.

Brielle had physical therapy and speech therapy back-to-back and tolerated it well. We took a break for lunch and then went to aquatherapy. These Fridays were very long days indeed, even for Ashley who eventually spent the day at preschool and extended daycare. However, making a change in speech therapists and investing the time, energy and money into traveling to Rockford was well-worth it.

MORE ABOUT....
The Costs of Private Therapy

The most overwhelming expense with a medically stable special needs child is therapy. The cost for each one-hour session was once about $125, but increased to over $300 over the years.

The Department of Rehabilitation Services (DORS) is Illinois' leading agency that serves people with disabilities. Through some creative interpretation of the rules, a local agency representative qualified many families, including ours, for pediatric developmental therapy services.

Brielle qualified as disabled and although the application and approval process did not review family income, there were financial asset limitations.

DORS benefits funded Brielle's private therapy for several years. However, when the stock market grew our investments, we were no longer eligible and had to rely solely on our health insurance, which did not fully cover the cost of Brielle's therapies.

The Evolution of Therapy

As Brielle started elementary school, the therapists discouraged me from being in the room during therapy. They told me older children often got more out of the sessions when their mothers were not in the room. I hated to admit it, but I eventually realized they were right. Instead of constantly looking to me for approval and attention, Brielle focused on the activities and formed closer relationships with each therapist without me there.

This care model was in stark contrast to my earlier experiences with Martha. Although this change was a major adjustment, I learned to back off. The therapist came to talk to me about our week and things we had tried at home. Then, Brielle went happily back to the treatment room with her as I sat alone in the waiting room.

Over time, I learned what a gift that quiet time was. It was an hour to read a book, flip through magazines, or step outside to call a friend without a child at my hip or household demands beckoning me. At the end of her session, the therapist came out with Brielle to explain or show me what she worked on and what we could do at home.

When she got into her preteen years, Brielle got past the point of thinking therapy was just for fun and realized it was to help her. She rarely complained, worked hard at each therapy session, and was eager to please the therapists as well as me. Although she was never in true pain, she gave it her all.

Brielle received therapy from many different therapists over the years. Learning to make decisions about therapists in Illinois became a valuable skill when Brian's job moved us around the country again and again. We moved from Illinois to Austin, Texas when Brielle was six years old, to Toledo, Ohio when she was 10 years old, and to Atlanta, Georgia when she was 12 years old. Each time, we had to restart our lives, find new houses, new friends, a new church, new doctors, and a new set of therapists. It all became easier with each new experience.

I learned to be very good at researching therapists' experience and background, interviewing them, and doing test runs before committing to regular appointments. Each therapist had his or her own strengths. Each played a formative role in Brielle's development and the development of my unique mothering skills.

At different times in Brielle's development and progress in each area, I found therapists that had a specific set of skills that she needed.

MORE ABOUT....
The Need for Insurance Coverage for Pediatric Therapy

In the fall of 2000, when Brielle was four years old, we received our health insurance benefit options for open enrollment for the following year. We quickly realized the new plan would only cover therapies for injuries like a twisted ankle or recovering from knee replacement, not pediatric developmental therapies.

Since we no longer qualified for DORS benefits, there was no way we could afford to continue her therapies.

When Brian talked to the benefits manager at his office, the manager said he had no idea the change they made would have such a deep impact on families such as ours. The benefits executives immediately changed the coverage for the entire company including the countless other families with special needs children. Brian felt a real sense of pride about helping make that change in his company and so did I.

The plan changed several times over the 17 years Brian has been with the same company. No organization is immune from financial pressures. What Brielle once received as unlimited therapy sessions is now limited to 60 sessions per year for all three therapy disciplines (speech, occupational and physical) combined.

When Brielle started elementary school and needed to be able to do school work, I found an occupational therapist that focused on handwriting. After Brielle had major surgery in middle school to lengthen the tight muscles in her right leg, I found a physical therapist that focused on rehabilitation and could work with Brielle in a therapy swimming pool as well as in a more traditional way. When the hope of Brielle ever speaking was eventually lost when she was a few years old, I found a therapist that knew some sign language and could work with Brielle on her language skills based on signing.

Each therapist had something new to offer, his or her own special skills as well as weaknesses. Some were better at working with Brielle's unique physical limitations and personality. Some directed all of their communication to me while others preferred to focus their attention on Brielle as if I were not even in the room. Although the kindness and sensitivity of the EI therapists in Freeport was exactly what I needed at that time, I later did not need therapists to have exceptional bedside manners. What they could do for Brielle became more important.

With experience, I realized therapists were not all knowing and were not always right. When Brielle was just over a year old, the EI team told me to start working with our insurance company to finance the purchase of a wheelchair because Brielle would never walk. Brielle was just a toddler and we were already being told what she would and would not be able to do. However, Brielle started walking independently shortly after her third birthday. It was initially awkward and unbalanced, but she eventually became quite agile.

The second most poignant example of a therapist being wrong was about Brielle's ability to speak. When Brielle was about 18 months old, Arlene told me to be patient, that Brielle would eventually start talking, maybe by the time she was about eight years old. Brielle never learned to speak. I realize it is difficult to make predictions. However, the ones that offer up so much hope only to fall so dramatically short are the most painful.

Sometimes, there was a huge success during a therapy session that resulted in meeting a milestone. Other times, progress accumulated so slowly that achievements snuck up on us. Often, people who did not see Brielle daily, like her grandparents, were able to recognize and point out fundamental improvements we did not notice. When progress truly did stall, I became discouraged. Sometimes my days were only as good as Brielle's. Other days, I found the strength to dig deep and press onward toward the goal knowing that the long string of therapy sessions would eventually help her.

Formal Therapy Ends

Special equipment prescribed by therapists once filled our home. Clunky wooden chairs with straps and headrests, bath chairs made of blue mesh and white plastic PVC pipes, walkers, and therapy mats were essential tools for her progress. We also had an array of small equipment such as special cups, utensils, scissors, writing utensils, zipper pulls, knee immobilizers, leg braces, hand splints, and wrist weights.

Now that she is 17 years old, only a few of these objects remain. She still uses a bib and sippy cup for meals at home. She sits in a simple bath chair we purchased at the drug store for bathing. She occasionally rides in a wheelchair that looks more like an oversized stroller when we go places with a lot of walking like the zoo or amusement parks. The other pieces of special equipment are things of the past.

As Brielle's progress started to level out in her teen years, we reduced the frequency of her therapy sessions. By the time she was 17, we stopped therapy altogether. Therapy could only take her to a certain point. Instead, life itself would become her next best teacher.

Although we traded the sports and music activities that most kids have with therapy appointments, Brielle had opportunities to participate in modified activities specifically designed for special needs children. Along the way, these activities provided informal opportunities to help her development and lessen the impact of her cerebral palsy. Once therapy ended, they continued to benefit her.

Brielle has played Miracle League baseball for six weeks in the fall and again in the spring since she was about seven years old and has become one of our family's favorite activities. The specially designed field is completely flat to allow children with mobility impairments that might use wheelchairs and walkers to go right over the painted-on bases. The dugouts have wide entrances and are extra wide inside to accommodate multiple wheelchairs or kids who just need a little extra personal space. Each player patiently gets as many pitches as necessary to hit the ball. Playing baseball improves her balance, hand-eye coordination, and arm strength. Teenage volunteers help players throughout the game as needed and offer peer interactions the special needs players might not often get. The peer buddies often get more out of the experience than the players, such as a new perspective on people with disabilities and competitive sports.

Since she was eight years old, Brielle has bowled with Special Olympics each winter. An adult volunteer helps carry the heavy bowling ball to a metal ramp in front of the ally. Brielle must line up the shot on her own before she pushes the ball down the ramp towards the pins. She is not allowed to use the bumpers and must follow all other bowling regulations. The highlight of the season is the final tournament. Players from all over the state come together to compete in a huge event with a medal ceremony resembling the Olympics. Bowling helps her balance and hand-eye coordination as well.

For several years in her mid-teens, Brielle participated in special needs cheerleading and dance. The team practiced weekly year-round and competed in state and national competitions. It amazed us how Brielle learned the routines and took to the stage without any fear at all. Although she loved this activity, the rigorous schedule simply got too difficult to maintain.

TOPSoccer is a sport she first joined in her late teens. Peer volunteers help the players run drills that help improve their kicking power, aim, and control as well as agility. The players also play modified games with a much smaller field and a more cooperative approach to the game. Brielle's success at soccer was a real surprise to us. It gives her a fun way to improve her gross motor skills including balance, leg strength, ability to jump, and stamina for running.

Brielle participated in several other activities specifically designed for special needs children and teenagers. When she was younger, she attended a week or two of summer camp. She went to dances that were alternatives to homecoming and prom. She performed dance routines for talent shows at her high school. The most memorable activity was participating in (and winning!) a local beauty pageant through an organization called Miss Amazing. Although these activities may not add much therapeutic value, they are a great boost to her ego and are fun experiences for the whole family.

Other things in life provided additional natural benefits. Using sign language improved her fine motor skills. Her signs were not perfect, but I insisted Brielle attempt two-handed signs that helped strengthen her right hand over time. Carrying her plate to the table or her laundry basket to the washing machine improved her right hand as well. Gently petting our small dog taught her to control her fine motor skills. Playing tug-o-war with him strengthened her upper arm muscles as well as her grip.

The time for therapists passed. Moving through our days and increasing her independence naturally provided opportunities to stretch her physical abilities as well as her communication skills. Those steps to independence started in our earliest days of therapy, especially with Martha's urging to back off and let Brielle fail. I truly became my daughter's own personal, amateur therapist. Only at this point, I am not such an amateur anymore and certainly neither is Brielle.

Whatever your hand finds to do, do it with all your might...

— ECCLESIASTES 9:10 (NIV)

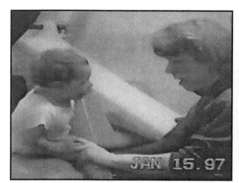 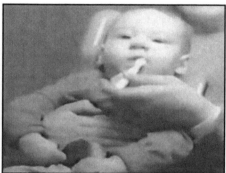

CHAPTER 17

Hospitals Smell Funny

I stroll into the hospital with 16-year-old Brielle to visit a friend of mine who is in the final stages of ALS (Lou Gehrig's disease).

"Not me," Brielle signs, then cups her hand over her mouth and takes exaggerated breaths.

"No, not you," I tell her. Brielle endures so many procedures at hospitals that she automatically associates them with breathing anesthesia.

"Not this time, Sweetie," I reassure her, taking her hand.

Brielle's Collection of Medical Professionals

Before Brielle was born, I spent little time in doctors' offices. Routine visits to the pediatrician with Ashley were my only experiences outside my own annual visits. That all changed when Brielle entered the world.

Other than the cough and congestion and the short hospitalization with pneumonia when she was an infant, Brielle has been generally very healthy. She rarely even gets a cold and only sees her pediatrician once a year. Her medical history is complicated simply because of the sheer variety of specialists who provide care for her because of her disabilities, more specifically her cerebral palsy.

Appointments dot my calendar with people whose titles end in "ologist." We visit one doctor and he or she suggests we see one or two others. It is a pyramid scheme. It starts with her pediatrician, but then connects us to multiple tiers of other specialists until we are tumbling in a sea of people with initials after their names.

Each doctor has his or her own agenda as they treat one small part of my child's body. Sometimes I think I need a chart with an outline of Brielle's body and each body part color-coded to designate which professional works on which part.

Of course, when one doctor refers us to another, it may be weeks or months until their first available appointment. I am grateful for the smorgasbord of health care professionals available to us. However, bellying up to the buffet so many times has given me my fill.

Despite modern digital medical charts, the specialists never seem to coordinate their efforts well. Moreover, they do not communicate directly with one another. It becomes my job to bring information from one professional to another.

Ready for Battle

Annual visits to Brielle's dentist, eye doctor, or pediatrician are unremarkable. In contrast, other health care professional visits ratchet up my anxiety.

I wonder if Brielle's doctors ever consider what it takes to get us to his or her office – the planning, coordinating, preparation, emotional energy, time, and physical endurance. Staying organized keeps me focused on the process so I do not have to think about the strain medical appointments puts Brielle through.

When we are anticipating a decision about a major procedure, Brian takes off from work to meet us at the physician's office. Outside those few visits, I am on my own taking Brielle to her doctors' appointments.

After circling around the overcrowded multi-tiered parking deck for a parking place (which we have to pay for by the hour) as well as navigating the elevators and maze of hallways, we arrive at a doctor's office. There is no chance we will not wait. After all, it is called a waiting room. Then there is the additional waiting once we get to the examination room. Despite going in armed with a creative bag of tricks to keep Brielle busy and cooperative, sometimes it is only a matter of time before my little angel becomes cranky.

I try not to be overly protective, worrisome, or combative with the doctor. Each assaults me with a battery of questions, first on endless forms and then in person, sometimes first with the nurse and then again with the doctor. In order to efficiently and accurately answer their questions, I keep a cheat sheet with a list of Brielle's conditions, medications, allergies, previous procedures, and current medical professionals including the date we last saw each one. I am also armed with a list of questions and concerns as well as a pad of paper to take notes.

How we care for Brielle in every way is under scrutiny. They ask how often and by what process we floss her teeth, stretch her leg muscles, and wipe her bottom as well as a myriad of other dignity-violating questions. I sometimes stretch the truth to maintain my façade as a parent in complete control. Other times I hide the truth for my daughter's sake. Just because Brielle is disabled does not mean she lacks modesty.

Our time with the doctor will most likely be a 15-minute visit, during which he or she gives a cursory exam of Brielle after peppering me with questions. The doctor rushes to get us out so that he or she can move on to the next patient. Despite his or her hurriedness (after the long time we spend waiting), I take my time asking questions and make sure Brielle gets the appropriate care.

When a doctor says, "She'll be fine" or "There's nothing to worry about," I refuse to let him or her trivialize my concerns. Surely, the doctor did not go to medical school just to spew those sorts of platitudes at me. A refreshing, yet all too rare response from a doctor is, "I don't know the answer, but let me investigate that for you." That answer to my toughest questions will earn them my deepest appreciation.

When a doctor says, "It could be worse," I realize, for the doctor, his or her statement simply means, "I've seen this before, and it's no big deal." This child is uniquely ours and everything about her is a big deal to us. Trying not to consider how much worse it could be, I also try not to imagine normal since that image is so painful.

No matter how much time we spend with Brielle's doctors, they are not my friends. A good bedside manner is not required as long as they treat me with respect and Brielle with kindness. The best of them speak directly to Brielle, especially as she gets older.

I Am Not Invisible

During appointments, doctors often address me as "Mom" as if I have no name or identity separate from my child. I realize this label is easier to use than looking at the chart for my name. However, its generic nature is frustrating. Using the label instead of my name is an especially common practice when the doctor brings in a student.

The doctor sometimes asks to include medical students in our daughter's care. Of course, I want future physicians to learn from Brielle, so I permit it. During a student's interaction with us, I am polite and explain what I can. Sometimes, I need to conceal my amusement from the rookie who is timid about examining my daughter or might ask something he or she presumably learned to ask from a textbook. One day, this student will naturally and confidently treat patients, but not on this day with Brielle and me.

As the physician and medical student talk, their doctors' language and smattering of acronyms slide right over my head. I try to listen and process their hushed voices searching for more clues about my child's health. However, their mumbling morphs into something resembling the indiscernible voice of the teacher on *Peanuts* cartoons and "Mom" becomes invisible to them.

Doctors learn, train, and practice for years to prepare for this one visit with my child. I respect that, but I (along with Brian) have the sole ability to make decisions about Brielle's health care. We do not let them rush us into hasty decisions. Doctors cannot ignore our knowledge, experience, and opinions since we are the experts on our child.

Non-Traditional Medicine Can Work

When Brielle was a toddler and preschooler, we tried some alternative medicine practitioners at the urging of Pam, her EI physical therapist. I trusted Pam and figured it could not hurt, other than purging our wallet.

The acupuncturist used electrical stimulation and acupressure (not needles) to stimulate each zone. The ancient theory of traditional Chinese medicine suggests that stimulating these points can correct imbalances in the path through which the life-energy, known as "chi," flows. The treatments gave immediate results (better balance, more energy, and improved digestion) and we believe that they helped her overall health, immune system, and muscle coordination.

Her chiropractors have battled her slightly curved spine and misaligned hips since she was an infant. They use an activator, a device that provides low force to adjust the vertebrae (rather than manual adjustments). The payoff has been better balance and a smoother running gastrointestinal system. She still sees a chiropractor and even her physical therapist recognizes when it has been too many weeks between adjustments.

The first chiropractor Brielle had also provided us with nutritional suggestions and homeopathic supplements, natural supplements designed to help the body heal and regulate itself. Six months after following the homeopathic routine, Brielle's pediatrician tested Brielle's urine to see if she was still shedding CMV. Although it can take up to eight years to clear a CMV infected child's system, at two years old, Brielle's urine tested negative for the virus. I give at least some of the credit to the alternative medical treatments we tried, especially the homeopathy.

Giving Bad News, Or Not

Although I am sure it is something they hate doing, doctors must deliver bad news from time to time. We have certainly received our share about Brielle over the years. The talks with our gynecologist and the perinatologist are engrained in our memory. Her pediatrician had to convince us that 18-month-old Brielle needed leg braces. Her orthopedic surgeon had to tell us we should not wait any longer for 11-year-old Brielle to have heel cord and hamstring lengthening surgery.

Then there are those situations when the doctor did not deliver the bad news. Doctors never told us Brielle was technically intellectually impaired (also referred to as mentally retarded). That news came from school personnel who administered I.Q. tests as part of their annual testing. Doctors never told us that Brielle had cerebral palsy. That diagnosis came to us in a very unexpected way.

For several years, a little boy had the appointments with Martha right after Brielle's two days a week. He was just a few months older than Brielle and their bodies seemed to have the same issues, although something other than CMV caused his delays. The mother and I naturally became friendly since they often walked in Martha's small therapy office before we left.

One morning as we were getting into our van, I saw the mother crying as she got out of her car. When I approached her and asked her what was wrong, she told me her son's pediatrician told her the day before that her son had cerebral palsy. I comforted her as best I could, but all I could think about was Brielle.

She and the little boy were the same age (around two years old), had trouble doing the same things, and even had the same pediatrician. Did Brielle have cerebral palsy? What did that exactly mean? Would the doctor tell us the same thing at our next visit?

When we eventually returned to Martha's office later that week, I told her the mother had confided in me, since I assumed the mother talked to Martha about it as well. Although Martha never shared anything personal, she expressed concern for the mother and how she was coping with the new diagnosis.

"Does Brielle have cerebral palsy, too?" I asked her.

"I can't diagnosis that," she replied. "A doctor is the only one who can do that. Maybe you should ask at your next visit."

Her answer was disconcerting. Brielle's next visit was months away. I was anxious and wanted to know right then and there. Martha could not tell me anything specific about Brielle, but I asked her what cerebral palsy really was. She tried to explain it, but I was not as ready to hear it as I thought I was. Her words went in one ear and out the other and my mind raced in disbelief. I knew Brielle had delays and was disabled. However, cerebral palsy was a term I did not understand and did not associate with our daughter.

When I was better prepared to hear about it a week later, I asked Martha again. She did her best and explained that there is no real test for it, no blood test or anything like that. A doctor can diagnose it based on feeling how loose or tight a child's muscles are. She also gave me a video about CP to watch with Brian that explained it in more detail.

In that video, Brian and I learned that there can be many causes of CP and that the diagnosis is usually secondary to whatever caused it. Therefore, Brielle's congenital CMV is her primary diagnosis with

CP secondary since the CMV caused the brain damage which manifested itself as her muscle impairments, also called CP.

We learned that different terms describe if the muscle impairment is on one side or both. All four of Brielle's limbs are impaired, although the right side much more so.

There are also different terms to describe if the muscles are too loose or too tight. Brielle's muscles tend to be too tight rather than loose.

The one description that really clicked with me was that saying someone has cerebral palsy is like describing someone as a brunette. Ashley, Brielle, and I all have brown hair, but there is a huge difference in the shades of hair that qualifies each of us as being brunette. The video explained that the same could be said for someone who has cerebral palsy. A person with a diagnosis of CP may have a minor impairment of one hand that may go unnoticed by most people or have all four limbs very impaired leaving the person unable to physically do most things. Brielle is somewhere in the middle.

We took in the information in mostly a clinical way. We did not get upset or cry as we came to terms with a word that most likely described our daughter. We waited for a doctor to deliver the bad news, that Brielle had cerebral palsy. None ever did.

It was a year later that I noticed a diagnostic code and the word "cerebral palsy" on a medical form. There was no big sit-down or fanfare about it. It was just there on a form. By the time I saw it, we knew she had it and had come to terms with it. She had not caught it like a cold, chicken pox, or CMV. It was just a description of her body. It was one of the effects of congenital CMV.

What's Up Doc?

When the first doctor placed Brielle in our arms, we had reason to believe Brielle was a broken child, just how broken, we did not know for quite a while. We sought out the tools to fix her as best as we could.

Medical professionals are important equipment in our toolbox, but excessive importance is not placed on her doctors. They are human, not magicians or miracle workers. Although they may know much about their field of specialty, they do not know all there is to know about our child and we, her parents, are ultimately responsible for her care.

Brielle has experienced a steady stream of doctors. It started with the neonatologist who cared for her in the first hours and days of her life. Through the years of changing medical needs, literally dozens of medical professionals across five states have treated Brielle. Some were wonderful and made remarkable contributions to her health, physical abilities, overall well-being, and quality of life. Others will not easily be remembered.

Her body bears a permanent collection of war wounds, essential artifacts from her most memorable procedures. Matching scars line each underside of her jaw where her ENT removed her salivary glands when she was seven years old to help control her drooling issues. Scars line the back of her right knee and ankle from where her orthopedic surgeon performed a hamstring and heel cord lengthening procedure when she was 11 years old that significantly improved her gate and eased the strain on her ankle, knee, and hip. If you look closely, you can see a tiny divot out of the bottom lid of her left eyelid from where her ophthalmologist removed three small cysts.

Other procedures did not leave their mark. Over the course of several years, her orthopedic surgeon gave her three rounds of Botox injections in her legs and right hand to relax the muscles. After each, she wore a leg cast and wrist splint for several weeks to hold the stretch in place. Her gastroenterologist performed an endoscope to exam her esophagus for reflux after several months of gagging incidents. He also ordered a swallow study to ensure that she could properly move food into her stomach. Twice, her neurologists have attached electrodes all over her scalp to assess her brain waves using an EEG. She also endured several MRI's to evaluate the structures of her brain.

Brian particularly struggles with the decisions we make for her to endure these procedures. It is difficult to put so much trust in a doctor and hand over your child to him or her. We ask so many questions before agreeing to something, but always wonder if we asked enough. We want the doctor to give us specifics about how the proposed procedure will help her. Brian wants percentages, piles of data, and the doctor's unwavering opinion. He rarely gets that.

Sometimes I think about how we prepared Brielle for each doctor's visit and procedure. Did we explain it to her in a way she understood? Did she realize how important the procedure was? Did she know how each would help her despite the fright and pain she would endure? We will never know. And yet, she never questioned any of it. She trusted us.

Brielle has endured countless tests and procedures. She has been under anesthesia almost a dozen times in her 17 years of life, twice for major surgeries. Opening her mouth and saying "ah" is almost as routine as brushing her teeth. She seems to expect medical personnel to pull on her legs and push on her stomach. Brielle is a pro at blood tests and actually watches the needle go into her arm with curiosity. Swallowing two or three pills at a time is an easy ritual for her.

For gym rats and tattoo enthusiasts, pain is mostly voluntary. Physical pain has been part of Brielle's life as well, but she never volunteered for any of it. Doctors are the ones who most often inflict it. My feral instincts are to protect my child from any discomfort. However, pain has sometimes been part of the processes that helped her the most. At each event, I need to justify in my own mind why I signed her up for pain. After all, I am the one who signs those hospital consent forms.

Although some were better than others, we are lucky enough to be able to boast that we have not had a bad health care professional or one that treated Brielle poorly. I cannot place blame on any doctor, including mine, for the shortcomings in Brielle's circumstances. Instead, I am confident that each one has cared for her in the best way that he or she could. If only Brielle did not have to have so many "ologists" in her life.

> *Strengthen the feeble hands, steady the knees that give way; say to those with fearful hearts, "Be strong, do not fear; your God will come, He will come with vengeance; with divine retribution He will come to save you." Then will the eyes of the blind be opened and the ears of the deaf unstopped. Then will the lame leap like a deer, and the mute tongue shout for joy...*
>
> — ISAIAH 35: 3-6 (NIV)

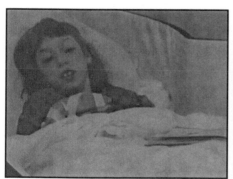

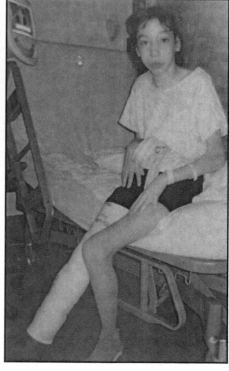

CHAPTER 18

Communication Matters

My 15-year-old stands in the bathroom watching me put on makeup one evening after dinner. "Where you going?" Brielle signs to me.

"I'm going to teach a man and his wife sign language," I say, snapping a tube of lipstick shut. "The lady is sick with something called ALS. Her mouth doesn't work right because she is sick and she can't talk now."

Brielle watches me brush my hair as she processes what I told her.

"She's like you now," I explain as I put down the brush to sign to her. "She can hear, but now she can't talk, just like you."

Brielle looks perplexed. "I talk. I use sign language."

I look at my daughter's sweet reflection in the bathroom mirror. "Yes, but you can't use your mouth to talk. You can't talk like Mom or Dad or Ashley. You have to use sign language with your hands because you can't talk with your mouth. Just like this lady."

> *Brielle looks at me as if I told her something she never realized. Then she looks at her hands as if they were detached from her body.*
>
> *"Sign language good," she finally signs to me, and then promptly walks away, leaving me staring at my own reflection in wonder.*

First Words

When Ashley first began talking, we showered her with praise and recorded her first words in her baby book. When she repeatedly mispronounced "zebra" as "bee-dra" or used improper grammar like "I eated all my peas," we chuckled at her mistakes and corrected her pronunciation or grammar like other parents might do.

When Brielle did not attempt to speak her first words as a toddler, we were concerned. Although we hoped that she would eventually speak, her speech therapist in Rockford told us our daughter might never be able to speak. The therapist explained that Brielle lacked the complicated coordinated ability of breathing, lip closure, and tongue dexterity needed for speaking. It was a slow coping process, but we came to grips with the fact that the cerebral palsy that affected her body affected her mouth and her ability to speak most of all.

Brielle tries to make sounds. Like most mothers of young toddlers, I can discern a small handful of her sounds that mean "Mom" or "home" or "Ashley." From the other side of the house, I can tell the difference in her voice inflection or a string of vowels that means "Help me" verses "I'm coming" signaling she is on her way to the dinner table. In recent years, Brielle attempts to mimic facial expressions with great concentration while she looks in a mirror. She might stick out her tongue just past her bottom teeth, but that triumph will never lead her to an ability to speak.

A Sign of Things to Come

With little expectation for Brielle to speak, her therapists introduced sign language when she was about 18 months. Hand over hand, they made her fingertips of both hands come together as they repeated the word "more" aloud. It took weeks and lots of repetition, but Brielle finally learned that first sign. Slowly, word by word, the therapists introduced more signs and Brielle learned to use them. She was so excited to have others understand what she wanted. Moreover, we were excited to see her finally communicate.

In the beginning, it was difficult to tell when Brielle was simply flailing about and when she was actually trying to communicate. When she attempted to sign, her movements were awkward and her signs muddled because of her fine motor skills. For example, her signs for "ball" and "cookie" initially looked very similar. The two have the exact same hand shape, although there is a slight twisting motion when signing the word "cookie" (like twisting open a sandwich cookie). Just as a toddler initially might sound like he has marbles in his mouth but learns to enunciate, Brielle's signs became more distinctive.

Brielle first learned individual signs and then began connecting them into phrases and sentences like stringing beads together. As her sign vocabulary grew, we soon realized that some signs had to be adapted. Each sign had to be left-handed (where the left hand does the primary movements) since her right hand was more impaired. Certain, more complicated, signs we simply had to get used to being imperfect, since there was no hope for clarity.

I initially kept a running list of words Brielle knew how to sign, a record of her accomplishments, like a mother records her child's milestones in a baby book. I wrote down the dates she learned the signs, numbering each one, and kept adding to the list of words on page after page of a yellow pad of paper. By the time the list reached three or four hundred, my preschooler was learning signs faster than I could make note of them.

Her hands were magical. They had the ability to convey meaning, to communicate her thoughts. We just had to keep up with her.

Learning to Speak With Our Hands

Our family initially learned signs one at time from the therapists or a sign language dictionary. When Brielle was three years old, I took a sign language class at the local community college. It was odd to be back in college. I felt both nervous and excited trying to mimic the signs the teacher taught. The next semester, Brian took the same course from the same teacher. We practiced together and tried to sign with Brielle as much as we could.

At first, we learned signs in American Sign Language (ASL). This is the language system deaf adults in America use and what you might see actors like Marlee Matlin use in movies or on television shows.

One sign in ASL can represent several spoken words. For example, there is one sign that represents multiple good feelings including happy and joyful. Small words such as conjunctions and affixes are implied and not usually signed at all.

ASL also has a different word order than spoken English. A sentence like "I saved my money for three weeks then I bought a new bike" is signed "money save three week finish bike new buy."

When Brielle was about four years old, teachers at her school for the deaf introduced us to Signed Exact English (SEE). SEE is a complete sign language system designed to represent each word in the spoken English language. Children who use SEE tend to be better writers since they are writing the exact words in the exact order they sign. It made more sense for Brielle to use SEE while she was young and still learning language.

MORE ABOUT....
The Development of Signed Exact English (SEE)

In the mid-1970's, researchers discovered deaf children who used ASL were poor writers. At that time, a group of parents and researchers developed SEE to help those children perform better by designing it to more closely follow the English language.

Over seventy percent of the signs used in SEE are based on ASL signs. SEE follows the word order, prefixes and suffixes, grammar, and syntax of spoken English.

As deaf children who use SEE grow and have more exposure to deaf adults who use ASL, they begin to transition to ASL. SEE is not intended to be a substitution for ASL, but as a means to help children understand spoken English more completely and also become better writers so that they can experience academic success.

Ashley's second grade teacher, Sarah, previously taught at a school for the deaf and knew both ASL and SEE. She tutored our whole family in SEE once a week for several years while Brielle was in preschool and early elementary school. Brielle's best friend, Audrey, wanted to learn, so she joined the group as well. While Ashley, Brielle, and I learned fairly easily, Brian had a more difficult time. Sarah did her best to keep the pace slow enough to include him and fast enough to keep the rest of us challenged.

As my signing progressed, I attended my first weekend workshop in Indianapolis offered by The SEE Center while visiting our family in Illinois. The 100 participants included speech therapists, special education teachers, and classroom aids, but most were parents of deaf children. The SEE teachers broke us into separate groups based on our skill level. I was overwhelmed as they bombarded us with new vocabulary, activities to practice our skills, and homework each night, but doubled my vocabulary in just those few days.

I returned to that weekend workshop in Indianapolis two more summers. Each time, I moved up to a more difficult class level, stretching my skills. However, it was not until I attended a full-week workshop in Dallas that my sign vocabulary grew exponentially.

During that week, we were not allowed to use our voices at all for one of the days. Classrooms and hallways were silent, but hands were busy signing. At lunch, we had to order our meals at the hotel restaurant by pointing to the menus and writing down specific requests like "no pickles" or "add cheese." Although it was meant to give us as much of a deaf experience as we could have, it gave me the exact experience my daughter had with the ability to hear, but not speak.

Living for just a day in part of Brielle's world was an eye-opening experience. My heart broke in new ways when I truly understood what her frustrations interacting with others must be. I also had new appreciation for her ability to overcome communication obstacles and still keep a positive attitude.

MORE ABOUT....
The SEE Center

The SEE Center (The Signed Exact English Center), a nonprofit organization established in 1984, works with parents and educators of hearing impaired children and provides educational materials, DVDs, webinars, and other support opportunities. Their instructors provide the only organized trainings of SEE at about a dozen weekend and weeklong workshops offered throughout the country each year.

Although there is no formal certification available, The SEE Center offers Educational Signed Skills Evaluations, which rate the expressive and receptive skills of signers.

I returned to that weeklong workshop in Dallas the next two summers. They were physically and mentally taxing weeks. However, growing my sign vocabulary justified why I spent the money and time away from my family.

Brielle and I continue to learn new signs almost every day when we read a book together, work on homework assignments, or just do our daily activities. We look up words we do not already know how to sign in a sign language dictionary and look for ways to integrate the new vocabulary into our everyday language.

Some language skills are still challenging for Brielle, especially idiomatic expressions such as "raining cats and dogs." We need to get creative with words that do not have specific signs, refer to new technology, or words like "zoom" and "whoohoo." Dr. Suess is a nightmare.

Sharing My Skills

When Brielle was 10 years old, the girls and I began attending a friend's church in Ohio. The pastor approached me the third or fourth time we attended services, introduced himself, and asked about our family.

"I see you and your daughter signing the songs here Sunday mornings. Would you be willing to sign the whole service in front of our church each week?"

"Uh," I stumbled over my words knowing I was not ready for that. "I could maybe sign the songs with some practice, but I don't think I could keep up with your sermons."

"Really? I write out my sermons and speak from the script almost word for word."

"That's really still beyond my abilities," I held my ground as my stomach did nervous flip-flops. "But, like I said, I could probably do the songs."

"Deal," he said as he firmly shook my hand.

What had I gotten myself into? I signed with Brielle and had taken plenty of classes by that point. However, getting in front of 150 people to sign was a completely different experience. Although I was very nervous the first night I went to Praise Team practice, I was glad my new friend was one of the singers.

"No one in our church is deaf. No one will know if you're not doing it right anyway," one of the guitar players tried to reassure me at the first practice.

"I realize that," I replied. "But, I'll know the difference."

After that first Sunday church service when I nervously signed the three opening songs and one closing song, several people approached me to compliment and thank me for doing it. Their praise and support eased my nerves.

As the weeks passed, I started to love being up there and having an outlet to perform. Clearly, "holy" and "crucified" were not signs I regularly used with Brielle. However, other new words helped me expand my everyday sign vocabulary.

There has never been a deaf person attend a service that I interpreted, at least not to my knowledge. However, that really is not important. Seven years later, I still look forward to Sunday mornings largely because of the challenge to improve my skills and have the opportunity to share sign language with my church.

Most people are intrigued that we use sign language. Some even ask how to sign a greeting or pleasantry like "Thank you" or "You're welcome" so they can interact with Brielle. I taught several classes at my church in Toledo and Atlanta so that parishioners who wanted to understand my signing could learn about it. I tutored a half dozen people in sign, including a lady who now signs at my former church in Toledo, several of Ashley's friends, and, more recently, the lady who had ALS and lost her ability to speak (she passed away in 2012, just 18 months after I started tutoring her). I truly enjoy teaching and am excited to see others be able to communicate independently with Brielle.

MORE ABOUT....

The Role of Signing and My Faith

Although I previously went through the motions of "checking the box" that I had gone to church each Sunday, signing at my church in Toledo started me on a new journey. Being forced to think about the words in the contemporary Christian music, I began to study God's words and re-evaluate what I believed.

With the additional input from the pastor at this nondenominational church, participation in a small Bible study group, and my growing friendship with the friend that attended the same church, I slowly began to develop a personal relationship with God.

Although I had been baptized by being sprinkled as a child, I was baptized in a full-emersion ceremony in 2009, recommitting myself to God.

Signing in Isolation

In order for Brielle to be able to communicate with others in any meaningful way, I must act as her interpreter. Brielle must be reminded to look at the person when she signs so it more closely resembles a real conversation. Brielle often drops words and needs prompts to sign full sentences. If she wrongly assumes people know what she is talking about, I encourage her to fully explain herself or I have to fill in the gaps and explain what she is really trying to communicate.

Understanding and being able to interpret Brielle's communication is often like trying to figure out a riddle. I must watch her hands carefully, decipher her muddled hand movements, read between the lines, and infer her intentions when she drops words or makes assumptions about what someone might already know about her. I try not to assume too much or sell her short by assuming too little. It is a delicate balance of reading her signs and conveying her thoughts. I do not edit what she signs, but let her words speak for themselves.

As Brielle's sign language vocabulary grew, fewer people could understand her. Some of her speech therapists and teachers knew a little sign. However, few other people in her life knew any sign language at all. For most, it was not about their eagerness to communicate with Brielle. It was about the daunting task of learning another language.

Brielle's grandparents only know a few signs. With no one to sign with on a regular basis (other than visits with us a handful of times a year), the hours spent learning sign language seemed overwhelming to them. At first, I was hurt that they would not even try. My mother later told me how guilty she and my dad felt over the years for not trying harder in the beginning. Now, with Brielle's signing skills so advanced, there is practically no hope of them learning fast enough to catch up to her.

Despite this gap, they find a way of communicating. Brielle can nod and shake her head to indicate "yes" and "no" and eagerly uses the "thumbs up" to communicate a number of positive responses. When Brielle reads books with my mother, Brielle signs the words and my mother slowly reads them aloud so they can both participate in the activity. It works for them, but it is not an ideal communication relationship.

Ashley learned sign language through those tutoring sessions and was at least an intermediate signer at the time. Although I never see her sign to Brielle now, she understands more than half of what Brielle signs to her. Brielle automatically turns to me to interpret, but I remind her to sign to Ashley and only step in to interpret when necessary. The sisters have a limited range of topics they talk about and they never get into long conversations, so they are able to communicate in their own way.

It is painful to know that they do not have the typical sister relationship most teenagers have. It is just not possible with Brielle's cognitive delays, understanding of the world around her, and their ability to communicate. There are no late night talks, gossiping, or sharing of secrets. However, there is a special bond between them that goes beyond communication.

Brian struggled learning sign language and lost most of what he learned by not using it. He is a smart person and, although he did not attend any additional sign language workshops with me, he was there for our weekly tutoring with Sarah. Perhaps he did not learn as easily because he was not convinced it was the best choice of communicating since so few people know sign language. Perhaps his signing skills are put on the back burner because I interpret too much for him. Not being forced to sign with her allows him to know less sign language and still maintain the same communication relationship with her.

He now knows only a small amount of Brielle's signs and never signs back to her. Brielle automatically turns to me to interpret when she is communicating with him and I do it without a second thought, most of the time. Other times, I get frustrated that he does not know sign language better, especially signs for things that are so important to her. His lack of fluency in sign language limits the scope and depth of their conversations. I believe it also encourages him to interact with her at a much younger age level, rather than the highschooler that she is. Although she still loves interacting with her dad the same way she did ten years ago, it can get under my skin. When she is 40 years old, will they still be communicating at the same level?

On the few days when I am away with friends, Brian and Brielle manage just fine. He understands when she needs help with her headphones or needs to use the bathroom. He understands if she wants popcorn or pretzels with her lunch. However, is managing in this way good enough?

I worry about how they would communicate if something happened to me. Moreover, I worry that she would have no one to really talk to, no one that really understands her when she wants to talk about more complex things. What would her life be like? How much smaller would her world become? Those thoughts are truly disturbing.

I assume that she would rely more heavily on other communication methods, but will that be enough?

Alternative Communication Systems

Since so few others know sign and I am not always with her to interpret, sign language will never be the perfect communication system for her. School systems have specific rules about how much hearing loss a child must have before they will provide a sign language interpreter. Brielle, who has no hearing loss at all, never met their requirements. Sign language may be the most important system Brielle uses to communicate, but without an interpreter, we have had to try other ways.

Voice Recorders

The technology specialist in our Austin school district gave her a voice recorder to use at school when Brielle was in kindergarten. This small device buckled to her wrist like a watch and had three buttons she could press to play brief greetings. Although other children in her class were initially intrigued, they quickly became bored with its limitations. For a child with a vocabulary beyond three phrases, these pleasantries were extremely limiting for Brielle as well.

Voice Output System

When I made our frustrations known to the technology specialist, she invited me to her office one day to test drive two more complicated communication systems, both the size of a classic TV dinner. The one I chose for Brielle to use, called a DynaVox, had a touch screen system with about 30 icons on the main screen. If she tapped the icon for verbs, another screen popped up with icons and their corresponding words for a dozen common verbs. Other buttons were labeled with icons for other categories of parts of speech or noun categories such as food, toys, and animals. By touching a particular series of icons, she could generate a sentence such as "I want to eat waffles." With another tap, a synthesized voice spoke the entire sentence for her.

Although Brielle loved the DynaVox and quickly learned how to navigate the system, it was a painstakingly slow process to get her thoughts out. The batteries never lasted the whole school day and the machine was heavy and cumbersome for Brielle to carry. Dropping the $8,000 device was a looming possibility, even a probability. The technology specialist assured us we were not financially responsible for the device. However, we still had concerns since a broken device sent back to the manufacturer for repair meant that Brielle had no voice for a week or longer.

MORE ABOUT....
Capturing Brielle's First Words

As any proud parent might do when their child first begins to speak words, I captured Brielle's first words using the DynaVox system on video.

"I went to play outside yesterday."

The joy and pride in her expression are second only to the feelings I had behind the video camera.

Word Processing Programs

One of Brielle's strengths is her ability to spell. From about second grade, she could type out what she wanted to say on a basic word processing program on a computer using the one finger hunt-and-peck method. However, a computer is not always available to her, such as at lunch, in gym class, or out on the playground. Even if she was in her classroom, someone had to come over to the computer to be able to read what she wanted to say.

Pencil and Paper

When she was about 13 years old, Brielle's handwriting finally started to improve enough to be somewhat legible. Spiral notebooks never run out of batteries, are virtually indestructible, and are portable. Although her handwriting is still sometimes hard to discern, the old-fashioned writing method bridges the gaps when her voice output system is broken or low on battery power.

Cell Phones

A few years ago, a friend at church youth group let Brielle type words on her small slide-out cell phone keyboard. The friend spoke back to her and deleted the text before Brielle inadvertently sent it to someone. Although we rarely use this method, it has come in handy once in a while.

Apps

Although there are a variety of apps available, an app called SpeakIt on her iPod allows her to input words and then press a button that will speak what she has written. Her iPod is in a sturdy case and hangs from a lanyard around her neck, so it is both portable and protected. The batteries last almost all day when she is not playing games or watching videos on it, but it is still a slow process.

Between several alternative communication methods available to her, Brielle now has a voice when I cannot be there to interpret for her. In the future, she will have to rely more and more on technology. None of her communication alternatives is a perfect method in all situations. When I am with her, we rely on signing almost all of the time. Signing may not work in dark movie theaters or when our hands are full. However, it is what works best for her at this point in her life.

Special Connection

I am Brielle's full-time interpreter and language conduit through which she expresses nearly every word. I am eager to be Brielle's voice when she has no voice of her own. Sometimes I wonder what kind of relationships she would have with others if I were not there to be her ambassador.

Brielle's ability to hear and lack of ability to speak is a unique situation. Few typical kids befriend her for what I can assume is a variety of reasons. Her lack of ability to speak is clearly a barrier when she is at social events with other disabled children and teens who can both hear and speak. Although she has had few experiences with anyone who is deaf, I often wonder if she might ever be welcomed into deaf culture because of her other disabilities and her *lack* of hearing impairment.

Brielle tells me she dreams only in sign language. I get very excited when I have a dream in sign language, but wake up tearful when I dream about Brielle using her voice in a way I know I will never hear.

Despite how overwhelming it is, sometimes I think about what life would be like if Brielle could speak and I never needed to learn sign language. Signing with Brielle, signing at church, and teaching others to sign are part of who I am now. I use sign language every day of my life and cannot imagine a day without it.

Communication can take many forms other than the spoken word and is not unique to humans. Birds sing to find a mate or chirp when danger is near. Lions roar to defend their territory. Ants leave messages through pheromones so other ants can follow their trail to a food source. Our dog, Cooper, responds to voice and sign language commands, as do many dogs.

However, it is at least partly people's ability to use our complicated verbal communication system that makes us so different, so human. Despite texting, email, and social media, in terms of connecting people, no invention is as effective as the human voice, something Brielle does not have.

We know that Brielle will never be able to speak. This does not leave her powerless. With her use of sign language and technology, she speaks volumes through her magic hands. In the end, I realize that it is just as much about us teaching her how to speak as it is us learning how to listen.

> *The Lord said to him, "Who gave human beings*
> *their mouths? Who makes them deaf or mute?*
> *Who gives them sight or makes them blind? Is*
> *it not I, the Lord? Now go; I will help you speak*
> *and will teach you what to say."*
>
> – EXODUS 4: 11-12 (NIV)

CHAPTER 19

Preschool: Finding a Place to Belong

Brielle reaches up and puts her whole hand flat on the glass of one of the two framed pieces of priceless art hanging in our hallway.

"Mine," she signs.

"Don't touch it," I tell her. "You'll smudge the glass."

These two pieces of art are not paintings by Picasso, Rembrandt, or Monet. Our girls made them. This pair of purple flowers made from their handprints is special because it is one of the few things they did equally well in school.

"That's not yours anyway," I say. "The other one is."

Without their names carefully printed in small handwriting on the bottom by their preschool teachers, we would not be able to tell which one is whose.

"Oh," Brielle signs stepping a bit closer to read the names. "Right. Both cute."

The End of Early Intervention, The Beginning of School

When Brielle turned three, she aged out of Early Intervention services. She was then eligible for special education preschool provided by the public school district. We continued with her private therapy schedule, but she would also receive additional therapy services by the district therapists while in school.

A week before Brielle started preschool, I visited the classroom. In many ways, the room looked similar to Ashley's preschool. Brightly colored posters decorated the walls. Children's names taped to the rug on the floor formed a semicircle in front of the chalkboard. A door led to a bathroom with short toilets and low sinks.

Brielle's classroom was also somewhat different. A small walker was parked at the classroom door next to a red wagon filled with toys for playing outside. A pair of wheelchairs lined the edge of the colorful rug for circle time. Stacks of diapers and wipes sat on a sturdy therapy table stretched out in a corner.

The juxtaposition of typical preschool paraphernalia next to equipment designed for special needs children was striking. It made me uncomfortable seeing it all together and realizing that this was where Brielle now belonged.

On the first Monday after Brielle's third birthday, I dropped Ashley off at her preschool as usual and then drove to Brielle's preschool where her new teachers were waiting for her. Brielle's name, printed in bold red letters, hung over a peg on the wall where other children's names and coats hung. In the same bold lettering, her name was taped to a spot on the rug as well as on one of the short tables. After a brief exchange of instructions with the teachers, I gave Brielle a hug and walked alone to our minivan.

Some moms cry on those first days of preschool. My tears were from exhaustion, not sadness or sentimentality. Five hours of peace finally interrupted the long days of running from one therapy or doctor appointment to another, and one meal or diaper to another.

Our empty house had a library-like silence. After a luxuriously long bubble bath, I slept. No bustling around with laundry, house cleaning, or shopping on that first day of preschool. No guilt about wasted time. Just Zen-like relaxation and sleep.

After that first day, we established our new routine. Brielle spent four mornings a week at the special education preschool while we continued our usual Friday therapy schedule in Rockford. She had therapy sessions with Martha two mornings before going off to preschool. Other days, a doctor's appointment might interrupt her day at school.

Household duties filled most of my mornings, but I also finally had a chance to meet a friend for breakfast or read a book. I felt like I imagined most stay-at-home mothers felt, did what they might do. For those hours without Brielle, I felt normal for a change.

Brielle's teachers wrote short notes in a spiral notebook, sent back and forth in her backpack. They reported our daughter's eating and pooping habits. They occasionally wrote about something they were trying to teach the children – colors of the rainbow or sounds farm animals make. Compared to what Ashley did in her preschool class, we were completely unimpressed by the amount of teaching in Brielle's.

Adding to my frustrations, Brielle often came home filthy. Drips of chocolate milk, splotches of applesauce, and dots from markers (not the washable kind) were my nemeses in the laundry room each week. These stains complemented the mysterious scratches, bumps, and bruises that decorated her face and limbs like confetti. Although a certain amount of dirt and boo-boos of unknown origin are expected (especially since Brielle was just starting to walk at this time), we were concerned that our daughter was not getting the care we assumed she would get.

A few unannounced visits to the classroom confirmed our suspicions. Those visits allowed me to see exactly where those gaps in care and teaching were. With so many other children in the class, a few so impaired that they needed constant care, Brielle was getting little attention and limited teaching.

Hunting for a New Preschool

Although we wanted to find a different preschool, which one would accept Brielle? Finding part-time childcare for her the previous fall so I could have a few hours of respite had been difficult. The Christian daycare where Ashley attended on Fridays turned Brielle away. The facility claimed they could not meet Brielle's needs and that their liability insurance would not permit them to care for a disabled child. Rejection felt more personal when the daycare at my own church refused my daughter. Their explanation was that they could not provide for her needs, specifically citing that, despite being three years old, she needed to be spoon fed like an infant and was not yet potty trained.

Although Brian was disappointed that the daycares rejected Brielle, he thought I went off the deep end when I contacted the state regulating agency to investigate them.

"Can't you just let this go?" he asked one evening as I reviewed the laws and highlighted sections in a copy of the state rules for daycares.

"I can't," I said emphatically. "How can they turn her away?"

MORE ABOUT....
My Faith in the Face Of Rejection

Although I was hurt by two church daycares rejecting Brielle, my faith changed very little since it was still in its infancy. It was difficult to face the decision-makers in my own church every Sunday, but I sensed they were as uncomfortable as I was.

"But, how can we ask them to change their rules about being potty trained? They expect that from any kid her age that attends their daycare."

The state cited those same guidelines and ruled that there was no violation since she was not potty trained. I eventually conceded and had to let it go. However, it was a painful process. Feeling deeply wounded and furious at those daycares, a funk overwhelmed me for weeks.

MORE ABOUT....
Ashley's Tender Words

Ashley was very concerned when she saw me crying repeatedly after the rejections from the Christian daycares. I eventually told her in simple terms why I was crying.

"Maybe someday they will learn and understand she's a nice girl," my preschooler said with such innocence and simplicity. My heart ached as I wondered if they ever would.

I eventually found an in-home provider to care for Brielle for a few hours each week. It was a different situation than the large facility we had become accustomed to over the years with Ashley. However, the woman was kind and provided excellent care at a time when I really needed a few hours to myself.

Six months later, we faced Brielle's only preschool option. If no other daycare would accept Brielle, what preschool would? It was difficult to imagine Brielle continuing in her special education preschool. Even more grim was the thought that she would always be in that sort of classroom. But, what choice did we have?

After Brielle had been attending the special education preschool for about two months, the local newspaper printed an article about a preschool that received a large grant to purchase new outdoor playground equipment. Part of the equipment would be accessible to children who use wheelchairs because the grant specified that the school must accept all children. The preschool was 30 minutes away, across the Wisconsin state border.

With the sting of rejection still fresh, the thought of a typical preschool declining Brielle worried me. I decided it could be worth the commute to the Wisconsin preschool and hoped the guidelines of the grant might change things for her.

Strategically scheduling a tour while Brielle was at school, I pushed my apprehension aside as I entered the preschool. I was delighted to see how well planned and structured the day was and how clean the school and children were. When the teachers asked if I would like to complete the initial paperwork, I filled it out on the spot and wrote a check for our deposit. Exchanging pleasantries before leaving, I casually mentioned the newspaper article.

"It was quite exciting for our preschool to get that grant," the lead teacher replied, beaming with pride.

"What impressed me the most," I added, "was that you now accept children of all abilities."

Blank stares paired up with their pasted-on smiles. Suspecting they knew what was coming next, I informed them about Brielle's abilities and needs. I also conveyed my willingness to help in the classroom to bridge any gaps. Bracing myself for their reaction, I could not help glancing over at our application and deposit check already neatly tucked away in a folder on the teachers' desk.

"We would be so pleased to have your daughter with us." The lead teacher's response seemed genuine and after a few reassuring exchanges, I felt confident they would truly accept Brielle.

Relief and elation overwhelmed me. Sitting in our minivan, I sobbed deeply, letting all of those emotions out that still clung to my heart from the daycare rejections. Wanting to share my triumph, I called Brian. When his office assistant said he was in a meeting, I called my mother, blurted out my good news, and cried more tears of joy with her on the phone.

Brielle's acceptance into that preschool was a turning point. Between therapy appointments, doctor visits, special equipment, leg braces, and special classrooms, Brielle's life at three years old was so very different from Ashley's. Attending this preschool for a few hours several days a week, gave her a small window of normalcy in a life filled with so much that was not normal. That was something that I ached for, not just for her, but for me, too.

Our busy days got busier that fall as Ashley began kindergarten and Brielle started an even more complicated schedule. She continued therapy with Martha two early mornings a week and therapies in Rockford on Fridays. She attended special education preschool two days a week and her preschool in Wisconsin the other two days a week. The 30-minute trip each way across the state line was long but easy enough. We boogied to tunes in our family minivan with Ernie singing about his rubber ducky and Barney singing about some creature called a kookaburra.

I stayed with Brielle for the first few weeks in the Wisconsin preschool to help her color within the lines, cut up her snack, or occasionally change her diaper, but slowly began to hang back. By Thanksgiving, I was able to drop Brielle off at the classroom door, which gave me time to do some shopping or just sit in the minivan reading a book. Returning a few hours later, my happy, clean child proudly showed me macaroni necklaces, birdfeeders made from pinecones and peanut butter, and purple flowers on pink construction paper made from her handprints. Brielle signed to me about her friends and I often watched her play outside with her classmates on the accessible playground.

This was a time of great success and happiness for our family. Ashley thrived in kindergarten. Brian received a promotion. Brielle was happy at preschool, walking independently (finally), and expanding her sign language vocabulary daily. I was a busy, but happy mom. We finally left the days of worry far behind.

Time for Something New?

In the spring, I met a woman and her young son who was deaf. We struck up a friendship and I told her about our great year at the preschool in Wisconsin. Although my new friend was supportive, she questioned why we did not send Brielle to the preschool for deaf students in Rockford to help support Brielle's growing sign language vocabulary.

I never even knew there was such a program, but the idea intrigued me. I imagined Brielle signing back and forth with her teacher and new friends. No more, "What is she saying?" or "Why can't she talk?" from kind but curious classmates. Rockford would be a long daily drive for a four-year-old, but she was used to those long drives.

First, we had to convince our school district officials to send our daughter there. Brielle was neither deaf nor had any hearing loss at all. Therefore, she did not automatically qualify. Nevertheless, we knew attending this school would benefit her language skills.

Although the preschool in Wisconsin was a wonderful experience, her special education preschool was more like a glorified daycare. Moreover, Brielle could not communicate with anyone in either setting. How could the public school district continue to send her to a classroom where no one could communicate with her?

Fighting for Her Place

The first meeting with the school district representatives was disastrous. I had gone alone. Brian agreed with me and wanted her to attend the preschool for the deaf, but he was unable to take time off from work. The school officials turned Brielle away, citing qualification rules. Not deaf meant no school for the deaf. Those same feelings of anger and hurt I had when the Christian daycares denied her bubbled to the surface once again.

After crying, I got angry. Acceptance at the preschool in Wisconsin had given me a good dose of courage. This new rejection transformed into a call to battle. The warrior in me was ready to fight back with renewed vigor.

An advocate from an independent social service agency helped prepare us. She informed us of relevant state laws and advised us on what evidence we needed. When we requested another meeting with school officials, we were ready with our formal arguments, supporting documentation from her pediatrician and speech therapist, the experience of the advocate, and our secret weapon, Brielle.

As our daughter happily colored pictures and looked at books, Brian and I sat at a large conference table at the local school board office. Along with our advocate, there were 10 school officials including therapists, teachers, a secretary to take notes, the school principal, and the director of special education for the entire school district. The full house was intimidating.

After I presented our case with calm conviction, one of the school officials immediately began to recite the qualification rules.

"She simply does not qualify," the woman stated, furrowing her brow in frustration. "Frankly, Mr. and Mrs. Stull, I don't understand why you requested a second meeting. The rules are clear."

My heart pounded and blood rushed to my face in anger as I took a deep breath to start reiterating our case. Before I could speak, Brian's business-like voice filled the room with facts from our documentation, details about Brielle's sign language skills, and the potential benefits of sending her to the school for the deaf. I was taken aback by his assertiveness. His professional presence made him a much more formidable opponent than I was as a passionate mother.

In contrast to Brian's demeanor, Brielle smiled and giggled to herself as she pointed to pictures in her books and spontaneously showed off her sign language skills. It was a stunning contrast of power and innocence.

The woman scowled without any attempt to hide her foul attitude. "Mr. Stull," she chimed in as soon as Brian had restated Brielle's case, "That still does not change..."

"Hold on," the director of special education said, abruptly cutting her off. The room fell silent as all eyes turned to him. In a most dramatic way, the man slowly leaned forward asserting his undeniable authority.

"How can we make this happen for this family?"

His decision, not so subtly cloaked in a question, rang out like a clanging bell at a boxing match. Ding, ding, ding. Technical knockout. Fight over.

The school officials looked at one another in disbelief as our advocate stifled a triumphant grin.

In a matter of minutes, the group began to discuss how and when to make the transition from the special education preschool to the preschool program for the deaf. Miraculously, someone produced a form for us to sign, authorizing the change in schools. We filled out the details of Brielle's new school plan in a new Individualized Education Plan (IEP), a document which outlined her skills and delays as well as goals and plans to help move her along, much like the IFSP did during Early Intervention.

"School for the Deaf" was written in the box labeled "placement" on the front of her IEP. I smiled thinking of something the advocate had told me just a few days before.

"The term 'IEP' should also remind you to continue to be an 'Involved Educated Parent'," she said encouragingly. "School officials are the least prepared for those sorts of parents. If the spirit of the law doesn't move them, surely your preparations will."

Although there were handshakes all around as we stood to leave at the end of the meeting, it was clear that the woman felt sideswiped by the power play of the director of special education. Her anger and embarrassment were palatable as we put our daughter's things into her Barney backpack.

"Let me walk you to the reception area," the director offered casually.

We walked down the hallways making the turns in silence until we reached the building's front door. The director stood in front of it, pausing for a moment before pushing it open for us.

"I just couldn't look into your daughter's smiling, beautiful face and tell you parents, 'No'," he stated almost in a whisper.

"Thank you," was all that we could say as we offered our grateful smiles and another round of handshakes.

In the privacy of our minivan, I finally let out the huge breath I had been holding in for so long. The tension oozed out of my pores and evaporated.

"What just happened?" Brian asked in shock as we drove out of the parking lot.

"I'm not at all sure," I replied, still bewildered by the sudden turn of events. "I think we had a guardian angel on our side in there."

"I don't believe in angels," Brian stated. He turned to the backseat where Brielle happily looked out the window from her car seat. She was completely unaware of what transpired and how it would change her life. "At least I don't believe in any other angels except for her."

Although I drove Brielle the 60 minutes each way to and from her new school on the first day that next fall, I let her ride school transportation after that. I lifted my little four-year-old into her car seat by 7:30 each morning and had to wake her up from a sound nap most days when she arrived home at 4:30. Brielle, my friend's son, and another boy in fifth grade with a grumpy attitude rode together in an SUV driven by a quiet man in his early 60's. No more songs on the road about rubber duckies or kookaburras.

Brielle's new teacher and I wrote notes back and forth in a notebook, similar to how I communicated with the teacher at the special education preschool. Her new teacher's long notes full of details about Brielle's day were reassuring. Even more exciting, Brielle signed to me about her new friends and fun activities as her vocabulary blossomed just as we had hoped it would.

Another Move Brings More Change

A year later, when Brielle was five years old, Brian got another promotion and transfer to Round Rock, Texas, just north of Austin. After living in Freeport for nearly five years, we finally were able to call this small town home. I was saddened leaving the place where so much of our girls' little lives happened. My heart ached leaving Martha, Bobbi, and my other friends. Although we enjoyed being just a few hours from our families, we were eager to move to this new city with four times the population where we would be close to a major city and have plenty of services to meet Brielle's needs. It was the right move for many reasons, but it was still a tough move emotionally.

Federal laws required the school district in Texas to follow Brielle's existing IEP. She would attend a school program for the deaf and there would be no fight.

Brielle attended the Texas preschool program in the mornings with children who were deaf. In the afternoons, she went to a typical kindergarten class with her morning teacher there to interpret and help when needed. Although Brielle would again ride school transportation (a big yellow school bus this time, much to her delight), the school was just across town.

Brielle made friends quickly and thrived in this sign language immersion environment with a wonderful teacher. Although we used the same notebook exchange system, Brielle's teacher often called me to give me more details than she could write.

Brielle's teacher opened up a whole new world to me by talking with me about issues facing deaf children. She talked with me about the difference between American Sign Language and Signed Exact English. Brielle was quickly learning new signs in SEE. Although we had begun tutoring with Sarah, Brielle's teacher encouraged us to attend workshops hosted by The SEE Center to stay a step ahead of our daughter's growing vocabulary.

She was also the first person to educate me about deaf culture. She talked to me about how Brielle might not fit in with her deaf peers since she was not deaf. Brielle's physical and cognitive disabilities might also be barrier to acceptance. These were tough words to hear, but it was something we would need to eventually face.

Another Year, Another Battle?

As the first school year in Texas came to a close, Brielle's teacher told me that the school administrators would not allow Brielle to continue in her class. Instead, they planned to send her to our neighborhood elementary school where Ashley went. The dreaded qualification rules struck again.

We now had a decision to make – to fight or not to fight.

In a classroom with children who were deaf, Brielle's development amazed us daily. There were no classes in our school district designed exclusively for children who were deaf past her preschool classroom. Those older children simply gathered together to attend one particular school in the district with interpreters in each of their classrooms. If we fought and *if* we won, Brielle would be in those classrooms as well. However, there would still be no immersion classroom like the one she had experienced in Rockford and again here in Austin. The class would be just a typical classroom, like classrooms Ashley attended.

We thought about how it might be nice to have her closer to home at the same school where Ashley attended. I was at the school often volunteering with the PTA. In addition, Sarah was a valuable resource as a teacher at our neighborhood school.

Either way, our daughter would be in a typical kindergarten class. However, if Brielle attended our neighborhood school, she would not have an interpreter because she would not be in the school where all of the children who were deaf attended.

Brian and I had many discussions about our options. We were torn. There was value in both classroom situations. One thing was certain. If she went to our neighborhood school without an interpreter, it would be very difficult to fight to get her back to the other school later if we changed our minds.

We had been very lucky in our battle the last time in Illinois, but only because of the opinion of one administrator. What were our chances of success in another fight? Moreover, I was not sure I could handle another battle, especially if it led to another rejection.

We also considered the counsel of Brielle's teacher about deaf culture. Brielle could continue to use sign language, but other deaf students might never accept her. Without a way to communicate, I wondered if other children with disabilities would accept her either. She needed to learn to communicate with other peers, no matter who they were.

The scales of decision tipped in one definitive direction when Brielle's teacher introduced me to the technology specialist who eventually gave Brielle the DynaVox, her communication device. Although the device was not perfect, it gave her an alternative to signing. Brielle took to it immediately and learned to use it even easier than anyone expected.

We worried we were backing off too easily, but having the communication device helped us make the decision to send her to the kindergarten class in our neighborhood school. Sign language would no longer be Brielle's only way to communicate with others in the classroom. Her new communication device would allow her to be in a kindergarten classroom just as Ashley had been in with at least some sort of ease. Attending our neighborhood school was the start of a new adventure for her.

> *You make known to me the path of life; you will*
> *fill me with joy in your presence, with eternal*
> *pleasures at your right hand.*
>
> — PSALM 16: 11 (NIV)

CHAPTER 20

Elementary School: Struggling to Keep Up

"Audrey will love it," 8-year-old Brielle signs, tapping the brightly wrapped birthday present in my hands as I help her ascend the stairs. Brielle's classmates rarely invite her to birthday parties, but Audrey is different. They are best friends.

As Audrey's mother opens the door for us, a small group of girls squeals and races to the door.

"Hi, Brielle! How are you?" Audrey signs. She has been coming to our tutoring sessions with Sarah each week, learning to sign right along with the rest of our family.

The other girls ask what she is signing and what Brielle is signing back. They run off as one pack to the living room where pop music is playing on the stereo. I stay to help Brielle with the party games and birthday cake, assisting Audrey's mother with what I can as well.

"We are so happy Audrey is learning so much sign language," she tells me.

"We're glad she can join us. She's getting to be a good signer," I tell her, watching the group of girls dancing to the music in a nearby room with Brielle. "And I'm so glad Audrey and Brielle are friends. You can never know what it means to us."

Time for the Big Show

Our family's school experience changed in many ways when Brielle started kindergarten at our neighborhood school in Texas. Brielle previously boarded her bus early, allowing Ashley and me to walk together to her school. That 10-minute walk each day to and from school provided time for Ashley to have my undivided attention. Precious chatter about schoolwork, playground games, cliques in the lunchroom, and cute boys who smiled at her filled our walks.

Brielle could not walk the distance to school and I did not want her to have the stigma of being pushed in the wheelchair that we typically used only for long walks at the zoo or amusement park.

Brielle complained about not riding the school bus that she loved so much. Car rides to school with the girls were very different from our previous routine. Unlike our leisurely walks to school, we now had to navigate traffic with soccer moms chugging coffee, crossing guards wearing brightly colored vests, and school drop-off lines jammed with minivans and SUVs. Afternoon chats over milk and a snack replaced my walking conversations with Ashley. I sensed her sadness about the change, but she never complained.

Brielle was in a typical kindergarten classroom but needed extra help with certain tasks. Two part-time aides or paraprofessionals (sometimes called "paras") helped Brielle complete classroom activities such as cutting along the dotted line, squeezing the glue bottle, and going hand over hand to count blocks. They also helped Brielle stand up from the floor at circle time, get seated at the cafeteria table for lunch, and navigate around the playground for recess. They helped her eat her lunch and snack, spoon-feeding her if necessary, and changed her diaper when needed.

MORE ABOUT....
Ashley and Brielle Attending the Same School

Although Brielle attended our neighborhood school in Texas for five years, Ashley was only there for three of them since she moved on to middle school. I was very active at their school and on the PTA Board. It was heart-warming to see them in their classrooms and occasionally interact with one another at school events. Those three years were the only time they attended the same school together.

The woman helping her in the morning was the best aide Brielle ever had. Shirley was warm and funny, but she made Brielle do as much for herself as she could. Shirley joined us each week for our sign language tutoring sessions with Sarah and expanded her sign language vocabulary quickly.

We hoped the afternoon aide would be a good match for Brielle since the woman was severely hearing impaired. We quickly learned that, despite her hearing loss, she did not know much American Sign Language and was unwilling to learn any Signed Exact English at all. To make matters worse, the teacher often clashed with the afternoon aide personally and professionally.

Although this kindergarten class was designed to be an inclusion class, one that included special needs children, Brielle was not always treated as a full member of the classroom. The teacher was well loved by her students and came with glowing reports from parents. However, from Shirley's reports and my own observations while volunteering in the classroom, it was clear that her teacher rarely interacted with Brielle and delegated any additional teaching responsibilities to the aides.

We trudged through the year and did the best we could with the situation. I was thrilled when Sarah told me the principal planned to move her from teaching second grade to first grade. Therefore, she could be Brielle's first grade teacher the next year. Sarah even arranged for Shirley to become Brielle's aide full-time.

The DynaVox communication device, although helpful in certain situations, mostly collected dust during first grade. As Sarah taught, she signed and interpreted for Brielle as well. Sarah worked hard to make Brielle just one of the other 20 students in the classroom. She treated Brielle the same and held her accountable to the same expectations. Moreover, Sarah knew how to connect with our daughter and get her to understand new concepts. Brielle made huge strides that year in a classroom situation that was as close to perfect as we could hope for.

The Less Than Ideal Elementary School Years

Although Brielle's year with Sarah was the best she ever had, she had a blur of well-intentioned, but average teachers over the next three years. Those teachers did well with other students. However, for the most part, they did not understand Brielle or how to meet her academic needs in their mainstream environment. They made little effort to accommodate her skills, which fell further and further behind her peers.

Beginning in the second grade, Brielle went to a resource room for part of her day. In this separate classroom, students could receive one-on-one instruction. The teacher there could help explain classroom materials or give extra time to complete regular classroom assignments. We hoped this type of focused instruction would help bridge the gaps in Brielle's understanding and give her more academic success.

I eventually learned that the resource room teacher assigned to Brielle was not a certified teacher, did not have any specific training to help teach children with learning issues, and did not have a college degree. Instead, she was grandfathered in from an old system and kept on by school administration friends for the previous 20 years. Her background in and of itself did not necessarily alarm me. It was the fact that she made no progress with Brielle at all that put me on high alert.

I started keeping detailed records and observed the resource room teacher with Brielle on several occasions. Every time I was there, they spent more time playing Candyland than any learning activity. When I met with the school principal to present her with my logs and observations, she had no choice but to review the situation. Within two weeks, the principal transferred the woman to a non-instructional job in the school and assigned a different resource room teacher to Brielle.

The new resource room teacher was better, but by the end of third grade, Brielle was overwhelmingly behind her peers. She was still doing kindergarten and first grade work in most subjects. It was clear she needed more than a regular classroom with portions of her day spent in the resource room. A self-contained special education classroom was the only alternative.

With visions of her preschool in Freeport running through my mind, I worried Brielle would be lost in the shuffle of another special education classroom. Although I knew she was well-below her peers, I did not want to face the true extent of her limitations. In my eyes, she was just Brielle.

Evaluations, Reports, and Difficult Meetings Over the Years

Brielle's classroom teacher, resource room teacher, therapists, school administrators, and I had to work together to write a new IEP each year. The document had to include evaluations and reports from her teachers and therapists, progress made on the previous year's goals, and goals for the new school year. The process was always the same, from preschool through high school and culminated with the IEP meeting.

It is a good idea in theory, but, in my experience, IEP meetings were always a grueling ordeal. I wanted to trust the system. After all, it served literally millions of students and was governed by national, state, and local laws. However, instinctual anxiety settled over me from the moment the date and time were set.

Each year, her teachers and school therapists (PT, OT, and speech) evaluated Brielle's academic and physical abilities by using standardized testing. In addition, every three years as federal law mandated, the school district completed detailed cognitive, social-emotional, and behavioral testing for Brielle prior to her annual IEP meeting. Just like a mouse in a lab, she endured the testing treadmill. This long process took days to complete.

The full evaluation completed every three years started with the evaluator from the school district questioning her teachers, aides, school therapists, and us. Her job was to ensure that the evaluation included a clear and complete picture of Brielle. It never did. How can you sum up a person in numbers and words?

When it was our turn, the woman assaulted me with a barrage of questions over the phone about Brielle's medical history and our home environment as well as about Brielle's abilities to take care of herself. She asked questions in rapid-fire succession about how Brielle ate, took a bath, got dressed, and even how she went to the bathroom. The stranger's questions were an invasion of our privacy and, yet, I had to answer them just the same because her report had to include Brielle's need for care.

This evaluator also attempted to test Brielle's intelligence. Most IQ tests were based either on manipulating puzzle pieces or on language skills. Both kinds of tests were problematic because of Brielle's fine motor and communication skills. As a result, the evaluator pieced together one section from one test and one section from another to come up with a score.

Beyond my concerns about its accuracy, I pondered what use that number would have on how someone might teach Brielle. Brielle was eager to cooperate with the test activities, but was oblivious to the consequences. There would be consequences. What type of classroom and what would be taught were directed by that number. It was just a number. It was not Brielle. I hated that number.

A week before the scheduled IEP meeting, Brielle delivered a thick packet of papers in her backpack with the reports and all of the evaluations. They were full of numbers, percentiles, and age equivalencies. It took hours to thoroughly review, but Brian and I both read it cover to cover. Then there was the delightful added bonus of hearing the results of the testing line by line at the meeting.

Since Brian's work schedule was so demanding, he rarely attended the meetings. He helped me write our list of questions and concerns to share at the meeting and always gave me a pep talk the morning of the big day. When I returned from the meetings, he read the reports and IEP document and asked me questions if something was not clear. If I needed him to be at the meeting to bring out the big guns for some major dispute, he would be there. However, most years, there were no big issues.

Over the years, I became a pro at handling the meetings on my own. I knew they would not necessarily be any easier to endure with him there. Therefore, I usually sat alone at the school conference room table surrounded by a room full of school officials.

By its simple design, the IEP meetings were inherently adversarial. Mom against them. I do not know why they had to be like that, but no matter where we have lived and how many I have been to, they always were.

One by one, the participants read their reports aloud. Each began pleasantly highlighting Brielle's strengths. Although rare, it was always a thrill to hear "normal" or "typical" and "Brielle" in the same sentence. Invariably, the short list of strengths gave way to the long list of things Brielle could not do.

The list grew longer with each year that passed. Nothing on the list was a surprise. I could not argue against the truth of their statements. However, the reading of the list stung as if it was a list of crimes of which I was personally accused, like somehow it was my fault Brielle was "less than." Of course, it was not and I did my best to try to rationalize that.

Just because someone read the charges with a smile on his or her face, they did not sting any less. As the teachers and therapists droned on with their lists, my internal dialog re-wrote the awful things they were saying with all of the simple things Brielle could do that brought such joy to our lives.

"Brielle cannot tie her shoe laces," the occupational therapist read from her report.

But, she can sign 'I love you' and really mean it, I thought to myself.

"Brielle cannot ascend or descend stairs independently," the physical therapist reported.

But, she can dance with incredible joy to music playing on her CD player, I considered, picturing her beaming face as she twirled.

"Brielle needs assistance using a calculator to do simple math problems," her teacher stated.

But, she will never have to fill up her brain with useless trigonometry problems that I've never used, I contemplated.

Their reports never pointed out the small successes I saw as so important. They did not reflect how she was finally eating better and able to put on a few much-needed pounds. They did not point out how she rarely had trouble transitioning from one activity to another like she did in preschool and kindergarten. They did not report how her interests were going beyond that of a preschooler and were becoming more age appropriate. They did not highlight her ability to make friends with some of her peers and the positive impact she had on those friends. They did not show how great she did in the school choir signing the songs with the other students singing. They did not even report when she finally got potty trained when she was eight years old.

The IEP meetings always ended with establishing goals that were just beyond her reach. Reading those simple goals made me feel even worse than before. The people at that table all had such low expectations for my daughter and it broke my heart.

The two-hour meeting unraveled my nerves. Signing my name on the last page of the pile of paperwork was a rushed ritual. Everyone was eager to move on to the next child whose parents were undoubtedly waiting outside for their appointment with the same nervousness I had before Brielle's meeting started. I was glad when I was finally able to leave, go home, and collapse in a chair.

This was how the meetings went, year after year. There were years when something in those 25 or more pages was important. We had certainly fought hard enough to get "School for the Deaf" on the front of her IEP back in preschool. However, as the years passed and Brielle's academic progress slowed, the IEP documents meant less because they resulted in little difference in her development.

Her IEP meeting early in the fall of fourth grade was one of the few that stood out. The reports that year confirmed our concerns about Brielle's progress. She needed to demonstrate progress towards her academic goals if she was going to stay on her inclusive track. However, the school team made it clear to us that they would most likely have to assign her to a special education classroom in a different school the following year for fifth grade. I dreaded the inevitable prospect.

Another Move

In the middle of her fourth grade year, Brian received another job promotion and transfer. We moved yet again, this time to a small suburb of Toledo, Ohio. Brian's new boss told him that he would be working in Toledo for about two years until the company moved the division to the new corporate headquarters in Atlanta. With so many divisions under the same roof, a future job change within the company would simply mean Brian moving to a different floor of the massive building instead of across the country.

Knowing that another move was looming over us was unnerving. Although we briefly considered having Brian move without us and commute back to Texas as much as he could, we dismissed the idea in favor of keeping the family together.

We lived in Texas for nearly six years. Ashley was in the middle of seventh grade and blossoming into a beautiful yet complicated teenager, active in gymnastics and volleyball with growing interests in fashion, pop culture, and boys. I had recently scaled back my volunteer work with the PTA and church, and was spending more time focused on our family. We had good friends in the community, at school, and at work. Texas felt more like home than any place had before.

And, yet, here we were, making another move.

Ask the former generation and find out what their ancestors learned, for we were born only yesterday and know nothing, and our days on earth are but a shadow.

Will they not instruct you and tell you?

Will they not bring forth words from their understanding?

— JOB 8: 8-10 (NIV)

CHAPTER 21

Middle School:
A Time of Transition

The girls and I walk through the mall when I notice a group of teenage girls walking toward us. One of them is beaming at us.

"Hi, Brielle," the girl says as she approaches with her friends. "How are you?"

Brielle eagerly greets the friendly teenager. The stranger doesn't introduce herself to me or Ashley.

"Who was that?" I ask Brielle once the girl and her friends walk away.

"I don't know," my teenager signs.

So many people know Brielle. We walk through a store or a movie theater and inevitably, someone, usually a teenage girl from school, greets Brielle. Most of the time, Brielle recognizes the person even if she doesn't know the girl's name.

*"Another one who mysteriously knows Brielle,"
Ashley mutters under her breath as we continue our
shopping at the mall.*

Another New Place, Another New School

The school system in the small community outside Toledo did not
have the option of a one-on-one teaching system like the resource
room at Brielle's school in Texas. Therefore, she attended a special
education classroom with other special needs kids who were in both
the fourth and fifth grade.

Her new classroom was decorated with colorful preschool-type
posters and furnished with special equipment, wheelchairs, and therapy tables. Painful emotions bubbled to the surface. It brought back
visions of Brielle's special education preschool in Freeport I thought
we had long since left behind. Brian was not as worried as I was and
encouraged me to give the new classroom environment a chance.

As the new school year began, positive notes from her teacher
or one of the two aides filled the notebook we sent back and forth.
Although Brielle used the same communication device she had in
Texas, the teacher sent home word lists from her classroom lessons
so that I could teach Brielle the signs for new vocabulary. Worksheets
with spelling lists and math problems came home on a regular basis.
Finding a colored picture or a sloppy but precious art project in her
backpack was a treasured surprise.

As the cold and dreary Midwest winter months broke free to
warmer spring months, I felt more at ease with Brielle's school placement. Nothing had changed. I had simply slowly learned to accept
that our daughter belonged in that special education classroom.

It had taken many years to make the transition from wanting
Brielle to be like other kids her age to realizing she was not. I watched
the gap slowly widen over her elementary school years as she fell

further behind academically, socially, and emotionally. As I looked to the future, I could not picture her interacting with middle school and high school students in a way similar to how Ashley did already. With wise counsel and support from close friends who had older children with special needs, my hopes slowly faded and I learned to create new dreams about Brielle's future as I settled into her new classroom placement.

Although Brielle was with the same teacher the following year for fifth grade, her other classmates moved up to sixth grade at the junior high and there were no new fourth grade special needs students in the entire rural school district. My first thought was that it would be wonderful for Brielle to have a one-on-one teaching experience. However, I worried that Brielle would be lonely without any peers in her classroom.

Despite my apprehension, Brielle made huge strides academically that year and the teacher did her best to help Brielle have more contact with other schoolmates. Brielle picked up attendance sheets from each classroom in the morning and took them to the office. She collected papers that needed shredding and put them through the machine. Students from the other classrooms played games with her or helped her work on projects. Brielle excitedly talked about her jobs at school, the nice ladies in the office, and her friends that came to visit her. Therefore, I stopped being concerned about her happiness in her solo classroom situation.

The Permanent Move

Although Brian's boss told him it would be at least two years before moving us to Atlanta, the new building was ready sooner than expected. The company moved us after living in the Toledo area for just 18 months.

Brielle adjusted to the moves easily, but we knew they were hard on Ashley. It broke our hearts to see our oldest daughter cry when we told her about the move. We had not prepared her for this to happen so quickly. We tried to reassure her that at least she could start her first year of high school in the new school.

Meeting a girl the same age in our new neighborhood soon after we moved helped make the adjustment to her new surroundings a little easier. Although Ashley made another friend on the first day of school, she struggled to feel like she fit in for the first few months. However, by homecoming, she had a boyfriend, found more friends, and settled into her new school.

Brielle started sixth grade in our northern suburb of Atlanta in a special needs classroom that was part of an elementary school. She used the same communication device, her new teacher focused on academics, and it was an uneventful year. However, Brielle's next year in seventh grade was very different.

A teaching veteran taught the combined special education seventh and eighth grade classroom at the junior high school. At Brielle's IEP meeting that fall, the new teacher told us the focus of school would shift to mostly life skills (cooking, cleaning, laundry, counting money, etc.). We saw very little academic work come home other than a weekly spelling list of six kindergarten sight words that were well below my daughter's abilities.

MORE ABOUT....
Teachers Over the Years

Although most of Brielle's teachers had a lot of teaching experience, that did not automatically make them good teachers or a good fit for Brielle. Some had plenty of experience with special needs students like Brielle. Even then, that experience did not always translate into a good teacher. Individual differences in teaching styles and willingness to learn how to best connect with Brielle were the best predictors of a good fit.

I asked the teacher for a vocabulary list for whatever they were learning academically, hoping to be able to teach Brielle any new signs as I had in the past. Although the teacher said she would get me a list, she never did despite my constant reminding. Guessing some of the words Brielle might need to know from things she told me was like throwing darts at a target in the dark of night.

"Brielle is using her communication device to learn and talk about our new unit," the teacher tried to assure me when I continued to prod her for the vocabulary list. "She understands what we are learning. Trust me."

We were not convinced Brielle was learning anything. Whenever visiting the classroom, remarkably, I always seemed to arrive when they were neither doing academics nor working on life skills. Sure, there were cooking items on the counter and a broom in the corner of the classroom. However, we never got any reports about our daughter's ability to cook or clean. Brielle only told us about her friends, movies she watched, games she played on the computer with friends from other classrooms, or what she ate for lunch.

We were frustrated, but Brielle was happy. I wondered if that was enough. In my heart, I felt it was not.

The Not-So-Funny Incident

"I just had to call to tell you a funny story about Brielle," her teacher began to tell me in a phone call in early February. "It happened when we were getting ready to go to the thrift store this morning for our monthly outing, you know, to teach them how to shop."

All I could think about was how the five dollars I sent with Brielle would inevitably result in a used preschool movie that was too baby-ish for my teenage daughter, not to mention it would be a VHS tape. Who still used a videotape player anymore in 2010?

"I sent the girls to the bathroom while I got the boys on the bus," the teacher continued with her story. "When the other two girls got back from the bathroom, they got on the bus, too. The classroom aides were packing up the shopping bags when all of the sudden, Mr. X *(the male aid)* noticed Brielle standing at the classroom door with her pants and underwear down around her ankles."

"What?" I gasped in horror. "How did that happen?"

"I guess Brielle couldn't pull up her pants in the bathroom, so she shuffled back across the hallway to get help," her teacher surmised flippantly.

"Why weren't you or Ms. Y *(the female aide)* in the bathroom with her?" I asked as calmly as I could. "You know Brielle can't pull up her pants let alone button and zip her jeans."

"Ms. Y was getting our shopping things together and I was settling the other kids on the bus. I guess our little Miss Brielle just couldn't wait for someone to come help her."

I was silent as I pictured "our little Miss Brielle" at 14 years old, fully in the midst of puberty, shuffling down the junior high school hallway, naked from the waist down. My pulse quickened, my face got hot, and my hands slightly shook as I stood there holding the phone. My knees felt weak and I knew I should sit down, but all I could do was pace the planks of the hardwood floors in our living room.

"Don't worry," the teacher tried to reassure me. "Brielle wasn't the least bit embarrassed. And no one was in the hallway when she walked back to the classroom. We checked."

I could not fathom what her teacher thought was so funny about this incident. Was she serious? Did she think I would laugh? Had she laughed about it? Or was she just trying to smooth it over before I heard from some witness at the school?

"How could this...? Why weren't you...? You know what could have...?" I struggled to utter a complete sentence.

"Mrs. Stull," the teacher's voice cracked for the first time. "I can assure you..."

"I'm sorry," I said abruptly. "I can't process what you have just told me and I certainly can't speak to you right now."

With that, I hung up. I longed for the days when I could slam down the phone receiver with a loud thud heard at the other end of the line. Pressing OFF on the cordless phone was hardly satisfying.

Funny story. Funny story.

Her teacher's words clanged in my head like a gong as I let the cascade of emotions wash over me. Brielle could have easily tripped over the pants around her ankles and gotten hurt. Any number of teenage boys could have seen her half-naked and said or done who-knows-what. As it was, the male aide saw her standing in the doorway.

Considering my options, I continued to pace as my fingernails dug deep into my clenched fists. Brian left the house that morning already stressed about his packed schedule at work, so I did not want to interrupt his day. Swooping into the school to take Brielle home early could be reassuring, but would not change anything. The principal or the superintendent of special education could get a very irate call, but I was too angry to be coherent. A call to one of the many lawyers who would surely be willing, even eager, to take on a case like this could help us file a formal complaint, but that seemed extreme.

Paralyzed by the shock of the situation, the hours before Brielle arrived home on the school bus ticked past at an alarmingly slow pace. She stepped off the bus as happy as she was on any other day. She signed to me about her pizza lunch and trip to the thrift store. Yes, another prized preschool videotape was in her possession. She was safe and happy. All was fine in her mind.

"What can we do about this?" Brian stormed when I told him the teacher's "funny" story that evening. "They were clearly negligent. You know what could have happened?"

I knew. My mind had raced with the potential outcomes all afternoon. I could see the frightening headlines in the local paper and the news anchors solemnly reporting the "incident that occurred at a local school." Although the possibilities horrified me, nothing bad had happened. She was not hurt. She was not upset. No other teenagers saw her.

Although we could have contacted the local media or filed a formal complaint through an attorney, those options were quickly dismissed. The only alternatives we really considered were confronting the teacher and reporting it to school officials.

The only witnesses were the teachers involved. Brielle could not tell us anything useful, even when we prodded her with questions about her day.

"I got help in bathroom," Brielle signed to us. "My teacher helped me."

A major factor we considered in our decision making process was that the teacher and aides would be in Brielle's classroom for the rest of the year as well as another year after this. This was her only placement option since there were no other special education classrooms in the district at the junior high school level. Without a positive relationship, the teacher and aides could subtly take it out on Brielle in ways we would never know. Our daughter had no way of protecting herself and might not be able to tell us about it either.

What could we accomplish with anything other than letting it go? We tried to convince ourselves that this was just an unfortunate circumstance of miscommunication between the teacher and aide about who was going to help Brielle in the bathroom. We had to assume that they would be more careful in the future.

With much restraint, we swallowed our fury and kept our mouths shut. This is one of the few choices we made that I second-guessed. Considering the best possible outcome, in the end, nothing could beat Brielle being OK and putting the whole thing behind us. We needed to salvage the situation for our daughter's best interest.

MORE ABOUT....
Handling "Incidents"

Things like Brielle's bathroom incident could happen to any special needs child. Although we chose not to do anything, we should have documented the event by taking detailed notes and insisting on a written report. If additional "incidents" occurred, we would have had that documentation to fall back on to report it to the principal or file a complaint.

Academic Evidence

With my stifled anger lingering over the bathroom incident, I eventually confronted the teacher with zeal about the lack of academics or life skills instruction. At least with that issue I could gather some evidence that might result in a positive change.

"I'd like to see all of Brielle's schoolwork," I requested over the phone on a Friday afternoon in early April.

"I have to keep it all in her file to add to her annual report to the state," her teacher replied hesitantly, obviously a little taken aback at the direct request. "So, I can't just send it all home."

"Then I can come to the classroom and look it over," I casually countered, not missing a beat.

"But," she stammered a bit. "I'll be out of the classroom next week for a conference. So, it will have to be after that."

"Fine. I'll come in a week from Monday. I can drop off Brielle at school myself that morning instead of sending her on the bus."

As soon as we made those arrangements, I could not help but wonder if the extra days would help buy the teacher time to pad Brielle's schoolwork file. I wished I had just shown up in the classroom with the request instead of doing it over the phone.

Arriving that Monday morning as planned, the teacher chatted endlessly about everything but the papers I came to see.

"I'd like to see Brielle's schoolwork now," I eventually interrupted her, not so subtly changing the subject to the agenda I came for.

A folder appeared from a locked filing cabinet in the back closet. It was tidy and organized into four paperclipped sections, one for each academic quarter. There were no reports or documentation about life skills activities. Some of the papers included dates, but most did not. No handwriting analyst was needed. I recognized Brielle's sloppy printing on some of them, but could not be sure of others. Some of the worksheets simply required circling the correct answer or filling in a bubble, so the true author of those was not discernible.

More than 160 days of school culminated in a stack of papers about an inch thick. Meager results, but noteworthy evidence. Even in first grade, Ashley would come home with stacks of worksheets and other busy work. How could there be so little in Brielle's file if nothing came home to us? I did not expect to see much documentation for life skills instruction. However, it was clear that academics had not been part of the teacher's daily schedule either. What did the teacher do with her all day?

On the ride home, I contemplated Brielle's future. How could Brielle survive, let alone succeed, in this world without both academic and life skills? She was already years behind her peers in so many ways. She needed basic knowledge and the ability to do things for herself. Clearly, her teacher was not preparing her. I pondered what we could do for our child in the years to come. We had to make a drastic change.

Start children off on the way they should go, and even when they are old they will not turn from it.

— PROVERBS 22:6 (NIV)

CHAPTER 22

Homeschooling:
The Great Success

Music from Brielle's iPod stereo blasts lyrics from Big Time Rush, her favorite teen idol band. I knock on her door and turn down the music. My 15-year-old is sitting on the bed with her doll, Daisy, on her lap and about 150 addition and subtraction flash cards scattered around. Brielle holds up a flash card, punches the numbers into her calculator, and shows it to Daisy.

"I am teacher," Brielle signs to me. "I am good teacher. I teach my baby math."

I smile and tell her to teach her baby good things so she gets smarter.

"You my teacher," Brielle signs with a huge smile. "You teach good things. I smart. Good job, Mom."

Hard Evidence

As Brielle finished that school year, I thought back to all of her previous school experiences and the teachers she had over the years in the different places we had lived. When was the last good year she had? First grade with Sarah? How had things gone from such a wonderful year to what it was now in middle school? With the lack of instruction, her current classroom more closely mirrored a daycare situation, not a seventh grade class.

Other parents of special needs teenagers told me things only got worse at the high school. No academics at all. A few life skills. Lots of field trips. Mostly more fun and games. Even Ashley reported often seeing the special education kids just milling around the halls during class time.

I felt betrayed by the public school system that should have been helping Brielle. Reviewing that meager stack of papers from her teacher was the last straw. School was not preparing our daughter for life. The evidence was stacked against them. The verdict was clear. Guilty as charged.

Could We Wear Fuzzy Slippers at School?

For years, I vaguely considered homeschooling. Surely, I could do a better job teaching Brielle than any of her teachers had done in the last six years. No more cumbersome communication devices. I could teach her signs to go with each lesson designed just for her. We could do it our way, even in our pajamas.

I did my best thinking over coffee. Sitting on our back deck one morning in May, I thought more seriously about homeschooling than I ever had. I thought about a few of my acquaintances who homeschooled. I tried to recall details they shared about their experiences. What were the rules? How much time did it take? What troubles did they have?

Then I heard it. My inner little self-deprecating voice whispered in my ear, *"You can't really do it."*

Sipping my coffee, I took a shot of confidence. Shoving those feelings of insecurity to the far reaches of my mind, I reminded myself of my qualifications and successes.

Every mom is a teacher. I taught Ashley how to read her first book, write her name, and tie her shoes. I helped her with math and science before her homework started going over my head in high school. (OK, I'll fess up. Ashley's homework started going over my head in junior high.) Since moving away from Texas, I taught Brielle every new sign she learned and tutored quite a few people in sign language as well. I taught Sunday school to young children for several years and was the co-leader for Ashley's Girl Scout troop in elementary school. On top of all of that, in my previous life in graduate school, I taught Introduction to Communication and Public Speaking to college freshman. I could do this.

That little voice whispered in my ear again, *"What about Brielle's friends?"*

Despite the lack of academics, all of the fun activities she had in school encouraged friendships with her peers. Most days, Brielle's greatest enthusiasm came out when she talked about things she did with her friends, including buddies from other classrooms.

Considering our options, I thought about how we could still pick up her best friend, Victoria, for a trip to the mall or a movie. Brielle could still have activities like Special Olympics bowling and Miracle League baseball to be with other special needs kids. Sure, she could still have friends.

"You'll be with Brielle all of the time. All of the time," my inner voice pointed out to me.

I stared at the last few drops of confidence that lay cold at the bottom of my coffee cup. Could I manage being with Brielle all of the time? Would it drive me crazy? Although things had become easier over the previous few years, the basic care for her more closely resembled that of a three-year-old. I had to prepare all of her drinks and food, get her dressed, bathe her, brush her hair, and even wipe her bottom when necessary.

Her care is exhausting and yet all done on autopilot. Thinking about it for too long, I could easily spiral into a self-pity fest.

Those more difficult times seemed to come in waves. At any given time in her life, for a day or two at a time, she drove me crazy. Every single thing my daughter needed felt like a burden and I easily slipped into the role of the martyr. Then for a week or more, I could not get enough time with her, just to be with her and enjoy the glow from her innocent ways and positive attitude. Of course, too much togetherness could stir up bad habits in any relationship. This was a definite concern.

"If Brielle is with you all of the time, you won't have time for yourself," that pestering voice clanged in my ear yet again.

Although once a full-time working mother, I had been a stay-at-home mom for the previous 13 years. Running Brielle to therapies and medical appointments kept me busy those first few years. Volunteering helped fill my days for several years while she was in elementary school. However, by this time, I had more discretionary time than most. There was freedom and flexibility in the lifestyle of a stay-at-home mom. I selfishly wondered how my personal activities would still fit into our schedule if homeschooling responsibilities were on the agenda each day.

Let's Make a Deal

Over many cups of coffee across several days, I circled around Brielle's school issues, searching for clues that might reveal a solution. As I mulled over the possibility of homeschooling, my inner, self-doubting voice slowly faded away. There was no real light bulb moment.

No instant when it became clear all at once. No epiphany. I eased into my decision like slipping into a warm bathtub. I wanted to try homeschooling.

I approached Brian with my proposal one evening in late May as we sat together on our deck. A glass of wine was now my liquid confidence.

"Really? Are you sure you want to do this? This would change everything for you," he said.

"I know I can do this," I pleaded my case.

"I know you could teach Brielle and do it well," Brian reassured me. "But, I worry about you. It's a lot of responsibility with no breaks. You know how things might be for you two. And what about all of the other things you like to do? What about the book you're writing?"

My husband was questioning the very things I had. It was as if he heard the little voice in my head.

"I'll tell you what," I smiled as I put my hand over his. "Let me do a test run with Brielle over the summer. I'll do everything as if it was the middle of the school year and we'll decide after that."

Brian gave me one of those all-knowing looks encoded by 20 years of marriage. He had seen that resolve in me many times before. Finally, he flipped his hand over to hold mine.

"Deal," he said shaking my hand firmly. "But, it needs to be a real try and we'll need an honest discussion about it. If I think it's not working, I'll veto it and she'll go back to school for eighth grade."

Although an observer might consider our discussion more of a business deal or that Brian was the sole decision maker, it was all with a familiar lightheartedness and not unlike how we made other major decisions. I had used veto power several times in our marriage and so had he. Veto is what Brian and I call one of the informal rules we agreed upon in our marriage. With any major decision or purchase, we each have veto power. If someone does not agree with the other, status quo prevails and things continue as they are.

"Deal." I agreed to my husband's terms, pleased that he decided homeschooling was worth a try.

We discussed a few more of the details including how exactly I might balance my personal interests, the demands of the household, and Ashley's needs. We agreed this might not be a long-term solution and that it may be beneficial to send Brielle back to public school at some point. However, we knew that most details would be worked out along the way by trial and error.

The Ultimate Test Drive

After researching the requirements on the internet and attending a local homeschooling conference, knowledge and genuine confidence propelled me forward. I was eager to start our new experiment. When I told Brielle we would be doing schoolwork together, she was eager as well, but clearly had no idea what homeschooling really meant.

Determined to make it a success, I planned the road ahead. However, my inner voice was right about a few things. There were definitely some roadblocks to navigate around. First, and foremost, I had to teach Brielle. She needed time with friends. We still needed a life with some of my favorite activities. In the end, I had to keep from getting too frustrated with the whole process.

A trip to a teachers' store and the library resulted in a diverse supply of books and teaching materials. Brielle was technologically savvy and loved using the computer. I began to bookmark websites for addition drills, episodes of *Schoolhouse Rock*, and science experiment videos. As for teaching her, I decided the best approach to getting the most out of her abilities was to start with the basics, build on what she knew, and expand her sign language vocabulary.

There were things I realized Brielle already knew. With other things, I understood how to follow her logic because I knew her life experiences and point of view about the world. During one of those excruciating IQ tests the school performed, the evaluator asked her what a carrot was. Not having the sign for carrot in her vocabulary at the time, she signed rabbit. The tester marked her answer wrong, but clearly, she had an understanding of the orange vegetable.

A few weeks of homeschooling produced inches of worksheets and stacks of pictures of Brielle gaining new life skills. However, what Brielle was learning could be more accurately measured by what she eagerly told her dad each evening.

"What did you learn at school today?" he asked. It was the question asked across many family dinner tables. The list she excitedly shared was long. I could not help but to beam with pride as I interpreted for her.

Every Friday evening, I laid our homeschooling binder by Brian's chair for him to review. He studied it with great intent. Although he rarely commented on it, I felt confident my husband recognized the progress Brielle was making.

"How do you think things are going?" Brian asked about a month into our test run.

"It's going well. How do *you* think it's going?" I asked, anxiously awaiting his approval.

"Well," he started to share his opinion. "The household is still running smoothly. Brielle is definitely learning. And you seem to be in a good mood. I'd say, so far, so good."

Without a reason to disagree, I hid my delight and gave him a hug. Inside, I was doing a happy dance.

I searched for opportunities to help Brielle have more interactions with other teenagers. She joined a special needs cheerleading and dance group as well as an American Heritage Girls troop, which was roughly like a Christian version of Girl Scouts. Victoria's mother eagerly let her daughter join both activities. The girls were thrilled to be able to spend time together each week and it gave them both a chance to be with other teenagers.

The women in my Bible study group and other friends I met weekly for lunch were happy to have Brielle tag along. In addition, I could still sign at my church each Sunday, attend my writers' group two nights a month, and go scrapbooking one Saturday a month with other friends.

Household duties became opportunities to learn real life skills. Brielle learned to fold washcloths and small towels for me. She helped load and unload the cart at the grocery store. She learned how to dust furniture and clean mirrors. Helping prepare food, especially sweet treats, became one of her favorite tasks.

MORE ABOUT....
Our Daily Study of Faith

Our homeschooling routine included reading a daily devotional designed for young girls. It was difficult to know what Brielle believed about God. However, it gave us an opportunity to discuss morals and values as well as provided another opportunity to do reading comprehension activities.

In addition, she learned to do more for herself. Little things like taking out the donuts for her breakfast, carrying her plate to the table, and pushing up her own sleeves before washing her hands helped make routine tasks easier for me. The more I asked her to do, the more I realized I could expect from her. Although there would always be things I would have to do for her, she could do more for herself each day.

Being a mother to a special needs child did not automatically make me a more patient parent. However, our enthusiasm and positive energy together while doing schoolwork spilled over into even the most monotonous tasks of meeting Brielle's needs. We formed an even tighter bond over addition drill sheets and videos about how plants grow.

During that summer, I was able to keep up with the housework without many issues. Like before, I rarely had to do any tasks at night or on the weekends, so our family time was still available. Ashley was about to be a junior in high school and had little time for us that summer. She was busy with her boyfriend, friends, and a part-time job at an ice cream and sandwich shop. However, we still enjoyed a short trip to the beach, a few afternoons at a neighbor's pool, a bar-b-que with friends for The Fourth of July, and popcorn at a few movies.

We convened a family meeting one evening late in July. We spoke freely and honestly about life for our family during our test run. Even Ashley had input regarding how things seemed to be going. Brielle was happy and learning more than she had in years. The self-doubting little voice in my head was no longer whispering things to me. Ashley gave me a few words of encouragement and Brian put his stamp of approval on it. We were officially homeschoolers.

The Power of Emancipation

After filing the proper paperwork with the county, I called Brielle's school the week before she would have returned to begin the eighth grade in the fall of 2010. After I informed the school secretary of our plans to homeschool, I asked to speak to Brielle's teacher, the same one who allowed my daughter to walk half-naked across the hallway. Despite my lingering negative feelings, I could not burn bridges. I restrained my desire to say something vengeful, but still took great satisfaction in her former teacher's shock at our decision.

Our typical homeschooling day started with coffee, breakfast, and a little internet surfing while watching a morning news show. Teaching began around nine o'clock. Still wearing our pajamas, we sat on the sofa to do a short devotional, review our calendar, check the weather, and read a chapter of a book. We moved to the kitchen table to work on handwriting, language arts, social studies, science, and math. While she completed some of the work independently, I did a few household chores. We took a break for lunch before she worked on a few composition exercises and wrote e-mails to her dad at work and a few other family members. We might also talk about composers or painters. Most days included some sort of activity to work on life skills (such as laundry, cleaning, cooking, or shopping). The rest of the day was ours to do what we wanted or needed to do.

Measuring Success

Brielle learned something new every day and had plenty to tell Dad each evening at dinner. Over three years, she advanced at least two grade levels in each academic area, bigger gains than she ever made in public school in the previous six years.

When we started, Brielle could not add two single digit numbers, read or comprehend beyond simple picture books, comprehend simple science concepts other than about weather, or understand the role of government.

Within three years, she was able to:
- write much more legibly
- add and subtract triple digit numbers
- count coins
- read and comprehend fourth grade chapter books
- identify and properly use most major parts of speech (such as nouns, verbs, adjectives, and pronouns)
- comprehend a variety of science concepts (such as life cycles, the human body, environments, the solar system, magnets, and others) at a third grade level
- understand the role of the government and many U.S. historical events

In addition, she knew:
- the works of many famous painters and sculptors
- the works of many famous composers and musical concepts

- more stories from the Bibles and standards of moral conduct (beyond good manners)
- her address, home phone, and the phone numbers of all family members

She also learned to:
- shop for things we needed and wanted including how to make a list, use coupons, and compare prices
- sort, fold, and put away laundry
- clean the house including dusting, cleaning mirrors and windows, vacuuming, and emptying garbage cans
- bake and cook from simple recipes including measuring, stirring, setting the oven, and being safe in the kitchen
- navigate the computer even better including logging into her email and Facebook accounts as well as looking up information and videos

She truly learned more than even I expected. She matured more in those three years as well. She learned how to be more patient, manage her free time, and be more independent with her daily routine and activities.

Although I thought I had a good education, it surprised me how much the homeschooling process taught me as well. In our quiet moments, I realized that teaching was my calling. Although I taught public speaking while in graduate school and sign language to dozens of people over the years, seeing Brielle learn new concepts and have those "aha moments" was incredibly rewarding. Her success made it all the sweeter to prove to the school system, and me, that I could do it better.

I think back to those years she was in school not really learning anything. Sometimes, I feel guilty for not homeschooling her sooner. She nearly slipped through the cracks of the limitations of the public school system. With her improved academic skills and understanding of the world around her, I know that she is much better prepared for her future.

MORE ABOUT....
Homeschooling in America

Recent statistics show that homeschooling rates are at about four percent and rapidly growing, particularly in primary grades.[7] Specific reporting for special needs children is not required. Therefore, it is difficult to determine what percentage of homeschoolers have special needs.

State laws vary. However, at the time we homeschooled, Georgia laws mandated:

- A Declaration of Intent to Homeschool form filed with the county within 30 days of the start of the school year
- 180 days of instruction within a calendar year (parents could set start and end dates of that year)
- four and half hours of instruction each day
- instruction to include (but not be limited to) reading, language arts, mathematics, science, and social studies
- an attendance form sent to the county each month reporting specific days of instruction (a check in a box for each day)
- an annual report summarizing the child's progress kept in the parents' file (no format was specified)
- all records kept for three years

At any time, the county could request a review of our records. Therefore, I kept careful documentation of each day's work.

Although special services (such as therapies) were still available through the county school district for Brielle, we refused any services and simply continued with private therapies.

The Down Side of Homeschooling

We missed very few things about public school. The overpriced school picture. The school bus rides she loved so much. The surprise of handmade gifts at Christmas and Mother's Day. The list was short and relatively meaningless.

There was an adjustment to certain things. Just as expected, I did not have any real flexibility to do things on my own during the day. I could not leave Brielle home alone for very long since I could not be sure she could handle someone ringing the doorbell or some sort of emergency. Therefore, Brielle had to tag along to my doctor and dentist appointments. I had to ask friends if it was OK to bring Brielle to lunch or schedule evening time together instead. I could not go to the grocery store just for those few items I forgot on our weekly trip.

On the other hand, homeschooling gave us more flexibility to plan things Brielle and I did together. I could schedule her medical appointments at any time. We could take days off when we needed or wanted to for traveling to see family or just a random day off. Cleaning house, doing laundry, cooking, shopping, and certain other field trips could all be considered instructional time as long as Brielle was participating and learning. However, all of those activities took much longer and were more complicated when I involved her.

There were days when the monotony of our routine made me less than enthusiastic about my teaching job. Some days, it was clear that Brielle felt the same way. A few days spent on life skills or on field trips renewed our energies and we were ready to tackle academics once again. She got irritated with me on days when we did not do homeschooling. Never wanting to miss out on school, on those days off, she stayed busy playing school and teaching her dolls.

There were certain concepts that I could just not get Brielle to understand. I thought she would never move beyond adding single digit numbers. Then, after months it just clicked with her and she was able to move on. Other concepts were more frustrating. After days of trying to teach her how to use a ruler, I gave up, returned to it months later, only to be frustrated again.

Homeschooling is not for everyone. We are blessed with the financial circumstances for me to be able to stay home, the education and experience to teach, and the support of my husband. Moreover, Brielle and I are a good match to spend so much time together. I understand her needs and learning style. The same cannot be said for all mothers and their children.

"There's no way you could have ever homeschooled me," Ashley said emphatically from time to time during those first months of homeschooling.

I was not sure whether to take that as a criticism, a teasing prod, or a simple observation. Between Ashley's abilities and our personalities, I agreed with her. Homeschooling would not have worked out so well with my older daughter. However, for three years, Brielle and I had a positive experience.

The Edge of a New Experience

Although Brian and I originally discussed that there would probably be a time when Brielle should return to public school, the success we had homeschooling made it difficult to imagine what could prompt us to do that. However, as she approached what would have been her final years in high school, I began to wonder what she might be missing. Watching Ashley go to football games with friends, try on prom dresses, and walk across the stage at her graduation ceremony made me yearn for similar experiences for Brielle.

A friend who taught at the high school where Ashley attended, the same school Brielle could have attended, talked to me just before Brielle's seventeenth birthday.

"There are now two separate classes, one for lower functioning students and another for more mildly affected students," my friend explained. "The new special education teacher is experienced and has changed the format of the higher-level classroom. It has a more rigorous routine including more academics."

Since Brielle was doing fourth grade level work in most academic subjects, I surmised she would probably qualify for the classroom with the new teacher. I still had worries that the academics there would not be enough. There was no policy that would allow my daughter to split her time between public school and homeschool. Since she would not get home until nearly four o'clock, I could hardly expect her to endure homeschooling lessons after a full day of school. However, maybe there could be time to fit in a few lessons on the weekends and on other days when she did not go to school.

Her ability to communicate was still a lingering concern. My friend said the new teacher knew some sign language. That would not be enough to keep up with Brielle's fluent skills, but at least it showed a willingness to learn. Brielle would still need to use a supplementary communication device. With the advancement of technology in those three years, perhaps there were better options for her.

One of the biggest benefits of sending her back to public school was to gain work experience. The many businesses that the school collaborated with gave special needs high school students the opportunity to do simple jobs in the community. Several days a week, Victoria performed cleaning tasks at a pizza place and straightened shelves at a drug store. We had many concerns about Brielle's future and her ability to be employed. The school could help bridge this gap.

Attending public school again would allow Brielle to form new friendships with other special needs students as well as with other high school students who volunteer to be classroom buddies. She would get to spend more time with Victoria and we knew this would bring great joy to both of them.

Special needs students qualify to stay in public school until just before their twenty-second birthdays. If Brielle attended school, she would have something to do each day for the next five years. However, if we did not send her back before her eighteenth birthday, she could not enroll after that. It was one of those "now or never" types of situations.

After much deliberation, we decided to send Brielle back to school in the fall of 2013 when she would be a junior in high school. As she started her new adventure, I began a new one as well. With my days free, I started new projects and found new activities. It was with some anxiety that we moved forward. However, we could return to homeschooling and, no matter what, I would always be my daughter's teacher.

> *We have different gifts, according to the grace given to each of us. If your gift is prophesying, then prophesy in accordance with your faith; if it is serving, then serve; if it is teaching, then teach; if it is to encourage, then give encouragement; if it is giving, then give generously; if it is to lead, do it diligently; if it is to show mercy, do it cheerfully.*
>
> – ROMANS 12: 6-8 (NIV)

CHAPTER 23

Someone Is Always Watching

After shopping at one grocery store, we are outside another store collecting more empty reusable bags from the back of my SUV. Brielle's 16-year-old face is sad and sullen, so unlike her usually cheerful smile. I ask her if she feels sick.

"No, not sick," she signs to me.

"Then what's wrong?"

"People stare at me," she signs as we walk into the second grocery store.

Until this time, I did not think she noticed the eyes of people upon her that I have always seen.

"Who?" I ask, looking around the store.

"Ladies at other store," she signs. "I sad."

"Why does it make you sad?" I ask, taking advantage of the moment to find out what she is thinking.

She shrugs her shoulders.

"Why do you think they stare at you?" I ask, but only get another shrug in response. "Do you think it's

*because you walk a little different than other people
and have the cloth to wipe your mouth?"*

"Maybe," she signs.

"I'm sorry you're sad about that."

*"I OK," she signs. With that, she gives me a big smile
and asks for a hug.*

Why Do People Do it?

Wherever she goes, people notice Brielle and their gaze follows her. I would like to think it is because of her infectious smile, but I know they are looking at her because of her differentness. Life can sometimes be like a game of *which-of-these-things-is-not-like-the-others*.

I cannot expect people not to notice my daughter. With her right leg twisted out and dragging across the ground nearly like dead weight, she limps across the room. Her right hand is often awkwardly tucked up against her body. Despite medication to control it, the cerebral palsy that affected her mouth makes some amount of drooling unavoidable. This part of her disability clearly disgusts some people in this germaphobic society. Even communicating using our hands draws the attention of others.

Curiosity is ingrained in people at a nearly instinctual level. Children often stare as if watching Brielle will help them figure her out, to make sense out of what they see.

When Brielle was about 13 years old, we sat in the busy waiting room of her speech therapists' office. A little girl about four years old stood in front of us staring at Brielle. I was patient, but annoyed that the little girl kept her gaze fixed on my child. Finally, the little girl spoke.

"Why does she have that rag?" she asked, pointing to the tan washcloth Brielle keeps on a retractable badge cord clipped to her belt. "Is it for when her mouth leaks?" she asked.

Her mother quickly came over and tried to redirect her child to look at a book.

"That's OK," I reassured the mother, waving the little girl back over to us. "Yes, she uses that cloth to wipe her mouth," I explained as I softened to the little girl's curiosity.

"Oh," she said, still staring at the cloth. With that, she smiled, waved to Brielle, and walked over to her very relieved mother. Her question was answered. No more curiosity. No more staring.

I believe some people look at us with feelings of genuine pity. I see people stare at my daughter until they notice I caught them gawking. They might offer me a weak smile and a tilt of their head. Occasionally, they actually mutter, "Awww..." or "That poor child" under their breath. Being the target of pity makes me uncomfortable and I am unsure of how to react.

Sometimes I slip into an egocentric mode and think that the staring people judge me, my daughter, or both of us. Therapists, doctors, and special education teachers evaluate Brielle regularly and naturally make conclusions about us both. Strangers' judgments can be more difficult to deal with since they know so little about our world.

When Brielle was younger, she had a terrible time making transitions from one activity to another. One afternoon after a long day of shopping, she went into a full-fledged meltdown right in the middle of Target. My seven-year-old stood in one of the main center aisles wailing, arms crossed against her chest, refusing to take one more step. Despite trying to explain that we needed just one more thing and then we could go home, she was beyond reasoning. She was too big for me to pick up and carry. Therefore, I walked away with the cart and let my stubborn child continue with her fruitless tantrum. Sometimes, it was the only way to break her cycle of stubbornness.

An elderly couple watched the scene unfold, clearly in horror. Perhaps any crying or misbehaving child in a public place would draw their attention. In this case, they literally stopped with their mouths gaped open. They looked from this poor disabled child to her heartless mother 20 feet away, as if considering how they should intervene. As suddenly as she started her fit, Brielle stopped crying, looked where I had once been standing with our cart, and then began running towards me. As I knelt down to dry my daughter's tears and again attempt to calmly explain the situation to her, the older couple continued to gawk. Despite no harm done to my child, I received distinct looks of disapproval from both of them.

Strangers do not always recognize us for who we are when they judge us. When Brielle was 12 years old, our family took a trip to Niagara Falls. The first day we went sightseeing, we did not anticipate so much walking and did not put Brielle in her wheelchair. By the end of the day, her strides slowed to a snail's pace and her legs were weak from the day's travels. The next morning, she could barely take even a few steps as we started to walk into an IHOP for breakfast. Brian swooped her up and carried her long, cumbersome frame into the restaurant. Immediately when we walked through the doors, a man at the counter gave us a nasty look as he eyed our whole family.

"Oh, lordy," the man said loud enough for everyone around him to hear, including us. "Look at this guy. She's not a baby, dude. Make her walk for Christ's sake."

As we ordered our breakfast, the man continued to watch us. His glares eventually softened as he watched Brielle eat, eventually realizing who she was. Disabled child in that party of four at the nearby booth.

What to Do

Anyone who believes looking never bothered anybody is mistaken. It does. The nature of someone's stares influences my emotional reaction and that influences my outward response.

It is like playing a card game when someone stares at my daughter. Which card should I throw down? Ignore the looks? Smile sweetly? Get angry? Defend her with some sort of explanation? Avoid the situation? I have a constant internal struggle as I navigate each interaction. Quite honestly, my response is sometimes unpredictable.

My initial reaction to stares when Brielle was little was often shame. That awful feeling still creeps up from time to time. Of course, I realize that I do not have anything to be ashamed of. It is not my fault Brielle is the way she is. It certainly is not her fault either. However, there are moments when I just want to curl up on myself until we are both invisible.

My first memorable experience with a stranger's gaze inducing embarrassed feelings was when we had just moved to Freeport. I took Ashley and Brielle to Wal-Mart to have their first formal pictures taken together.

"Just have the little one sit on the platform over there," the photographer said as she adjusted the lighting.

I felt a wave of panic. Brielle was eight months old, but could not sit up without assistance or support. I was barely coming to terms myself with how delayed she was. How was I supposed to tell this woman?

"Uh, um," I stammered, feeling my cheeks flush hot with anxiety. "Can we, uh, use that wooden thing to prop her up?"

"The triangle support is only for young infants. Your child is too old for that," the photographer stated emphatically as she tested the lights. "She'll be perfectly fine. You new mothers are just too protective."

"No, that's not it," I mumbled. "My daughter can't sit at all. She has... problems," I eventually managed to get out.

With that, the woman glared at Brielle, then at me, and then back to my child. I watched as the exasperated expression drained from her face and was replaced by something different. She continued the photo session saying as little as necessary, never touching Brielle, although she often turned Ashley this way and that to get the shots she needed. The pictures turned out well, but I avoided seeing her when I returned to shop at that Wal-Mart.

Sometimes the mama bear comes out in me and I am territorial. People who are more subtle with their stares might quickly turn away when I smile or glance in their direction. Others I might have to stare at a long time until they notice I am watching them watch us. By encouraging others to interrupt their focused gaze, my eyes have special powers to protect my child.

Anger is not in my nature, but I sometimes get frustrated or annoyed with the stares. There are times when strangers hit a raw nerve, those ugly feelings surface, and I simply feel provoked.

When Brielle was about 15 years old, we were standing outside a dressing room at a mall store while Ashley tried on some clothes. Two girls around age seven and nine were also there waiting for their mother changing inside a nearby dressing room. I initially ignored the intense looks both girls gave Brielle. However, when the older one began whispering and pointing at Brielle, I had to speak up.

I squatted down slightly in front of Brielle, shielding my child from the girls' inspection. Not moving any closer to them, but looking the girls straight in the eyes with my voice low and firm, I said, "You know, girls, it's not polite to point, stare, or whisper about someone, especially right in front of that person."

Both girls' faces went flush with embarrassment. I immediately felt guilty for being so direct and harsh with them without their mother right there. Nevertheless, no more pointing and whispering at my child. Maybe another disabled child would be spared in the future. Maybe.

More often than one might expect, the watchful eye of strangers can bring out positive feelings when my daughter's disability brings out the best in people. I might notice a teenage girl stare at Brielle and then make an effort to greet her with a smile or a kind word. When a little boy stares but then holds the door open for us, I have true appreciation for his kind gesture.

Sometimes the person's stares paired with his or her positive reaction makes me realize there is a teachable moment. We had just started to go to a new speech therapy office after moving to the Atlanta area. At each session, we saw a particular 10-year-old girl sitting in the waiting room with her mother. Her eyes were always on Brielle. The girl often smiled warmly or waved to us.

One day the girl came over to speak with us. "Excuse me, ma'am," she said in her most polite Southern way. "Does your daughter use sign language? I've seen her talking with her hands."

Aha! A genuinely interested member of the audience!

"Yes, she does. Her mouth doesn't work right so she can't talk," I explained. "She uses sign language to talk, but she can hear you. Her name is Brielle. What's your name?"

The little girl beamed as she gave Brielle a more enthusiastic wave, "Hi, Brielle. My name is Chloe. Do you think you could teach me some sign language?"

Other members of our family are not immune to the stares from others. Ashley certainly notices other people looking at Brielle. No matter what she may be thinking or feeling, she often just uses the staring back method and lets it go. However, Brian does not seem to notice staring much at all. He says he just does not care. I sometimes wish I felt the same way.

One of Us

When we are with a group of other disabled children at Special Olympics or some other event, nobody really stares at anyone. We all just get it. No impairment, physical oddity, or behavioral outburst would ever be on our radar as worthy of staring. Sure, we notice those things. However, they are not out of our norm. That differentness *is* our norm and tethers us together in a unique way.

Occasionally, Brielle will see other disabled children carrying a washcloth or using a bandana tied around their neck to wipe their wet mouths and will say, "They use same thing." The beauty of it is that she often says it with great pride and a sense of belongingness.

One evening when she was about 12 years old, we were all sitting together watching *Forrest Gump*. In the scene we were watching, Forrest was a little boy with bulky metal braces on both of his legs.

"Like me," Brielle signed, pointed at the television, and then tapped her own legs.

"Yes, he has leg braces that are kind of like yours," I replied. She paused for a moment, clearly in deep thought about that.

"I one, not two," she signed, pointing to her legs again.

"Nope," I confirmed. "You didn't have two braces, just one."

"I better. No leg brace now. Boy better, too. He runs fast."

The Undetected Gaze

There are many watchful eyes I am sure I never notice at all. One Sunday morning the girls and I walked into the elementary school cafeteria that served as the sanctuary for a church in Ohio. We had visited the week before for the first time and were eager to return. Before we could make our way to our seats, a middle-aged man approached us.

"Excuse me," he said, offering his hand to me. "My name is Steve."

"Nice to meet you, Steve. My name is Kerith," I reached out my hand to shake his.

He awkwardly fell silent and looked at me tentatively. "I'm not sure exactly how to say this," he began, stumbling over his words a bit. "I was sitting behind you and your daughters last Sunday."

"Oh?" I replied, not exactly sure where the man was going with this.

"I was… Well, I was in a really bad place last week," he stammered as he looked down at the linoleum floor. "I was depressed, angry, and feeling really sorry for myself."

When Steve looked up, his eyes were glassy from tears. "I was at my lowest low last Sunday, until I saw you with your daughters."

I looked at my girls. Eleven-year-old Brielle was oblivious to what this man was sharing. She was more interested in watching two small children running around the back of the cafeteria. On the other hand, Ashley was 13 and the look she gave me indicated she knew something was important about what this man was saying.

"I watched your older daughter help your other daughter take her coat off and get her in her seat as they laughed together. I watched you all smiling and doing sign language throughout the service," he paused a moment to wipe a tear. "All three of you seemed so... happy. Watching the joy and love for God come out of your family made me feel so ashamed of my petty problems."

I started to take a deep breath and open my mouth to speak, although I was not sure what I was going to say.

"I just wanted you to know," Steve continued. "You made a huge difference in my life this week and I'll always remember that morning watching you." With that, he abruptly turned and walked away.

Ashley and I just looked at one another. I was speechless. "Whoa," was all she could say.

The View from Someone Else's Shoes

Maybe you have done your fair share of staring at someone who was different. I can admit to doing it on occasion. I have been the person caught staring more than once. An unusual choice of fashion, people using sign language, and sometimes someone with a disability can garner my gaze. My experience being on the other side prompts me to satisfy my curiosity as quickly as possible and return to the task at hand.

There was an episode of *Oprah* with a woman explaining how she bought a pair of Oprah's shoes at a celebrity charity sale. The woman tearfully told Oprah how she often stood in those black high heels and imagined herself in the television star's life. That imagery gave the woman the confidence to move forward in her own life. Oprah was brought to tears and seemed truly humbled to know someone gained strength from standing in her shoes, literally.

I do not expect anyone to want to step into our shoes, to imagine our lives as their own. Strangers who stare get a peek into our world, at least the part that is visible. Brielle's outward disabilities will always be part of her. However, if that is the only part of her that others recognize, then they have only scratched the surface of who our daughter is.

I remind myself that you never know whose eyes God is watching us through. Sometimes the one who learns from that moment of watching and staring is me.

> *But the Lord said to Samuel, 'Do not consider his appearance or his height, for I have rejected him. The Lord does not look at the things people look at. People look at the outward appearance, but the Lord looks at the heart.'*
>
> *— 1 SAMUEL 16:7 (NIV)*

CHAPTER 24

Friends and Other Strangers

"Daisy is my friend," 12-year-old Brielle signs to me as I tuck her into bed. "She nice to me. She gives hugs."

"Friends can give good hugs," I say, giving my daughter a kiss on the forehead.

"We have sleepover tonight. Daisy best friend ever."

I hide my sadness with a smile. "I am glad you have a friend."

Daisy is a pitiful, bald-headed doll Brielle has had since she was two years old.

Longing to Belong

I spend a lot of time on the sidelines, watching other moms interact in close huddles at playgroups in church basements, PTA meetings in school cafeterias, and observation rooms at gymnastics and dance classes. As the parent of a special needs child, I often feel like the odd mom out, living on the margins of everyday life. I worry this is a foretaste of how Brielle might live her whole life.

When mothers see me with Brielle and her telltale signs of disability, they sometimes act as though Brielle's disability is contagious. People move to give us a wide berth. Sometimes, they look at us with weak smiles plastered on their faces. Some stare. Others avoid eye contact, staying busy with something so that interacting with the disabled kid and her mother is not an option. From many years of experience, I have sadly come to expect these things from strangers.

There might also be that fleeting moment when I see the mother's underlying reaction is, "Thank goodness that's not my child." Sometimes I find myself wondering what it would be like to be them, a mother of two normal children.

Wherever new mothers congregate, they use their babies' accomplishments as currency to pay for their membership cards to the mommy club. I cannot trade accomplishments. Brielle does not have the same kind of successes. Without the proper currency, I am not part of their club.

As the child gets older, successes often continue to validate his or her parents. Moms and dads boast about their child's accomplishments using phrases such as, "*Our* team won the championship" or "*We* got first place." Children sometimes become their parents' yardstick of success.

Although I hate to admit it, I fall into that same parent trap from time to time. I felt validated when Ashley brought home a straight "A" report card, excitedly posted on Facebook when she earned college scholarships, and used those plural pronoun phrases when her volleyball team won the local championship.

However, there are times when I struggle to cultivate those same feelings for my parenting ego from Brielle's accomplishments.

Teachers, therapists, and doctors fill her life and help her achieve much smaller successes that often go unnoticed by others. In addition, there are so many people helping her in life that I begin to wonder what contribution I had to even her smallest achievements. Was I simply the conduit? The chauffeur to and from appointments? The person writing the checks to pay the bills? My confidence as a mother waivers on those days when I start to question my worth.

Friends are optional, so is solitude. Having a disabled child sometimes erodes my self-assurance and I tend to isolate myself from others. Of course, this complicates my feelings of being forced to the sidelines. My mother often recited the old adage, "To have a good friend, you first have to be a good friend." She is right. I hate when she is right.

Making new friends was a priority after each of our moves. I am not naturally outgoing, but I had to be in order to make new friends. I learned to be more bold as well as open, instead of retreating into old patterns of self-banishment.

Sometimes I felt defeated trying to make good friends time and time again since they are so difficult to find and take so much effort to cultivate. After living in six different cities in our 23 years of marriage, it got a little easier. I did not necessarily get better at making friends, but got better at keeping in touch with the old ones.

However, I am only one person in the piece of the friendship puzzle and not in complete control of being part of their club. It sometimes feels like I have to go through rush then wait to get a bid before I can pledge and hopefully be initiated into their sorority. Only then do I get a chance to become close to those other mothers.

Twenty Questions Is No Game

Conversations about Brielle often begin before a new friend has even had a chance to meet her, sometimes before they even know that she is disabled. They might ask a casual question such as, "How many children do you have?" and then "How old are they? Boys or girls?" The questions that come next can raise my anxiety.

How do I respond to questions such as, "What sports does your daughter play?" or "What college is she hoping to get into?" Where do I start? How much do I share? What do I even say?

Brian finds the question, "What grade is she in?" particularly tough. Technically, grade levels are irrelevant in the special education arena. Schools often have special education classes with multi-age students. They move up to the next classroom or school automatically despite any acquisition of specific academic skills. When asked about Brielle's grade, should Brian report what grade levels she functions at for each subject? People probably do not want to hear that much detail. Should he just say she is in high school? Sometimes he finds it easier just to report her age and bypass the other complicating issues.

Over the years, I have fumbled around with answers. Some conversations were more successful and smooth than others. Some were downright failures, sending potential friends running for the hills as I described her body's limitations in too much detail.

Instead of flying by the seat of my pants each time, I developed a few well-rehearsed answers. With small tweaks, my scripts became foolproof, guaranteed to provide only the most necessary information in the simplest form.

When Ashley was in elementary school, I discovered she never spoke to her friends about Brielle and rarely even acknowledged Brielle was her sister even though they went to the same school. A huge revelation came to the surface when she told me through little girl tears, "Mom, I just don't know what to tell them about Brielle."

I helped Ashley write out her script for what she could say in those uncomfortable situations. We literally took out a sheet of paper and wrote it out word-for-word. It read something like this:

Brielle got sick when she was inside my mom's tummy. Now her arms and legs don't work right and she can't talk. But, she's really nice and she loves to dance and listen to music just like we do.

Similarly, for a long time Brian did not talk at work about Brielle and her issues. One night he finally confided in me that he had anxiety about how to talk with his coworkers about Brielle. Part of it was he is a private person and wanted to maintain a professional relationship with people at work. When it was a friend, he just was not sure of how to bring it up or how much to share.

"Maybe when people ask you how your weekend was, you could just mention that Brielle did Special Olympics bowling or Miracle League baseball," I suggested. "You could easily slip in there that you have a daughter with CP. If people want to know more, they can ask. If not, you can just leave it at that."

Over time, talking with others about Brielle and her disability became much more natural. Understanding and accepting her delays helped us be more comfortable with the issues before we even got questions. Having a planned and practiced script made the real difference, for all of us.

It takes a certain amount of bravery for friends to ask questions about Brielle. I expect to have some difficult conversations. Asking questions about my daughter shows me that a friend has an interest in my life, even those uncomfortable parts.

Aside from questions that cross the line of personal privacy, I would like to think there are no bad questions. In the beginning of a friendship, people know so little about our world that they could not possibly ask good questions. However, as they learn and feel more at ease asking questions, especially the tough ones, I might get an insightful one that I truly have to ponder to be able to form a response. In those instances, the friend and I might both learn something.

I rarely brush off questions, even from strangers. I try to keep my answers direct and simple even if the answer is not exactly clear in my own mind.

Others might think they are showing concern through their interest, but can sometimes come across as plain old nosy. They stumble over their words as they ask, "Will Brielle always live with you?" or "Will she be able to have children?" Questions like these from close friends, I can respond to openly. However, when they come from mere acquaintances, I often evade the questions and do my best to suppress my frustration at their invasion of our privacy.

At some point in their sequence of questions, a friend might offer a piece of unsolicited advice. I understand it is part of human nature to want to help as well as feel needed and appreciated for what we can offer others. However, some comments serve only to isolate me even further by highlighting the great divide between that person and me.

One of Brielle's preschool teachers in Wisconsin told me that a friend of hers put peanut butter on the roof of her child's mouth to help him overcome his speech delays. She suggested that peanut butter could help Brielle talk.

Really? I am certain that making a child orally manipulate something would help build muscles of the mouth. However, Brielle could not (and still cannot) stick out her tongue, close her lips, or make any sounds other than vowel sounds. Even the mere act of chewing is difficult for her. I love peanut butter, but Peter Pan will never make Brielle speak. Not even pixie dust can make that happen.

We all like a compliment or pat on the back occasionally. However, it makes me cringe when friends say, "I don't know how you do it."

Although they mean for that to be a compliment, they clearly never thought about what that particular phrase implies. Do they think I really have an option to do it or not to do it? To be Brielle's parent or not be her parent? In the day-to-day scheme of things, I cannot afford to wonder how I do it. I just do it.

I endure clichés and platitudes without much thought. Other times, it is a seemingly unrelated comment that cuts through my heart.

"Life is so hectic now that our kids are busy in high school with all of that college prep, isn't it?" a friend recently commented.

How do I react to things like that? Yes, our life with Ashley was busy with those preparations a few years ago. But, no, we are not doing any of those preparations for Brielle nor will we ever. My friend meant no harm and probably did not even see the difference between our lives at that moment. Nonetheless, her comment stung.

When Friends Hurt Us

In our unguarded moments, there are sometimes painful interactions with people we know. In second grade, Ashley's best friend would often walk home from school with us. As the three girls sat together at the kitchen table eating a snack, Ashley's friend would close her eyes, make a sour face, and literally turn her back to Brielle. My heart broke and Ashley's eyes filled with tears as her best friend turned away from her sister in disgust.

Ten years later, the scene with Ashley's best friend replayed itself, only this time, one of my friends was the leading cast member. I met two good friends for lunch at Subway once a week for several years. When I started homeschooling, I asked if Brielle could join us and they were pleased to have her with us.

A year later, unexpectedly and without any invitation or discussion, one of their husbands who worked from home started joining us. The three women chatted like hens, Brielle interjected with me interpreting for her, and then, awkwardly, there was the husband.

He came for about four weeks straight and then just stopped. We were relieved and never asked why he stopped joining us. We found out two months later when the wife of the missing rooster from our little hen party asked if Brielle ever drank anything else other than water.

"She usually drinks chocolate milk," I replied, wiping Brielle's mouth with a paper towel I brought from home. "I just bring this sports bottle with water for her to drink here since it's less messy, so she's not such a spectacle."

"You know," my friend started to tell me. "I don't want to hurt your feelings, but my husband just couldn't sit with us and watch Brielle eat. He literally got physically ill. That's why he doesn't come to lunch with us anymore."

I sat there bewildered. It was not what she said that shocked me. Despite my efforts, I knew Brielle was a messy eater with unavoidable poor table manners. What good could come from telling me about her husband's repulsion watching my daughter eat? Did my friend honestly think it would *not* hurt my feelings?

Saying "I don't want to hurt your feelings" did not lessen the pain. I hurt for a long time after that. My friend told me something I did not really need to hear. Making matters worse, I regretted being weak and polite instead of telling her exactly how I felt. I simply acknowledged what she said and did everything I could to swallow that lump in my throat and move on as if her comment meant nothing to me.

Death of a Friendship at a Funeral

In December of 2001, we received a call in the middle of the night. It was one of those calls people fear, unexpected bad news. Brian's mother had a stroke. She passed away four days after we arrived from Texas to be at her bedside.

At the ages of seven and five, we decided the girls were too young to attend the funeral. Although my parents were not good friends with Brian's parents, they shared many holidays, birthdays, and life events together with us over the years. Therefore, of course, my parents wanted to attend the funeral events and could not watch the girls for us. After being away from our hometown for over ten years, we had few friends there and those we had wanted to attend the funeral as well.

My mother asked her best friend to watch the girls for a few hours while we all attended the funeral. Her friend of 30 years hemmed, hawed, and avoided committing to help us. Finally, when my mother prodded her for an answer, the friend blurted out, "Ashley may come over and I can keep an eye on her, but Brielle can't. I just couldn't deal with her."

At a time when our emotions were already so fragile, the sting of rejection from my mother's best friend felt especially harsh. I had known this woman since I was a young child, saw her most Sundays at church, and occasionally played with her older daughters at family events. The pain my mother felt from her friend's rejection of her granddaughter was worse and I knew it. Their friendship continued to limp along, but never quite had the same vitality.

MORE ABOUT....
Family as Friends

Brian and I were both blessed with wonderful families. We can call all of them "friends" by choice.

Both Brian's sister, Tracy, and my brother, Jason, have always been good with Brielle despite what little contact they had living so far away from us. Although they might not understand her, they are open and fun with her. Brielle looks up to them both in special ways.

Our parents have always been supportive and respectful of our decisions and parenting of Brielle (and Ashley as well). The sameness of their interactions with her is comforting and reassuring. It takes us back to our own childhoods and reassures us that they see her with the same loving hearts we grew up with.

I am extremely close to my mother. Her friendship is the one enduring thread I have had over the years.

The Value of a Treasured Friend

Friends who accept and embrace Brielle are rare. I understand why. At least, I have a few theories.

I believe that previous experience with other children and adults with disabilities is the best predictor of how a person might initially interact with us. I also believe that it takes a curious spirit. People who are bold enough to ask respectful questions eventually tend to become more comfortable around Brielle and endear themselves to my heart.

Angie and I were in the same scrapbooking group and attended the same church in Toledo. From the start, she often nonchalantly asked questions about Brielle. She never started her questions with, "I hate to ask" or "If you don't mind me asking." She simply asked her questions, as if she was asking about what movies my child liked or what school she attended. I had no doubt Angie was genuinely interested in understanding my child, not only to know Brielle better, but also to know me better. Brielle and how she was different from other children, including her own, was simply no big deal.

I have other friends who interact with Brielle in special ways. When I talk on the phone with Dawn, a friend from Texas, she always tells me to give Miss Brielle a high five from her. Lee, another friend from Texas, greets Brielle with, "What up, kiddo?" and fist bumps. At church, Pastor Phil greets her with a hug, Pat never fails to ask her how baseball or bowling are going, and Dani sits with her to look at photos on her iPod. These small gestures of kindness mean the world to Brielle and they do not go unnoticed.

One thing that has truly surprised me over the years is how Ashley's friends interact with Brielle. When Ashley was younger, her friends mostly ignored or endured Brielle whenever forced to interact or play together. Although their reactions were probably magnified because of Brielle's disabilities, I am certain that this reaction is common with friends and younger siblings who tag along.

However, in recent years, as Ashley's friends became teenagers and young adults, several of them made an effort to befriend Brielle as well. They now greet her with hugs, chat with her on Facebook, respond to her emails, or text me to "say hi to Brielle" for them. Brielle thinks of them as her friends rather than solely her sister's friends.

Does Brielle Get the Birthday Blues?

When Brielle mainstreamed into regular classrooms in elementary school, I wondered what the other children thought of her. Although most treated her with respect, it was not difficult to see that other children thought of her as an outsider. Classmates did not include Brielle in playground games, welcome her at their table in the cafeteria, or invite her to their birthday parties. In fact, her best friend in Texas, Audrey, was the only one to regularly include her.

If Brielle knows what it feels like to be lonely, she never shows it or talks about it. She is just as happy playing by herself in her room as she is in a room full of classmates or hanging out with her family. Moreover, she knows what it means to have a good friend and how to be a good friend. She has had two good friends in her life.

Audrey was a typical child in her first grade class in Texas who immediately took an interest in Brielle. The little girl had plenty of friends, but Brielle became her best bud. It was common to see them walking hand-in-hand down the hallways of their elementary school. She learned sign language, which helped bridge the communication gap Brielle often had with other classmates. Even though we moved away in the middle of fourth grade, the girls continue to exchange e-mails, talk on the phone, and video chat occasionally.

MORE ABOUT....
How Brielle "Talks" on the Phone

The other friend or family member talks while Brielle and I are on speaker phone. They can hear Brielle laugh and make sounds while I interpret her signs for them.

Brielle's only other real friend is Victoria. They met in their special needs sixth grade class in the Atlanta area. She has a rare genetic disorder that affected her fine motor, cognitive, and social skills. Although she knows very little sign language, somehow these two friends have an almost magical way of communicating. They have spent countless hours together strolling through the mall, watching movies, going to school dances, and attending American Heritage Girls as well as cheerleading and dance.

Brielle has other acquaintances her age, but few qualify as friends who accept and appreciate her. A girl at church youth group was crying one evening about not making the volleyball team as a small group of young teenage girls sat around a table talking about their week. The other youth leader and I tried to comfort her, talked to her about challenges, and encouraged her to never give up. Brielle rubbed her back and just smiled at her the whole time we were talking.

The next day, the girl texted me, "By the way, Brielle is probably the best comfort I could have asked for. All she did was sit there and pat my back with her big smile. It's hard to keep crying when she does things like that. She's such a sweetheart."

Birds of a Feather

Over the years, we have met many other parents of special needs children. Some we encountered by chance, meeting in the waiting room at therapy or activities for special needs children. Others we met through friendships Brielle formed at school. We met a few through what must have been divine intervention to make our paths cross.

Friendships are rarely based solely on the commonality of having children with special needs. Like sorority sisters, even though we might all be part of the same club having earned our "mother of a special needs child" card, we cannot assume there are enough common interests to build a meaningful relationship.

When Brielle joined a special needs cheerleading squad in the Atlanta area, I was eager to meet some new people. However, the other mothers spoke in some sort of special cheer code, threw around unfamiliar acronyms and jargon, and talked about events and people I did not know. Their girls had been cheering together for years and these mothers knew each other's stories. I felt like an outsider in that room full of moms with special needs children. Although I slowly became close to those women, it was not automatic just because we all had special needs daughters.

My most precious special needs mother friendship is with Bobbi, my best friend from Freeport. That simple show of unity and frank conversation across her desk over her son's picture and mortgage loan papers led to a long and close friendship.

She is one of the few good friends with whom I can be completely honest about how life is with Brielle. I know that she not only understands, she also completely and wholly cares. She might share the woes of raising her son with Fragile X in one breath, then laugh at his antics and roll her eyes in another. At the same time, we do not have to spend our time only talking about our kids and their differentness. We both recognize that there is much more to the other than that.

The Mixed Benefits of Support Groups

There were many support groups available to us over the years. Brian and I tried a few of them.

With tissue boxes poised at the ready on every table and in every mother's purse, they often turned into crying sessions. Instead of sharing compassion and potential solutions for issues, parents seemed to almost joust over which family had it worse as they compared battle stories. They bragged about their children's shortcomings much like most parents brag about their children's successes.

While some families found this type of support helpful, Brian and I had different expectations. We wanted an uplifting experience filled with practical advice. Frustrated, we gave up traditional support groups for years.

In the summer of 2010, a friend of mine who worked at the CDC (The Centers for Disease Control and Prevention) in Atlanta invited me to a conference at her office about CMV. After connecting with one of the speakers who was the mother of twins affected by CMV, I learned about a Facebook group called CMV Mommies. This closed group has over 850 members, most of whom are mothers of children affected by CMV.

Despite CMV being so common, in fourteen years I had not met one other family with a child affected by CMV. I was initially conflicted about being welcomed into their group with phrases like "welcome to the family" and learning about their children with disabilities that were often far worse than my child's. Eventually, I found comfort in knowing that we were not alone after all.

The CMV Mommies group is incredibly active with 15 or more novel posts each day. Responses by 25 or more members to a single post is not uncommon. Worried moms ask advice about everything imaginable about caring for and advocating for their children. Nothing is off limits. Questions about firing a speech therapist, choosing a bath chair, stress from IEP meetings at school, navigating Medicaid applications, frustrations with extended family members, and results from medical testing are all frequent posts. The amount of support and information the group members share amazes me.

This cyber support group is something like a CMV Help Desk and what I always hoped traditional support groups would be. Although Brian is not part of the group, from time to time, I share something someone posted. He no longer seems to need a place to share his frustrations and concerns. Instead, the support we give each other is adequate for him.

When I find myself getting on the computer each morning even before I grab a cup of coffee just to read what my CMV Mommies are up to, I worry that my focus has gone askew. Real friends and family should be my soft place to fall, right? However, my friends in this group on Facebook are my comrades. More often than not, these cyber friends give me more compassion, support, and understanding than most of my face-to-face friends.

People might soon forget what you said or did, but never how you made them feel. Interacting with a disabled child seems to bring out the best and worst in people. We have seen extreme ends of that spectrum in full living color. People tend to be very consistent, seldom changing their approach to us after their first interactions. The rarest situation is someone who is completely accepting from the start. Those friends are the enduring treasures in our lives.

> *Two are better than one, because they have a*
> *good return for their labor: If either of them falls*
> *down, one can help the other up. But pity anyone*
> *who falls and has no one to help them up.*
>
> – ECCLESIASTES 4: 9-10 (NIV)

CHAPTER 25

The Ties That Bind

The early Saturday morning sun is just beginning to peek through the cracks in our bedroom shades. I feel eight-year-old Ashley's breath on my neck. She joined us in bed after a bad dream scared her a few hours before. I look over her to Brian, awake and smiling at me.

"Morning," I greet him in a hushed voice. "Been awake long?"

"Just watching my girls sleep," he whispers.

We suddenly hear the step-slide of six-year-old Brielle shuffling down the hallway in search of us.

"In here," Brian quietly calls out to her.

Ashley starts to stir as Brian pulls Brielle's long, thin body over him onto the bed amongst the rest of us.

"Good morning, family," she signs enthusiastically to us as she lies on her back. Ashley moves closer to me to make more room in our king-sized bed for her sister's flailing arms.

Without a word, Brian reaches up making a claw high above us. The girls immediately squeal and try to squish in closer to me. Swooping down like a dive-bombing hawk, Brian's clawed hand tickles each of the girls in turn. They laugh so hard, they almost stop breathing. I watch from the far side of the bed smiling, glad he can't reach past them to me. Tickles before morning coffee aren't my thing.

We lay there together giggling and talking for nearly an hour. Finally, it is time to seize the day. We throw back the blankets and struggle to our feet. Brian helps Brielle get her footing and she embraces him in a big bear hug.

"Love you guys," she signs before step-sliding down the hallway into the living room to watch cartoons with her sister.

Connections

Life is a journey not to be traveled alone. It is difficult to imagine roaming this world without the support of others, particularly my nuclear family. Friends can be wonderful. Family is forever.

Brian and I began our life together enthusiastic, hopeful, and with much love. We were partners from the very start and found a steady balance to our relationship. We made decisions and resolved differences without any drama. Sure, we might disagree or get short with one another from time to time. However, we have only had two shouting matches in 28 years.

Brian and I have different interests and that is ok. He loves sports, particularly golf, and I find them a complete bore. I like the arts and even recently took up acrylic painting. He would rather watch paint dry on a wall than go to an art museum. Despite those differences, we find common ground and are still fundamentally very similar. Time and shared experience is our glue.

In so many ways, Brian and I are a balance of yin and yang. Intertwined, interdependent, and complementary. Brian and I work together like a simple machine, all the parts moving together for a single purpose – the success and happiness of our family.

We each have our weaknesses, but play to one another's strengths. Brian is many things I am not and does what he knows best. His gentle roughhousing, teasing, and light-hearted exchanges give our girls interactions that are unnatural to me. My hyper-organization and way of getting into the thick of things balances his more playful side. His level-headedness balances my emotional tendencies.

Although I often initiate decisions for Brielle's life, I confirm them with Brian. I trust his instincts. We talk through our concerns and he makes sure that I see the issue from every angle possible.

Sustaining the Relationship

Creating and maintaining a close relationship in a marriage over time is a daunting task. Nearly half of marriages do not survive.[6] The complex responsibilities and stress of having a special needs child can further challenge a marriage.

Why has our marriage not only lasted but also thrived over 23 years? It is difficult to say. Brian and I came from intact families and never lived together, but married young and had children fairly early in our marriage. Our duties are clearly defined and we have clear expectations for one another.

In everything we do, we try to make life easier for the other person. It is often the little things that make a difference – making him his favorite meal, bringing me a glass of wine, or tiptoeing out of bed in the morning.

We have learned not to take life or each other too seriously. Even during intensely stressful situations, we try to find the lighter side. We can tease one another in lighthearted ways and realize it is an opportunity to shine light on our shortcomings in a non-threatening way.

Being around so many other families with special needs children, we have seen how situations can be worse. We are grateful for what we have and for what we do not have.

One of our unbreakable rules is that we take time for one another. We carve out the first ten minutes of our evening just for one another. When he comes home from work, I drop whatever I am doing and follow him to the bedroom where he changes from his work clothes. The girls know they are not allowed to tag along. It is a small slice of togetherness and this sacred timeout allows us to discuss our day, reconnect, and shift our focus to family time.

We make every effort to spend a night out at least once a month if not every other weekend. A few drinks and dinner out can recharge our relationship like no other time at home can. Although we do not often get extended time together for a week or weekend away, when we do, it is all about us.

Family Dynamics

Our family is not defined by Brielle's disabilities. They have changed us and the dynamics within our family, but they are not who we are.

It is difficult to balance parenting and attention to multiple children. Brielle's needs naturally outweigh Ashley's. However, that cannot mean she automatically gets more attention, certainly not all of the time. Brian and I have each spent both planned and spontaneous individual time with Ashley over the years. At numerous Girl Scout events, middle school volleyball games, high school senior year activities, and a few teenage bumps in the road, every ounce of attention was on Ashley. It was not and cannot be 50/50, but when it counted, the balance was there.

When parents say they love their children exactly the same, I wonder how that can be. Each parent and child has a unique relationship based on unique experiences together. Although it may not be a factor of more or less, that love cannot possibly be the same.

Although Brian and Brielle cannot communicate in sign language, they have their own way and stay connected in unique ways. Giving her loud raspberry kisses on her cheek or mimicking Scooby-Doo's laugh sends her into squeals of delight. He plays catch with her to warm up before her Miracle League baseball game and cheers with gusto at her soccer practices.

As Brielle got older, we decided it would be more appropriate if I took over all personal care such as bathing, getting her dressed, and helping her in the bathroom. If I am not home, Brian can and does certainly do what is needed for her and Brielle does not have any issues with that. However, in an effort to help her maintain her modesty, it just seemed better for me to do those personal things for her.

The early division of parenting duties we made helped make Brian and Ashley closer than most dads and their daughters. They spent countless hours watching cartoons together on Saturday mornings, throwing a ball back and forth, and dressing up for Daddy-Daughter dances. They attended many games of their favorite baseball and football teams and shouted at the television at home when referees made bad calls.

Their inside jokes and conversations about sports did not include me. For a long time, I was OK with that. I had no choice when Brielle took up so much of my time. Then, it got to me. I worried I had neglected my relationship with Ashley.

By the time Ashley moved into middle school, her interests started to shift. Talking with Dad about fashion, gossip, and boys was unnatural despite their close bond. She started coming to me and I was grateful for the opportunity to strengthen our relationship. We started to take long weekend trips to the beach when she was in high school. Respite from caring for Brielle and time spent alone with Ashley resulted in twice the benefit for me.

When Ashley went away to college, I sent her texts with a silly joke each afternoon. Those juvenile puns and knock-knock jokes kept us connected in a new way. Care packages with gossip magazines, yummy treats, and gift cards for overpriced coffee were a welcomed arrival. However, those texts were something special to look forward to each afternoon, something just between us.

Brian and Ashley still have their close bond. They talk about silly television shows, pop music, and sports that I do not pay any attention to. He counsels her about college and career plans. He still calls her by the nickname he started when she was just a baby. She still sits on the arm of his chair with her arm around him and calls him, "Daddy."

I look forward to helping Ashley get dressed on her wedding day. Brian will be a mess as he walks her down the aisle.

Although it seems Brian would be a natural fathering a boy, he never says he missed having one. Before we had children, we said if we had two children of the same gender, we would try for a third. When our second daughter was born, it was not the situation we expected. Brielle already demanded so much of our time, energy, and resources. We decided adding another child to our family would subdivide our attention even further. We made a permanent decision when Brielle was 18 months old and never regretted it.

Sister Act

Like many parents, before Brielle was even born, we tried to prepare Ashley for being a big sister. We read books about becoming Mommy's helper and talked about all of the things she could teach her little sister. As my due date approached, Ashley kissed my growing belly as she told it with great excitement and pride, "I'm going to be your big sister."

When we learned about the CMV and the risks to our unborn child, including the forty percent chance she might die, we had to prepare her big sister. Knowing that information would be overwhelming to a two-year-old, we simply told her that her baby sister was sick inside my tummy.

"Let's pray for her," I told Ashley after our bedtime stories. "We can ask God to protect Baby Brielle." We got on our knees and folded our hands as we did during our bedtime routine on any other night.

"Dear God," my toddler began. "Please protect Baby Brielle. Don't let her be sick. Bless Mom and Dad and my grandmas and grandpas. And extra bless Baby Brielle. Amen."

When we returned home a few days after Brielle was born, Ashley was completely unimpressed with the little bundle that was her sister. Within a few days, the little crying beast seemed to grow on her. She ran for diapers and burp cloths, put her dolls in the baby swing, and showed newborn Brielle the pictures in her board books.

As they grew up together, they spent little time playing together. Although they were only two years apart, Brielle's physical abilities made their age difference seemingly grow each day. They might have been in the same room, but they could not really play together. Instead, they continued in parallel play, doing activities side-by-side, but not interacting in cooperative play.

Although we never sat Ashley down to have a specific conversation about her sister's disabilities, we routinely talked freely about Brielle's progress and procedures. Especially as a preschooler, Ashley attended numerous therapy sessions and accompanied us on many visits to doctors and specialists. At some point, she must have recognized her sister's differences. However, she never talked about it. Instead, she wrote about it.

Captured On College Ruled Paper

When she was eight years old, Ashley wrote in her morning journal for school about the sister she never had.

If I had a twin, I would like a sister because I would like a talking one instead.

A year later, for the essay portion of state testing, she wrote that Brielle was the most important person in her life. She described her sister's differences in great detail and then how Brielle cheers her up.

I would sit on my bed and cry thinking how unfair it was that we moved. Then Brielle would come in, sit down, and give me a hug. Now I know that whenever I feel sad, Brielle will come in and cheer me up.

After saying such sweet things, she then wrote out her complaints about her annoying little sister for this same state test. At the end, she went on to write something that touched our hearts.

Well, she might bug me, but she's still my sister and I will always love her. That will never change.

While in her elementary school years, I started to see the influence of having a disabled sister on Ashley. Like any older sibling, I saw Ashley's frustration when Brielle tried to tag along with her and her friends. More than that natural reaction, I could sense Ashley's embarrassment, or at least uncomfortable feelings around her friends from time to time.

The writing prompt for an essay contest in fifth grade was "A Different Kind of Hero." Ashley wrote about our family. After describing Brielle's disabilities, she wrote about how it was not easy being Brielle's big sister.

Sometimes she's really embarrassing like any other sibling would be. But, she can be especially embarrassing when my friends come over and ask questions about why Brielle can't do something or why she's doing something most kids her age don't do any more.

She reflected on how having a disabled sister changed our family.

My whole family is heroic. We didn't choose to be this way. But, since Brielle is the way she is, we all have become more than

*just the average family. When we work together to make my
sister's life easier, we're a heroic family.*

Teenage Growing Pains

By the time Ashley started middle school, the gap between the sisters widened. Although Ashley was a good signer, they had little in
common and few things to talk about. Old enough to babysit, Ashley
began to care for Brielle in our absence on an occasional Saturday
night. Not wanting to burden her, we always asked if she could babysit
rather than making it one of her household chores. When she said
she had plans, we found some other teenage girl to stay with Brielle
or stayed in for the evening.

As Ashley started high school, she slipped into a somewhat dis-
tant, slightly moody period. For months, the only interaction she had
with Brielle was to tell her, "Good morning" and "Good night." It
broke my heart to see them this way. I wondered if things might be
different between them if Brielle were different. Although I never had
a sister, I had periods of strained interactions with my brother when
we were adults. I knew the pain of sibling issues and the joys of being
a sister as well.

One Christmas holiday when Ashley was almost 16 years old, my
mother confronted Ashley over a pot of boiling pasta. Although I
did not directly hear the conversation, my mother told me she had
never been so straight with Ashley as she told her how insensitive she
was being to Brielle. Ashley described the interaction as painful. She
could not believe her grandmother could be so angry with her.

It took several months, but Ashley eventually softened to her
sister. We began to hear Ashley ask Brielle about her day, step in to
help Brielle at meals, and even seem to freely reciprocate Brielle's hugs.

As her college move-in date approached, we noticed even bigger
changes. Out of the blue, Ashley started inviting Brielle to join her
for short errands to deposit her paycheck, to pick up something at
the grocery store, or to get ice cream. While Brian and I were out

one Saturday night, we got a text picture from Ashley. Ashley had straightened Brielle's hair and the two sisters were laughing together in a self-portrait taken in the bathroom mirror. It was so much like what we might expect from any two sisters.

Leaving our family to go out of state to college was hard on Ashley. There were tears all the way around as we drove off from her dormitory that weekend in August. While away at college, Ashley and Brielle exchanged emails every afternoon, simple notes about what they had for lunch and what they did that day. Brielle wrote Ashley snail mail letters each week so she could send her sister drawings or photographs.

When we returned to Ashley's university that September for Family Weekend during her first semester, Ashley asked if Brielle could spend the night with her in her dorm room. When we picked them up the next morning to take them out to breakfast, our hearts swelled watching them stroll out of the dorm hand in hand. They seemed so natural together, so happy. There was a sister bond there after all.

Extended Family Matters

Moving away from our parents from the very start of our marriage and living so far away from them during our girls' childhood was not ideal. Although it made Brian and me more self-reliant and independent, we longed for the sort of relationship Brian had with own grandparents growing up. It would have been nice to have the girls spend a night or long weekend with their grandparents giving us more time to focus on our relationship. What would it be like if we could gather together with our parents for a special meal on Sunday afternoons? What if my mother could have been there at a few important meetings with the school to take notes for me and provide moral support?

Despite the distance, the girls have good relationships with their grandparents. Brian's mother passed away when the girls were still in elementary school and it is difficult to know what Brielle remembers. However, Ashley has memories of them playing board games and jacks together and having elaborate tea parties. Brian's father is endearingly known as "G-pa" and is always eager to talk with the girls about whatever they are into. My mother and the girls have a long history of reading books together. My father endlessly teases Brielle with a point of his finger and a sideways look.

Although my brother, Jason, sees the girls only sporadically, he is a playful uncle and lavishes them with the girly attention he cannot give his own young son, Jenson. Brian's sister, Tracy, sees the girls even less, but does her best to interact with Brielle and stay informed about her progress. Tracy and Ashley look and act so much alike, one might think they could be sisters in some way. Jenson is the girls' only cousin they know, but they do not have much of a relationship.

Distance and opportunities to travel make these family relationships difficult. Email, social media, video chats, phone calls, and snail mail only bridge part of the gap. Brian and I are truly saddened to know that our decisions about his career so directly affected our girls' relationships with our family.

Unified

Some of our happiest memories have been spent together as a family. A random Tuesday evening shouting answers at an episode of *Family Feud*, playing card games on New Year's Eve, or doing one of our holiday traditions such as going to the pumpkin patch or Christmas tree farm. These are the things that unite us.

We are not the ideal family. Does that even exist? We have made the best of our circumstances by working together cooperatively.

There have been plenty of relationship bumps in our road. However, the bond in our family is strong, steady, and reassuring.

Despite our unexpected lives that feel startlingly foreign at times, they became familiar and comfortable because of our shared experiences. Home is our soft place to land because home is where we find our family, our greatest support system.

> *Peace and prosperity to you, your family, and everything you own!*
>
> – 1 SAMUEL 25: 6 (NLT)

CHAPTER 26

Transforming Faith

It is Sunday morning and I am sick in bed with a bad cold. Seventeen-year-old Brielle peeks in my room.

"You OK?" she signs from the doorway.

"I'm OK," I say, waving her over to me. "I just have a cold. But, we won't be going to church this morning."

Brielle hangs her head low and pats my head gently. "Feel better, Mom," she signs. "We go church next week. I love church."

"Why do you love church?" I ask with curiosity while reaching past the thermometer on the bedside table for a tissue to wipe my nose.

"God there. I love God."

"God is here," I say, pointing to her heart. "He is with us, all of the time."

"Jesus nice. He my friend."

My Walk with God

My parents raised me in a traditional Lutheran church. We attended services most Sunday mornings except during good weather when we usually spent the weekend on our sailboat. I participated in vacation Bible school in the summers when I was a child and went through confirmation classes in middle school.

I irregularly attended church services at Methodist churches through college and the first years Brian and I were married. When the girls were born, I started going to church more frequently and became more active. I read the Bible passages on occasion during services, visited elderly church members at a local nursing home, and helped with vacation Bible school.

As the girls grew older, I took Ashley to Sunday school, just as I had gone when I was her age. When Brielle was in kindergarten and first grade, I taught her Sunday school class. It gave me the opportunity to help tailor the class to fit her needs and help the other children interact with her.

After we moved to Toledo when the girls were preteens, the girls and I started attending a church where a new friend was a member. Things were different at this non-denominational church. I joined a small group where I met weekly with seven other women to study the Bible, discuss practical ways to put God's Word to work in our lives, and generally support one another with comfort and prayer. I also began signing the songs at services. This was the first time I began to develop a personal relationship with God and feel the power of this change in my life.

When we moved to the Atlanta area when the girls were young teenagers, we visited 13 churches before we finally found one that fit. I joined a women's Bible study group, began signing the songs at services, and helped with youth group to help bridge the gaps for Brielle.

This was a huge time of spiritual growth for me. I was pushed past religion and introduced to a living faith through a relationship with God. Less than a year later, I was baptized in a full-emersion ceremony.

After the transformation of my faith, everything in life seemed different. It felt as if I had been away on a trip and was, at last, home. This was unlike any home I ever knew. There now was a guiding force in my life, a new beacon of hope, and something that brought great meaning to my days.

My Lonely Journey

A steady source of prayer for me is the souls of the ones I love, especially Brian and Ashley who are not believers. I sit with only Brielle in the church pew next to me each Sunday. I wonder what it would be like for our whole family to sit together in church, discuss the sermon on the way to lunch, and bless our meal with prayer together. I long for a time when Brian and I might attend a couples retreat and grow in our faith together. However, this is not the life I have.

Brian never attended church as a young person. His parents' busy work schedules pushed church to the wayside. He never learned the simple Bible stories, traditional hymns, or even The Lord's Prayer. Without a childhood foundation, he found it impossible to believe something he could not know for sure.

When his mother unexpectedly died in 2001, his beliefs about life after death shifted. Although he still did not believe in heaven, he began to ponder the existence of an afterlife. That was still a very long way from becoming a believer.

Always respectful of my faith, Brian never complained about my absence on Sunday mornings. He supported my efforts to bring the girls up in my faith, sometimes asked what they learned in Sunday school, and attended special occasions such as Christmas programs to see them perform.

I wish Brian believed. I knew when we met he did not. Assuming that difference would not matter, I married him. For a long time, it was largely insignificant. When my faith grew from that of a regular churchgoer to someone personally connected to God, I unfairly changed the rules on him.

Somewhere along the way, Ashley lost her way as well. I fear she was never truly grounded in her beliefs at all. It was a difficult position for her to be in, between her mother who believed and her father who did not. Certainly, her father's path without the encumbrances of early Sunday mornings going to church and the responsibilities the Christian faith requires was more appealing.

Although Ashley defines herself as spiritual, she does not believe in a higher being, the existence of heaven, or the role of Jesus' sacrifice to save her from her sins. She believes in high moral standards. However, this too is a very long way from being a believer.

How does a family maintain its cohesion when there are such fundamental differences among its members? Faith. I continue on my path, present a good role model, talk about my faith when opportunities arise, and continue to pray for them.

Needing God

God continues to teach me how to trust Him for the care and protection of Brielle. At the most difficult times in my life, I pray and lean on my faith to get me through. Each medical procedure and crisis Brielle endures exercises and strengthens my faith muscles. Faith helps me grieve, cope, and understand. It gives me the determination to continue.

Despite my despair or frustration with my circumstances at different points in my life, I never got angry with God. Even in my most desperate moments, I never tried to make any deals with Him. He does not make deals. I know that I cannot ask God to make my child whole. Her spirit is already whole. Instead, I know God will provide for her needs.

Laying Down My Burdens

Imagine that we could all put our burdens in a pile. There in the heap lay debt, bad marriages, troublesome teenager issues, chronic back pain, and our children's disabilities. I consider looking in that pile and picking out a burden. Which one would I pull out? Would I pick something different from my original problem? I imagine most people would choose what they knew.

It is through my struggles that I gain an understanding of the topography of my limitations. Our weaknesses are God's opportunities.

So many times in my life, especially since Brielle's birth, others have told me that God does not give us more than we can bear. Does that mean that if I were a weaker person, I would have fewer or lighter burdens? It does not matter what my troubles are. I feel God with me helping me with my struggles.

When suffering found me, I eventually made a conscious decision in life to be positive and not wallow in self-pity. I am not always happy. Happiness is transient. Instead, I look for sources of true joy and try to maintain that in my heart, even when it is only the size of a mustard seed. I transform my pain into energy so that it can serve me instead of hurt me.

A Vessel for God's Work

Some may wonder why bad things happen to good people. How can tornadoes hit a town in Oklahoma three different times in 14 years? How can so many innocent people be among those killed on 9/11?

Sickness, disability, pain, suffering. None of this would have happened in the Garden of Eden before original sin. God does not inflict the innocent. That would be so clearly contrary to His character. Now, in this fallen world, our circumstances are filtered through God's hands and His sovereignty to make them something useful and beautiful.

Brielle was born different. It is not my fault she is this way. It is certainly not hers. I believe there was a reason, though the full magnitude of it is difficult to know.

God is much bigger than the physical body Brielle must deal with. However, I never asked God to heal Brielle or take away her disability. That is clearly not His will. Although I do not know His full purpose for her, I trust Him and find comfort knowing that Brielle will not always be like this.

My faith helped me see my disabled child in a different light. Maybe Brielle is here for such an important reason that she does not even have to be able to speak of it to be able to achieve it.

As different as Brielle is, I sometimes remind myself that God had a Son who was different, too.

God Had a Plan for Me

Brielle was woven into my destiny. Despite CMV ravaging Brielle's body when she was growing inside me, God created her and entrusted her precious life to me.

Although I still have many questions, I am at peace with my circumstances. Most of my questions will go unanswered until I can ask God face-to-face.

As frustrated and wounded as I may have been during parts of my journey with Brielle, I never asked God, "Why me?" Who am I to complain or question God's handiwork?

Why not me? If not me, then whom?

I began to realize Brielle's disability was an opportunity to demonstrate my faithfulness to God. As my faith deepened, I slowly began to ask God, "What do You want me do with what I was given?"

God wants us to be His hands and feet in this world. Just as the moon does not shine light and only reflects the light shined upon it, God is the light and we are the reflection of Him.

God sent each of us into the world for a unique purpose. He designed our lives for the complex good, greater than we can even fathom.

No one else can fulfill that purpose except for the one that it was given to. When we walk in our calling and commit to something greater than ourselves, we discover something extraordinary that was already in our DNA.

God gave me experiences and gifts of talent to prepare me for my purpose. I cannot let them go idle. I must use them.

Through prayer and study of His Word, I have discovered what I believe is His purpose for me. Although I could not see the entire path in front of me, I took the first steps, stuck to His path, and am intently working each day to fulfill it.

I know that, primarily, I am here to love and care for my family. My soul feels at peace and finds the most joy and contentment when I am doing things for Brielle, sharing my sign language skills, or talking to others about CMV and Brielle's disabilities. None of this could have happened unless my daughter was born the way she was.

I know that I am also here to help Brielle fulfill her purpose. I believe one of her purposes is to show people simple things that are available to anyone. Despite her body that does not work properly, Brielle has an unburdened spirit, pure joy, enthusiasm for life, and compassion and love for others.

Brielle is able to show these things in such simple ways and does it without any effort at all. A few years ago, we were in the grocery store seemingly following a man who was taking the same path and pace through the store as we were. Brielle smiled and waved at him after we passed by him several times. The man smiled and returned her greeting. At one point, he sneezed several times in a row. Brielle signed, "Bless you," and I interpreted for her. The man smiled at us both as he replied, "He already did today."

Faith is My Cornerstone

Like the five small stones David picked up to fight Goliath, I have picked up my stones to hurl at the giant I face each day. My stones of knowledge, support, hope, determination, and faith have served me well.

Although my faith was not always as strong as it is today, I found peace and purpose. My life was transformed by my faith and is better having followed God's Word.

> *Therefore, I urge you, brothers and sisters, in view of God's mercy, to offer your bodies as a living sacrifice, holy and pleasing to God this is your true and proper worship. Do not conform to the pattern of this world, but be transformed by the renewing of your mind. Then you will be able to test and approve what God's will is His good, pleasing and perfect will.*
>
> — ROMANS 12: 1-2 (NIV)

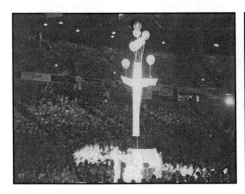 

CHAPTER 27

Thoughts from a Father

It's Saturday night and I just pulled a pan of lasagna from the oven. Ashley is away at college, but Brian and Brielle are nowhere around.

I follow the squeals into Brielle's bedroom where Brian is wedged together with Brielle onto her narrow twin-sized bed. Scooby-Doo is on and they are taking turns playing a game on her iPad.

"There you two are," I say to them. "Dinner is ready."

"Wait one minute," 17-year-old Brielle signs. "Dad play with me. He best dad ever."

These are Brian's thoughts on raising a special needs child – uncensored and unedited.

What memories stand out about the day we found out we were pregnant with Brielle and the weeks that followed?

The one thing that really sticks out is when you came in and said, "Bun." All I remember is being in the bedroom when you came in and said that. It felt like it was kind of anticlimactic. It seemed like an odd way of finding out we were going to have a baby.

I remember being happy about being pregnant with Brielle, but concerned even though we didn't really know if we had any reason to be concerned. I don't remember being distraught or overwhelmed with worry or anything like that in those initial moments. When we talked to the specialists, I remember it being a concern, but not an "Oh my God" concern. I remember it being something that could be a problem, but we didn't know anything at that point in those first weeks.

What memories stand out about when we found out about the CMV?

I don't remember how you told me. I honestly don't remember a lot about it. I remember being clearly more worried at that point knowing that there were all kinds of things that could go wrong.

Do I have specific memories? Did I feel this way or that way?

I think you can start to build concerns and go down a bad path if you don't have all the information you can get to help understand it. Once we had the information and understood the risks, I was scared, no doubt.

I remember the conversation around the table with the specialists and the abortion option being brought up. But, I don't think we ever seriously considered that. It was appropriate for the doctor to bring up, but I think we pretty much dismissed it right away.

What was the hardest part of the pregnancy?

I think the last month knowing that something was wrong was the hardest. If they would have been able to tell us "this" was going to happen, it would have made it a lot easier than dealing with "these are the things that could happen, but we don't know what it's going to be."

When you're going to have a baby, you think of that moment when you say, "Oh, we need to go to the hospital because you're having contractions." We didn't have that with either of the girls and I feel bad we missed out on that experience. And certainly with Brielle it was very pre-programmed at a certain date and time. It was more like a medical procedure than giving birth to a child.

I remember the night before when our parents were at the house and then driving over to Marshfield the next morning. We certainly didn't have any joyful feelings of having a baby. We had a countdown to the medical procedure and we had no idea how it was going to turn out and what we were going to be dealing with after she was born.

That, to me, was the hardest part, especially the last day. I don't remember anything specific, but I know how I felt. I felt like she was better off, safer, where she was than she would be a day from then when we would have to deal with whatever the issues were. When she was still in your belly, we didn't have to deal with it and, in one sense, she was safe.

When were you most scared because of Brielle?

That's an easy one. That was right after she was born and you were recovering. You were being taken care of and resting from the surgery. I distinctly remember sitting in the neonatal intensive care unit with all the surgical garb on and she's there in her little crib and there was an issue with her heart.

We kind of knew there could be stuff wrong with other parts of her, but we really didn't anticipate there being a heart problem. And then, they started talking about her having this heart irregularity and you could see it happening on the monitor. I remember sitting there literally by myself watching this beep thing go and hating it every time the squiggly thing came when her heart didn't beat right. I didn't know if she was going to have a heart attack and die right there. I didn't want you to worry about it at the time, but it was just awful watching that monitor.

I remember hating that machine and it was doing nothing but doing what it was supposed to do. It was just a damn machine. But, damn you, machine!

Part of me felt so alone because we weren't together and you weren't there to help and I couldn't help you either. I was just sitting there watching this thing with zero control over what was happening. Here I was a father and I couldn't do anything to help her.

For me personally, that was the worst time, those few days.

There were natural risks with the other surgeries she has had, but they weren't life or death issues. It was about quality of life, kind of fixing things.

What memory or feeling stands out most about Brielle's surgeries?
The biggest thing for me around the surgeries was I always wanted more certainty about what benefit there was going to be for her. You were more involved in the medical issues than I was and I know doctors will never guarantee anything, but there was frustration not knowing what the outcome was going to be.

I think we made the best decisions we could at the time and, for example, I get why we had her salivary glands removed for the drooling issue. Looking back on it, did it help? No, not really. It's just the frustration wishing those doctors gave us some sort of assurance of what was going to be the outcome.

Was there a time you were angry about having a daughter like Brielle?
Probably so. Probably more when she was younger, especially when she was colicky, even though I had no reason to be angry at her.

When she was young, I was mad about stuff she couldn't do and then I settled into that.

Not to go down the religion rat hole, but why would God ever do that to a child? Why would a creator do that? Put someone in a body that doesn't work right? It's part of what makes me question the whole God thing. If you have the ability to control this, even with billions of people in the world, why would you do this to an innocent kid? I get to some degree why things happen to adults. But, why an innocent child? I don't get that.

She's capable of more than her body allows her to do. Why she doesn't get pissed about it, I don't know.

Maybe I was angry early on that we weren't going to have that normal life. Probably still am to some degree today.

When was a time you were embarrassed by Brielle?

I think all of us wish her drooling issues were better, a way we could control it. I know we've all gotten used to it, but early on, it was a little embarrassing. At this point, I don't really care. It is what it is and she's gotten a whole lot better at using her towel.

I can't remember the last time she had a tantrum, but that was embarrassing a little.

I honestly don't pay attention to other people staring at us in public. I don't really care. I sometimes notice little kids because they are kind of obvious. But, I think they are just trying to figure her out. I never notice men and I only sometimes notice women. They aren't judging, at least I don't take it as that. I think they feel sorry for her.

When was a time you felt jealous of Brielle? A time when you felt like too much attention was on Brielle?

I don't think I ever felt anything like that.

I felt bad that how I handled the colic situation created the whole deal with "you take care of Brielle and I take care of Ashley." I can't imagine that we would have significantly altered that decision, but that was a key decision in our family that probably has in odd ways subconsciously set a dynamic in our family that is what it is. Those were hard times, but it was never a jealousy thing.

What is your favorite thing about Brielle? Do you think she would have that quality if she wasn't born the way she was?

The one thing? There's a lot of things.

Her smile clearly to me would be number one. I remember when we were doing the salivary gland surgery, clearly thinking that if they screw up her smile, that would be awful and I would never forgive myself for letting that happen. Not being able to see her smile would be painful.

I love her independence. As dependent as she is for many things, you can go hours in the same house and not know she's here because she's just doing her thing, entertaining herself.

Her whole spirit of how she can live with the challenges she has in life is amazing to me. She probably wouldn't be the same way if she were born normal.

I don't think she has an understanding of the world and she doesn't experience the negatives of this world to develop an "edge" like other kids do. The more you're exposed to the craziness of the world, the more cynical you can get. I don't think anyone can live in this world and be completely positive if you have a concept of what is really happening around you. She couldn't care less about the economy, unemployment, war, or any of those things. You can show her and explain it and she might get it, but she doesn't really understand it like a normal person. That keeps her happy like she is and to me that is a good thing.

What quality does she have that you wish you had?
I guess how she never meets a stranger and how she always seems to meet new people. People seem to always know her. Her positive attitude and how she is always happy and friendly is great.

I find it odd for someone in my line of work (human resources), *but it's difficult for me to meet people and make friends. Her ability to be open when she meets people is positive versus my approach. I don't really always want to talk to other people. I wonder what they want from me. That's just from my experiences.*

What do you think Brielle thinks about you as her dad?
I'm probably her definition of a dad, like you're her definition of a mom.

I hope that she thinks that she's loved by her dad and that he'd do anything for her and just wants her to be happy.

How did you feel about the extra responsibilities you had with Brielle?

Certain things are just what we do. I don't think a lot about the responsibilities that we had in the past or have today. I think what we had to do or have to do now have just become who we are and what we do.

Is it a pain that we have to get her dressed every day or still help her in the bathroom? Yes, but it's much easier, more natural, than it used to be. Do I spend even two seconds thinking of those responsibilities? Not really.

I am much more worried about how we make sure she is taken care of later in life and I certainly feel a huge burden to make sure we have all of that in the front and center of our planning, financially and otherwise. It is our job to make sure she is set. I don't want to pass that responsibility on to Ashley or anyone else.

How did you initially feel about learning sign language? And now?

I took the class and did the whole tutoring thing. But, frankly, that's my biggest failure, not doing a better job of understanding her sign language. That's probably the one parenting regret that I have. I know I need to do something about it.

It's not easy to have her always signing to you instead of communicating to me directly. But, it is what it is right now.

I don't need to sign to her because she understands fine. Frankly, at this point, I don't think she'll ever need us to sign to her because she's probably not going to lose her hearing. If I could just learn to understand her signs and her words and keep up with her vocabulary, I'd be fine.

I always kind of understood why the schools pushed so hard for some kind of communication device. The world does not sign. You might find a few people here and there. But, at some point, she's going to need to have some type of other communication system.

I don't know if that had anything to do with why I didn't go "all in" with sign. But, maybe it did. I assigned some importance to it, but I never fully committed to it. I think I always discounted it a little, because even to this day, when you're not around, we get along just fine.

I think I understand a reasonable amount of sign. It may take me much longer than it certainly takes you. And if there's something we just can't connect on, she can spell it and I can get it then. That's just kind of how we do things when you're not around. There's enough context since her world is pretty small. I can figure it out.

What is the hardest part about going to activities with other special needs kids? Good things?

Other than seeing what other families have to deal with for their kids, I don't find those activities hard at all. The activities are all really positive. I think that's why I really enjoy baseball, bowling, and soccer and when she did that beauty pageant. It gives her an outlet to participate in stuff. I don't know what she would do if she didn't have those activities. I know she'd miss them if she didn't have them.

I also know there's a benefit to those things for the buddies, for the regular kids that have interactions with the special needs kids. It could even be a greater thing for them longer term since those kids are going to be the future teachers, caregivers, maybe even parents of special needs kids themselves.

I think generations before ours were uncomfortable with the special needs kids. Our generation is better, but the kids today just don't get like that and it is great to see. If anything, I think the next generation will be more protective and watch out for their peers as they get older, at least I hope so.

Have you ever thought about if Brielle had a different or "worse" disability? What would be "worse?"

I think when you answer that question, you need to consider who would it be worse for.

Certainly, for us, it would be worse if she couldn't walk or feed herself. Remember when we had to do that three times a day for years?

I also think those interactions with other parents and kids at activities have made me comfortable with the challenges we have and thankful for those we don't have.

But, do I think about if she were like some of them? No, not really. She is what she is. It's hard to think of her being different in any way. And I certainly don't see her getting worse.

What is the hardest part about having a daughter like Brielle?

It's sometimes hard just thinking about it. I sometimes get lost in where she is in her life. I sometimes forget that she's 17 and not seven. I know that you sometimes think I baby her too much. I probably could do better treating her like her age. But, honestly, I'm not sure I really want to do that.

I think it's tough to think about how she would be if she were a normal child. I try not to think about it too often. But, there are times, like when she reaches milestone ages that it is normal to think that way. At 16 she would be driving, 18 and graduating, things like that. What her major in college would be, would she want to be a performer since she likes that so much already, or would she be an athlete or musician. Certainly, she wouldn't still be watching Scooby Doo *at this point in her life.*

I just have to try as best as I can to not go into that, at least not too often. Living with her day in and day out isn't hard at all. And then, of course, there's the long term responsibilities for her care and financial support. That's what is hardest to think about.

329

What makes you most proud of Brielle?

How she loves everybody and how she tries so hard. It makes me choke up just thinking about that.

She is the most positive person and kind, happy, gentle soul I have ever known.

I wrote in my self-evaluation for the leadership program at work that she is my hero and I mean that very much. To tackle what she does every day and have that spirit is amazing.

Have you ever thought about what it would be like if you were like Brielle?

Never have. I don't know why, but I've never really thought of it.

I'd like to think that her physical challenges and her mental challenges are on an even plane, that one isn't worse than the other, and that's why she doesn't get more frustrated. Whereas, if her mental acuity were much higher than her physical ability, then I think we'd get much more frustration from her.

I don't think we can put ourselves in her situation because we don't have that same balance. She doesn't know what she's missing since she's always been this way. We can't even think about what it would be like because we're too biased with what we know and have experienced.

What would you do differently with Brielle if you could go back to any time?

To me, my big miss is the sign language communication thing.

Did I make a mistake by not engaging more in her medical care? Maybe that.

If I had gone to more of her therapies, would she be in any different place? Probably not.

One thing for sure, I would have been more aggressive with doctors to give us some sort of more concrete scale of improvement on the surgeries she has had. I wanted to know more information and wish I would have pushed harder for them to tell us what specific percentage of improvement we could reasonably expect after the surgeries.

I don't know that there's too much else. Have we done it the model way? No. I'm not sure that there is a model way. I don't know what it would be. If there was one, we would have researched it and done that.

But, I go back to every kid is different. The only thing you can do is what you think is the best thing for them. If it turns out it wasn't the best, you can't change it, it's done and you move forward to the next thing and try your best again.

What are some of the things you missed out on the most having a daughter like Brielle?

I think I missed out on teaching her things, even simple things like riding a bike or driving and things like that. She'll never get to go on a date or to her prom. We won't have her grandchildren to spoil.

I think we missed out on being able to do stuff as a family without having to worry about if it was something she could do or if it was too hot for her or whatever.

Probably the one thing that hurts the most is we won't hear her voice. I would give almost anything to hear what she would sound like.

One of the other big ones is that we missed out on seeing the dynamic between Ashley and Brielle in a normal circumstance. It's been much better between them in recent years, but it's never been normal and it likely never will be. On the other hand, it could have been ugly, who knows.

Are there any benefits of having a daughter like Brielle?

On the lighter side, there's handicapped parking and going to the front of the line at Disney. But, those are small things.

More seriously, we never dealt with the teenager rebellion stuff with her. To this day the sun rises and sets with us in her world. I think you get unconditional love from her. She's not trying to read anything into it or manipulate anything, at least nothing significant.

I also think you gain a perspective about life. You know you can't take things for granted and that is a good lesson.

How do you think our family would be different if we only had Ashley and never had other children?

One, I don't think we'd be as happy. I think Brielle brings a whole dynamic that would be greatly missed, not that we'd know.

I think Ashley is very fortunate that we had Brielle. I think we could have applied a whole lot more pressure on her if she was our only child. I think we're the type that we would have gone full boar and pushed in all our chips if we had only one child. I don't think we did that with Ashley the way things were.

With your programming, the channel for attention you had to focus on with Brielle made that mother-daughter relationship with Ashley more bearable for her. I think your relationship with Ashley without a second child would have been very interesting. I don't know how that would have gone. I don't know if it would have been better or if it would have been worse. To me, it's a coin flip.

I don't think Ashley and I would be as close as we are if we had not had Brielle. Again, that goes back to how we had to split parenting duties to get through those months of colic.

How do you think you are different (for better or worse) because of Brielle?

That's a good question. I don't know exactly.

The first thing that popped into my mind will make you laugh. Maybe I'm more patient. I know I have my issues, but maybe it would be worse if it weren't for her.

I think I have a greater perspective of responsibility because of her. I think I would probably be more of a risk taker in some of the decisions we made, if we had a normal child who was going to be off our payroll in five years. I would likely have done something different in my career by now, something that would have been a more selfish choice for me.

How do you think our family would be different if Brielle weren't like she is? Ashley? Me?

I'm trying to think of a way Ashley would be different and I'm having a hard time thinking of something.

I want to think that she would have connected with a sister and they would have been really close. But, that's probably just wishful thinking.

Would Ashley like kids better? Maybe. I wonder if all of this experience with Brielle has influenced her feelings about having kids herself. Does she factor in the chance that she could have a child with special needs? This wasn't a genetic thing for us, but maybe being around other disabled kids planted that seed in her mind more than it would be otherwise.

Would Ashley have learned skills for handling conflict better because she would be fighting with her sister? Probably. Those are a few things I might wonder about.

You probably would be the most different of anybody. There's probably a laundry list of ways you would be different. You'd probably be working and doing who knows what. I'm not sure you'd have any of the same friends you have now because most of them are somehow connected to Brielle, the circles we run in because of her disabilities. You were just too busy to find other friends. I don't want to say you'd be completely different, but you'd probably be seventy percent different.

If you could go back to your younger self, what would you tell him about Brielle?

The one thing that's always been weird is why you had that job working with disabled high school students when you were pregnant with Ashley. That one, I can't answer. It's a little spooky.

As for my younger self, I would want to sit him down and explain, "Here's what you got coming and these are the things you're going to have to prepare for. There's going to be medical stuff that you're not going to be smart enough to understand. Don't trust the doctors. Make sure you understand what's going on."

I don't think I would do anything different from a financial stand-point. I think things worked out for us moving so much, but I'm not sure that was the smartest thing we did at the time. Sometimes I wonder if we should have made her the priority and stuck to one place. Knowing what we know now, it was fine. But, in those early years, we moved so much. Looking back on it, it was higher risk than was probably pru-dent at the time.

Do you think there is a reason or purpose Brielle is like she is?
I don't think so.

Is Brielle the way she is because if she wasn't maybe something else would be different in our family? Maybe there's a trade-off we don't know about. I have no idea.

She absolutely creates good in this world with her spirit and how she interacts with people. I think she has a big impact, even just with people in our family. I think she's a positive force in this world. Is she ever going to have a wide impact? Probably not. But, frankly, she al-ready has a wider impact than I have had with my life. Just look at the people around her.

What do you worry about most for Brielle and her future?
As I get closer to retirement, there's that whole burden of thinking about things other people don't have to think about, like retiring for three. We have to think about the long term future for her, have to plan for it. That's probably the biggest thing out of all of it that I worry about.

I don't have any problem picturing in my mind what she'll be like and doing as long as we're around. You see older people with an adult child that is a special needs person and they're hanging out with their parents. It's just natural she'll be with us.

I have a hard time picturing what her life is going to be like when we're not here. I can't imagine what it's going to be. Her purpose is so tied to us that I don't know what she's going to do. That is the biggest thing that makes my stomach churn. She could easily have thirty or more years on her own after we are gone. That is a sobering thought. I just never want her to be lonely. Having people to love is what makes her happy and I can't bear the thought of her being alone.

When and how do you tell or explain to your acquaintances, friends, or co-workers about Brielle?

Maybe it's gotten easier over the years. A lot of them know her because she's in the office sometimes with you, so it's not like I have to go into any great detail.

When I meet someone new, the family thing comes up. Then there's a whole thing like "How old are your kids?" and then eventually "Where does the younger one plan to go to college?" I have to go into how she isn't going to college and how she has cerebral palsy. I tell them what it is versus a generic term like she's a "special needs child."

I don't think twice about sharing now because it is who we are. I mean, who cares? I think the thing I've learned over the years is that so many people have a connection to a person with a disability and have an understanding of what it means. Whether it's in their family or through other friends, it is much more prevalent that it used to be. When I was young, I don't remember that ever being common. But, now it seems like it's more common or at least more kids get bucketed into "special needs." Maybe years ago they wouldn't have been diagnosed, just called something else, like hyper or slow or not behaved or something like that.

What do you wish strangers knew about Brielle? About our family?

I just wish they knew how much good she has in her heart and how much she just loves people and to meet and get to know people. I think people are probably hesitant to interact with her and us, to a certain degree.

My only hope is that others don't define us as the family with the disabled kid. We're more than that, but I'm sure that's how some people look at us.

Have you ever talked with another father of a special needs kid?
Well, Rick (husband of my friend, Bobbi, in Freeport) *back in the day. I don't remember anyone in Texas or anyone in Ohio. I probably spend more time talking to Victoria's dad* (Brielle's best friend in Atlanta) *now when we've been at the girls' dances.*

I've had other conversations with Jim (a friend at work who has a son with autism). *We've talked a lot about Miracle League baseball since his son does that. His wife has gotten big into the local and state autistic chapter and he's gotten into it more, too. From a technical knowledge of how the system works, Jim probably has a greater understanding of it than I do. Other than the discussion about the pressure or responsibility we have to make sure that whatever we have is going to last for our children for thirty or forty years after we're gone, we don't talk about it all much.*

But, I don't get into deep stuff with any of them. Dudes just don't do that. That's never going to happen. It's more about school stuff and what they like to do. Guys aren't going to get in on the same level that you and other moms get into. Guys never go there.

I don't think a deep conversation like that would have ever made a difference. I guess it could have. But, it just doesn't feel like that to me. Can't say I ever missed something by not having that sort of conversation with another father.

Frankly, sometimes I think you get too deep into that world. My inclination is to stay out of that world as much as I can. I don't think it's a coincidence that you are I are different on this issue. We sort of balance each other out on this one.

I don't remember support groups much. I don't know that I'm right, but to me, you have to either go in or stay out. There's no skirting around it. I don't know why. I don't think it's still a denial thing.

It just doesn't feel like it would be helpful. Maybe it would be, but it's not my gig.

What advice would you give parents, especially fathers, of special needs kids?

One of the things I've come to realize is that every kid is different in their situation. I'm not sure that any advice I would give would necessarily be helpful other than bucketing bigger things.

Nobody would have been able to tell me, "Dude, you'd better learn sign language because your kid isn't going to be able to talk." Nobody is going to know that. Would I have paid attention to that? I don't know.

That being said, I guess I can think of a few things.

Don't ever let them see you angry at them. When you're frustrated, you have to figure out a different way of getting that out that's not in their presence.

You need to be careful to keep things balanced in the house. I think it's easy when you have a special needs child to think that they won't know if there's a favorite child. You need to be cognizant of that balance. You need to love your child for who they are.

Pay attention to your marriage. It goes in one of two ways in families and couples. They either stick it out or they don't. When you have an extra challenge, you've got to work hard if you want your family to stay together.

Don't abdicate everything to the mother. Have a voice, be involved, and stay close to things. I think there was a time when I got away from that and I'm not sure I ever got that balance back again.

It wouldn't be easy to be fully involved because, whether we like it or not, the world is set up to treat dads differently. Even in normal situations, people assume you are not as capable of taking care of your child as their mom. That is only amplified with a special needs child. If I take Brielle somewhere by myself, women seem to be fascinated by us. I guess most people don't expect to see a dad alone with his special needs child.

Don't look at each thing as an end of the world thing. We pushed so hard for so many things. At the end of the day, did it really matter? I'm not sure that it did. I think you just need to allow certain things to roll off and say, "This is just the way it's going to be." Don't take everything as a win-lose situation and don't take every little hurdle as life and death because they're not.

I might say things like make sure you're plan financially because that road is really long, know all the hoops like limiting their assets and having your wills and a special needs trust.

What didn't I ask that you want to share?

I think it's such a special challenge. There's a certain honor having to tackle this. It's probably a really bad choice of words here. But, you can't look at it as a "Why me?" thing because if you do that then you're not going to embrace it and enjoy what you have. So, you might as well honor it and try to do the very best you can to make it the best you can make it.

I think it's of more value to live in today, more important to focus on figuring out the future, and more destructive to worry about the past. You can't change the past, so why focus on that? It just clouds your judgment and perspective and you need those to be sharp to plan and make the best life for your special child.

Thoughts From A Sister

"Look, Mom," 17-year-old Brielle signs as she thrusts a drawing upon me.

"We were talking in Sunday school today about the Twenty-Third Psalm," her teacher tells me. "We asked each child to write and draw something that helps them not to be afraid."

I look at the white chalk on the black construction paper. It reads, "I will not be afraid, for you are close beside me," in the teacher's clear penmanship. Below that it says, "Two sisters Ashley" with two stick figures, seemingly a representation of Brielle and Ashley.

"Not afraid. Ashley with me," Brielle signs and then points to the picture.

These are Ashley's thoughts on being a sister to a special needs child – uncensored and unedited.

What is your first memory of Brielle?
I think that my first real memory, not something I've seen in videos or heard you talk about, would be when we lived in Freeport. I remember her leg got stuck in the spokes of the rocking chair while we were playing in my room and she started crying. I didn't know what was happening and I remember being extremely scared when you said you were going to get a saw. I thought you were going to cut her leg off, not the chair spoke. I remember hiding in the closet crying and being really afraid that you were going to do something to hurt my sister.

Do you remember a time when we talked with you about Brielle being disabled?
I vaguely remember you telling me how to explain the way she is to other people. You told me to say she was disabled, she can't talk, but she can hear.

I remember never knowing how to pronounce 'cerebral palsy' as a kid so I mostly just stuck to the "she can't talk" explanation, even though that doesn't really answer the question.

I don't think I even understood what CMV was until I was in high school. As a kid, I didn't know what caused her disability other than "it happened in mommy's tummy".

How did you tell or explain to your friends about Brielle when you were younger?
I never brought it up willingly. Usually, I just waited until they asked about it after meeting her. I think I did that because I was always hoping someone wouldn't notice, but of course they always did. I usually just tried to give the shortest answer possible because I didn't want to just be the girl with the disabled sister. I would always try to change the subject.

Looking back, I may have been afraid that someone wouldn't come over to play with me or wouldn't be friends with me if they thought I had a weird family.

How did you tell or explain to your friends about Brielle when you were older?

I still don't bring up her disability unless I have to, but it's not because I don't think people will like me or that they will judge me. I'm just a little more selective of who knows about that part of my life because it is such an influential part of who I am.

After leaving for college and living so far away, it's less likely to come up with people who don't know my family. But, that also makes it harder for someone to imagine how Brielle is when all they have to go off of is what I say. It's just an awkward thing to bring up out of the blue, so I try to make it sound as nonchalant as I can and I go into more depth depending on the person.

I've always tried hard not to make it the defining thing about me when I meet new people because when I was younger, I just felt like I would be pegged as the girl with the disabled sister and it can still feel that way sometimes.

I went into a store with her once by myself and every time I go back, the same checkout guy asks, "You used to come in with your sister, right?" I don't like being that person.

When you were young, what did your friends say about Brielle?

When I was younger, my friends would always ask "What's wrong with her?" and then they would usually just leave the subject alone. It was probably because they didn't know what else to say.

I only remember a few times that a friend of mine would be grossed out by her and would openly show it. One time, in second grade, my friend came over and we were eating a snack at the table with Brielle. Of course, Brielle wasn't good at eating back then, so food was all over her. My friend wasn't very good at hiding her disgust, and I remember it hurt my feelings a lot. I didn't know how to handle the situation, so I just sat there ashamed.

That was a pretty extreme incident though. Most kids were more passive towards her. They asked their initial question and then moved on and just sort of ignored her.

How did things change over time with your friends' reactions to Brielle?

Now, my friends adore her. Sometimes when they come over to our house, she's the one they address first. They greet her with the first hug instead of me. They chat with her on Facebook and always ask how she's doing. One of my friends always says, "Say hi to Brielle for me!" every single time we leave each other. They go out of their way to be her friend, too.

I think as we get older, we're more exposed to kids like Brielle, so it becomes less of a shock when we meet people with a disability. At least, that's the way my friends explain it.

I remember when I first met Derick (her current boyfriend), *it was one of the first things to come up. When he came over to meet the family for the first time, his biggest concern was how to interact with Brielle. He asked questions, like how should he address her and what age level does she respond to.*

As I got older, everyone's questions got more detailed like that. My friends have even asked what your pregnancy was like, when you knew she would be disabled, what caused it, what's it like to be her sister, and just everything. I think once my friends became more curious about Brielle, so did I. And I began to actually realize what CMV was and what the disability itself was.

Did you ever wish someone else could have Brielle as a sister instead or even for a while just so they could understand what it's like?

No, never. I'm not sure I thought that abstractly as a kid. Plus, I was always so concerned with not making it a big deal that I just never thought about the other option of having people know what it's like.

Have you ever talked with another sibling of a special needs kid?
Only one time really stands out to me. There was a girl in middle school that had a brother with cerebral palsy, but we didn't talk about it for very long. She was way more open about it than I was. Her brother was very functional though. He could talk and understand things. Once I realized it was completely different situations, there wasn't much to talk about because I didn't feel like she was in the same boat as me.

I don't know that it would have helped me necessarily to talk to someone with a disabled sibling when I was younger because there are just so many different types of circumstances. I think it would have been hard to hear that my sister was worse-off than someone else's sibling and I would have felt bad for the other person if their sibling was worse-off than Brielle.

Maybe if I had been older when she was born, I would have been more aware of my feelings towards her disability and it would have helped to talk with someone. But, as a kid, I had no idea how I really felt about it. It's not really until now that I realize I had any opinion at all about it at the time.

When was a time you were embarrassed by Brielle?
Most embarrassed feelings that I have involving Brielle are just any time when the attention is brought to the fact that she is disabled. For example, when she throws a temper tantrum in public and we're stared at, it's embarrassing because most teenagers don't throw fits like that.

I feel more embarrassed for her or for my parents in those moments though, because I know people are either thinking, "What's wrong with her?" or "Those are bad parents because they're making their disabled child cry."

Also, any time when people stare at her just because she's disabled. When I was younger, I was embarrassed by it. Now, I just find it rude and I glare back until they stop.

When was a time you felt jealous of Brielle or a time when you felt like too much attention was on Brielle?

I feel like we got a lot of separate attention, like you were focused mostly on her and Dad would be the one to focus on me. That's why Dad and I got close when I was younger. As a kid, I always felt like it was you and Brielle and then Dad and me, especially when I was around 10 or 11 years old. I don't know if that was on purpose or if it just happened that way.

You and I still had our shared things, but it wasn't the same. I felt like it had to be just "Mom and me" alone to be able to actually get your full attention.

Once you and Dad divided, I don't think it ever shifted back to normal until a few years ago. It's not like anyone was a neglectful parent. I feel like I got a fair amount of attention, but so much of it was only from one parent so it seemed like less. I just never got full attention and for that I'm jealous.

Of course, there are times when the attention should be on her, like when she has surgery or when she's doing a sport. But, there were also times when the attention probably should have been a little more balanced and that's when I would get jealous.

When was a time you were angry about having a sister like Brielle?

I would never say I was angry. Maybe a little jealous of the kind of relationship you and I would have had if things had been different. But, I can't say angry. You can't be angry at something you can't change.

It's obvious there are some things that we're not going to have because of this, like I might never be an aunt. That kind of makes me sad.

There are things that have happened to me and, if she were a normal sister, she would be excited for me. For example, she didn't understand what being accepted to college meant to me, or what learning to drive meant to me. Or if I'm going on a trip, she can't really understand what that means, just that I'm not where she is. Or one day when I get married, she's not going to know the significance of that.

I know she's excited for me, but I think that's only because everyone else is excited for me. She somewhat understands what's going on, but it's not the same.

It's also that I don't have that extra wing of support beyond you and Dad, and that upsets me. Your parents are always going to be there for you, but it would be nice to have that other person that would always be there to support you. Sometimes I wish I had a sister to talk about things with.

In a lot of ways, it's kind of like being an only child. We'll never have that conversation of "Mom and Dad are driving me crazy" or "I'm doing something I'm not supposed to, do you have my back?" I just can't share those secrets that are only between siblings that I know my other friends have.

What is your favorite thing about Brielle? Do you think she would have that quality if she wasn't born the way she was?
I think she's really happy all the time and not many people are always happy like that. Other than her few little temper tantrums, she's constantly happy. I don't think she'd be like that if she wasn't disabled. She'd understand that things are not quite so happy all the time.

Things are sugarcoated for her because of her disability. You're not going to tell her that there are financial problems or that the 9/11 attacks happened. So, for me, those real life things might cause me to worry. But, for her, she doesn't understand what those things mean.

It's like when we were talking the other day that she didn't understand the concept of slavery. She's been protected from that concept and that entire social issue when all of us have had to deal with it and understand it. For her, she just doesn't know.

I think there are lessons you can learn from her, like that some things just don't matter, especially when it's a small thing. It takes a lot to shake her. Even though it's just because she doesn't understand certain things, it's still a good quality to have.

What quality does she have that you wish you had?
I wish I had the confidence or the ability to just say what I want when I want. She just talks about what she wants to talk about and she tells you what she's thinking no matter what it is. Heck, she'll talk to the lady at the nail salon about the Scooby Doo *episode she watched that morning. She has the ability to speak her mind freely and most people actually pay attention to what she has to say.*

What makes you most proud of Brielle?
The fact that she doesn't see herself as having anything wrong with her. She doesn't know any different, so she thinks it's normal.

For example, she thinks it's normal for her hand not to work properly or to not be able to talk. I'm not sure if she sees herself as different than other people or not, but she certainly doesn't seem to be phased by it if she does.

It's why I prefer the question "What does she have?" over "What's wrong with her?" Nothing is wrong with her. She's just my sister who has cerebral palsy.

How did you feel about learning sign language?
Years ago, the process of actually learning it was both a chore and kind of fun at the same time. Sometimes, I saw it as an extra thing that I had to know or deal with just because of her disability. But, I always liked language. So, for me, it was kind of fun.

Now, I think it's cool that I know it. I'm glad I do. I've even used it on my résumé before. But, I've never used it with anyone other than her.

It is something that I wouldn't have learned if she wasn't the way she is. I see it as something that I have to know if I want to have a better relationship with her, and I do want that, so I do it.

What do you most remember about Brielle's surgeries?
I remember visiting her in the hospital after her salivary gland surgery, but I think I was only about 8 or 9. I really didn't understand what it was, as in what a salivary gland was, or what they did to it. I

remember you said she wasn't hurt and that she was having it done so that she wouldn't drool so much. So, I thought, "OK, this is just another thing she does to make things better, like going to therapy."

Then, I remember the leg surgery when I was older. The main thing that I remember from that one was that we didn't go anywhere for Christmas that year because it would be too difficult. So, we didn't get to see family that year. It wasn't a bad thing necessarily, but it did affect what we would have normally done.

How did you feel about the extra responsibilities you had with Brielle?

I think that you and Dad did a good job of asking if I would mind helping out with things like babysitting her for a night or putting her in her pajamas. But, you always said it was OK if I didn't want to or felt uncomfortable doing it. I knew that it would help you guys. But, I never felt like it was part of my assigned chores. I did feel a little pressured to do those kinds of things, only because I always wanted to please you and Dad and didn't want to say no.

Obviously, I wouldn't have to do certain things if she wasn't like this, and I was always very aware of that. It's not fun having to take care of someone who normally would be fully capable of taking care of themselves. I would often get frustrated when I was younger and did things like dress her or feed her because I had no idea what I was doing and I knew other kids my age didn't have to do the things I did.

What is the hardest part about going to activities with other special needs kids?

I don't think there's anything hard about it at all. I'm just glad it's there for her since it's such a good thing for her to be around other kids with disabilities. When we're at those events I don't worry about her being able to keep up with the other kids like I do when she's with regular kids. I don't worry about her feeling left out or different or stared at. I think that's when she has the most fun, when things are on her level and she can just enjoy herself. It's a cool thing to see.

How do you think things would be different if you were the younger sibling?

I think if I was the younger sister and she was the older sister, attention would have been divided more evenly. I feel like maybe I would have gotten more attention because the youngest one usually gets more attention in general. But, having a younger sibling who also needs even more attention because of a disability was just double the attention that's on her and not me.

Have you ever thought about if Brielle had a different or "worse" disability? What would be "worse"?

Well, for me personally, I see any situation where she'd be in a wheelchair or couldn't do anything for herself as being worse.

I think of it as levels. At the top there's normal, where she wouldn't need any help at all. Then there's the level where she would need a little help, which is pretty much where she is now. Then there's that bottom level of not being self-sufficient at all, which is what I would consider worse.

It's going to be a lot harder to care for someone that you have to do everything for than someone who just needs help with a few things and can progress in what they can do for themselves. It would put a lot of pressure on us as a family and we might not be as close because it would limit us even further on what we can all do together.

What is the hardest part about having a sister like Brielle?

Not having someone there. The "normal" sibling. Somebody I could have fought with or wrestled with. Just kid stuff.

As a kid, I had that instinct to play and be a little rough. But, of course, I couldn't do that because I would have hurt her and I would have gotten in so much trouble.

I played by myself a lot, even if she was in the room, too. She couldn't be the other Barbie doll and little things like that.

If I had to include her, I had to come down to her level. A lot of times it felt like I was told to include her because she wanted to be included, which to me is like using "because I said so" as an argument. Also, including her was more like her including me because we always had to do her stuff since she usually couldn't do mine. So, I didn't always get to do what I wanted because my sister had to do it too, and she physically couldn't do what I wanted. I never got my way in those situations.

Now that I'm older, though, the hardest part is still not having someone there. I don't have the full emotional support of a sister and that's hard.

What are the benefits of having a sister like Brielle?

The little lessons you learn along the way. Learning to not judge people. To enjoy the little things in life. To not take things for granted. There are lessons I think I learned a lot earlier in life than most people because of having Brielle as a sister.

Being moved to the front of the line at Disney and getting tickets to see Taylor Swift wasn't too bad either, to be completely honest.

How do you think you are different (for better or worse) because of Brielle?

For better, I'm more accepting of things and people who are different. I'm more independent. I'm more sensitive about including others and making sure everyone is happy in a situation. I'm more patient.

For worse, it's more difficult for me to share personal things with other people because I don't have that one person who I can tell anything to and they will still love me no matter what. I'm more of an introvert because I always played by myself at home when I was younger and didn't have the typical companion that other kids had in a sibling.

What do you think Brielle thinks about you as her big sister?
I know she looks up to me and loves me. That's all I really need to know. As long as I am somebody she can look up to, I'm OK.

How do you think our family would be different if Brielle weren't like she is?
I think our lives would be very different.

I think you would have very different interests because a lot of what you do is centered on her. Maybe you'd be working.

I think Dad would be more open. He would probably also be less concerned about saving money for the future.

As a family, we would be more spontaneous with things like vacations. We aren't now and it's because of her and the planning that needs to be done for everything.

Do you think there is a reason/purpose Brielle is like she is?
I think that whatever the purpose of her disability is, it's a positive one. I don't see it as punishment on her or on us. She's affected too many lives in a positive way for her to be a punishment.

What do you wish strangers knew about Brielle or our family?
I know there are probably many strangers that see us out in public and think that Brielle is the center of our family and that we must have such a difficult life. Our life isn't easy because of her disability, but it doesn't create major issues either. She's not the only characteristic of our family.

I also wish people would see her as a person and not a disabled person. She has a personality and interests. In the grand scheme of things, she has the same qualities as any normal person. I think people tend to overlook that and just assume she spends her life being disabled.

Have you ever thought about what it would be like if you were like Brielle and she was like you? What scares you most about that?

I haven't. I don't know what I think about that. That's a really hard what-if scenario.

The only thing I wonder is if she would handle being the sister of a special needs person the same way I do or if there's something that I'm not doing that I should be doing. Something that she would do for me that I'm not doing for her.

What do you worry about most for Brielle and her future?

Hopefully, one day she will live somewhere other than with you and Dad. But, I hope that she gets the care she needs and deserves. I worry about her being neglected in a situation like that.

I worry about how she'll handle being on her own, emotionally speaking. I hope that she's never scared or feels like we've abandoned her because we want her to live independently and live as normal of a life as possible.

I worry that she won't have someone to care for her every day the way you care for her when you're gone.

What do you worry most about your responsibilities for Brielle and her future?

It's what I worry about most with Brielle. I worry about what's going to happen once you two are gone.

I worry about what role I will play in deciding what's best for her. I know that I will be the ultimate decision maker in her life. I also worry that I won't be able to be what she needs. I worry that she won't be properly cared for because of a poor decision that I make. I know that I will feel terrible that I won't be the one directly taking care of her, but I can't see myself being able to do that.

I didn't choose to be the one in charge of all this and she didn't choose me either. But, ultimately, I will be that for her one day. I worry that I'll fail her and something terrible will happen to her because of me or something that I failed to do.

What advice would you give parents of special needs kids about how to help their other children cope?

The biggest piece of advice I can give is to make sure your other children know and understand what the disability is. I hated not knowing exactly what to say when people asked questions. It made me feel like a bad sister.

Also, I think that siblings who clearly have such major differences should have something that they can come together for. If Brielle and I had had that one thing or interest in common, we may have had a better relationship then and now. It may be difficult to find something because there is such a huge gap in interests, but it's something I wish I had with her. It's important to have that sibling bond even in these unusual circumstances.

What advice would you give siblings of special needs kids about how to cope?

I think it's important to know your sibling as a person. Knowing their personality, what makes them laugh, and what is important to them. It helps to see past their disability and see them as the real person they are.

If you could go back to your younger self, what would you tell her about Brielle?

That Brielle is nothing to be embarrassed about, and that it is my responsibility to know that in order to help others see that.

What didn't I ask that you want to share?

I've always wondered if we would have looked more alike if she were normal. People say we look so much alike, but I have a hard time seeing it. I know you say it's all in the ears, but that's a little far-fetched. Maybe if her mouth worked right and she could talk and chew, her face and jaw might look different. If she could've eaten better when she was little, maybe she'd be as tall as me or even taller. I know that's a weird thing to think of, but I've thought about that over the years. I think it would have strengthened the bond I felt with her if I could physically see the family relation we have.

CHAPTER 29

The Road Not Traveled

"Tomorrow!" 15-year-old Brielle signs with great enthusiasm as she pulls off the last sticky note from the calendar. I take the yellow square from her that reads, "One more day."

"We'll be leaving early tomorrow, so get some rest," I say, folding back the sheets on her bed.

"I can't wait Grandma and Grandpa," she signs. "What time get there?" she asks, climbing into bed.

"Not until almost dinner time. It's a long drive to Illinois," I say, pulling the blankets over her.

Within a few hours, miles of road will lay out in front of us, our home in the rearview mirror. My parents have sold my childhood home. This will be our last trip to Illinois when we can stay in the same room I grew up in.

"What day come home?" she asks, pulling her doll close to her.

After looking forward to our trip for months, the day has almost arrived. And my daughter is already asking when we will be home, back to the familiar.

My Younger Self

In my early twenties, I had all the naïve hopes any young woman might have. Life was pregnant with possibilities.

I recognize that there were countless experiences designed to prepare me for the life I have now. Looking back at the person I once was, someone I used to be before Brielle was born, I wish I could prepare her even more, sit her down to tell her the truth.

Would I have the heart to tell her about the painful moments she would endure? Would it make a difference?

I would especially want to warn her that there was a virus lurking somewhere and tell her to be vigilant about washing her hands while pregnant. I wonder if that advice would make a difference. Would she listen and change her habits?

At the very least, I would want to tell her that there would be a detour in her life. She would never return to the original road. She would lead a life she has not planned for, a life almost entirely dedicated to one of her children. She would need to embrace the life she will be given and learn to let go of the one she dreamed of.

I would tell my younger self that despite what is to come, life would be OK. I would want her to know that she would survive and actually thrive. In fact, she will have many more successes and opportunities to help others than she ever imagined, and so would her daughter.

The woman I am now bears little resemblance to the young woman I see in old photo albums, different in almost every way – physically, emotionally, and experientially. As I stumble toward my fifties, I have different expectations than that naïve person I once was.

My hopes are more modest. I hope I can manage my responsibilities while still entertaining my passions. More than anything, I want my children to continue to be happy and live out many more days. I hope the same for myself, all with my husband by my side.

The Child Who Never Was

Sometimes I miss the baby I never met, the one who was never affected by a virus we knew nothing about. We will never know who Brielle might have been if CMV had not attacked her little body while she grew inside of me. However, I cannot help but wonder about that unlived life once in a while.

"What if...?" I catch myself thinking. Sometimes, I surprise myself that I even allow this thought to rattle around in my mind. When I do, I can only contemplate it for a few fleeting moments. I rarely allow those thoughts to tumble out of my head and on to my lips. I simply do not speak of it, at least not to most people. It is too terribly painful.

There are times when I cannot control my wandering mind. I have had a few dreams in my life about Brielle, not as she is, but as she could have been. I cannot control my dreams when I sleep. They intrude on my silent "What ifs?" with painful force.

When Brielle was a small child, I had a dream one night that she was in her crib. She was calling out to me, "Mommy, Mommy! Come here!" As I reached out to her beyond the edge of the crib rails, my small child pulled me into the crib with her.

Forget for the moment that there was no way I would fit in the crib let alone would have been able to climb over the tall rails with such ease. This was a dream. Weird things happen in dreams.

As my dream continued, I was laying on my side looking into her soft, brown eyes and stroking her silky hair. Brielle wrapped one of her arms around my neck and said, "I love you, Mommy."

My bubble burst when I woke up. I felt overwhelmed with joy hearing her voice and that particular phrase. However, my heart ached knowing that dream would never come to life. I would never hear Brielle's voice utter those words or any others.

The girl she could have been is like phantom pain from an amputation. That girl is not quite there, but sometimes feels as real as the memory of a dream that could have been.

Precious Experiences

Brielle has taught us so many precious lessons about life, unconditional love, and determination. It is difficult to know who we might be without her teachings.

Once in a great while, Brian and I talk about who Brielle could have been. We might have a full-blown pity party for about five minutes. Inevitably, it becomes too painful and the conversation naturally turns away from the laundry list of experiences we missed out on with her.

Instead, we might express our gratitude about things we will never have to worry about: drug use, teen pregnancy, binge drinking. However, this sort of discussion is just a diversion to hide our pain about the other topic.

Our conversation often drifts over to the many wonderful things about Brielle we might miss if she were not disabled. Brielle is pure joy, enjoying life without worries or fears. She sees only the good in people and often brings out the best in people as she teaches them in her own way about the truly important things in life.

There is beauty in focusing on the fragments of who she is rather than languishing on the whole of whom she will never be.

The Woman Within

I often see disabled adults within my community bagging my groceries, taking my ticket stub at the movie theater, or hanging clothes at my local thrift store. Perhaps, as a mother of a special needs child, I am more aware and observant. From what I see in that fleeting snapshot, I sometimes try to discern what the rest of their lives might be like.

I cannot help but to think about the disabled person's quality of life. What does he do each day? Does she have friends? Does he live in a group home?

My mind considers that this disabled person was once a child. This disabled person has a mother. What is life like for that mother now?

Then I stumble upon a difficult thought. One day, Brielle will be an adult. I will be the parent of a disabled adult. What will our lives be like? I cannot know, but I have hopes.

First and foremost, I hope Brielle will be healthy. She will always be disabled, but I pray that her body will continue to be healthy, free of seizures and other potential complications.

MORE ABOUT....
Concerns for Brielle's Health in the Future

We do not anticipate any unusual health crisis for Brielle, nor does she have a shorter life expectancy. However, she does have a few additional risks due to CMV and CP.

Due to CMV, Brielle could lose her hearing at any time in her life, particularly when her hormones change, for example, during menopause.

Because the CP affected her right leg causing her to have an unnatural gate, it puts additional pressure on her knee and hip that could eventually create more complications (such as arthritis or the need for joint replacement).

A close second hope is that she will be happy. Seeing her joyful heart now, when she is a teenager, it is difficult to imagine her not still smiling when she is 30 or 40 years old. Such small things make her happy – a quart of chocolate milk from the grocery store, video chatting with a friend, her favorite song coming on the radio, or her father doing his best Scooby-Doo impression. I anticipate similar things will continue to make her happy when she is an adult – family, friends, and her favorite things.

Maybe a man, maybe a man who is disabled, will love and accept her. Maybe he will want to marry her. Maybe I will get to help her get into her wedding dress one day. Maybe Brian will get to walk her down the aisle.

Other hopes feel so grandiose and unattainable that it is emotionally difficult to even see them here on paper.

The Road Yet to Be Traveled

Brian and I are realistic about Brielle's future as well as our own. Although we have expectations and plans, they are flexible and morph over time due to our circumstances and Brielle's abilities. Life throws everyone curveballs from time to time and we are not immune just because we have already been thrown a big one.

When a child turns 18 years old, he or she is a legal adult, independent of his or her parents. They can legally make all health, financial, and legal decisions on their own.

Brielle will not be capable of making most of those decisions. Therefore, about six months before her eighteenth birthday, we began the process of gaining legal custody of her. We will later go before a judge and prove that she is disabled and unable to be her own guardian. Then, we must petition for the courts to appoint Brian and me as her guardians.

Will Brielle have a job? What job can someone have if they cannot speak, have very limited fine motor skills, and have cognitive limitations as well? Even when I see other disabled adults working in the community, it is difficult to imagine Brielle able to work in any job.

We are realistic about Brielle's future, especially when it comes to her earning potential. When Brielle turns 18, she will become eligible for Social Security Disability Income (SSDI). We began the application process and started jumping through the government's hoops when she was within six months of her eighteenth birthday. Careful management of her assets throughout her life will be essential.

Will Brielle continue to live with us? Will she share an apartment with someone with the help of a nanny-style assistant? Or will we open a group home for her since the waiting lists for group homes are literally decades long?

Although we have several general ideas in mind, we do not have a specific plan yet for her future living arrangements. It will be based on where we will be living, what her abilities will allow her to do, and if she will be able to work.

Brielle will have her place in the world, and so will we. Brian and I once talked about becoming empty nesters. Now, I am not so sure we will ever truly have an empty nest, but that is not a bad thing.

No matter what happened or what the future brings, we know that we will continue to have parenting responsibilities for her entire life. However, we also hope to continue to be blessed with Brielle's precious spirit.

The past is sometimes painful to remember. There will always be worries about Brielle's future. We cannot know what will happen by the end of the year, month, or day. The only guarantee is this moment, right now.

The Obsolete Model

One day, I will be obsolete, elderly and not able to do things for Brielle. A newer model, perhaps a nanny or other professional caregiver, will replace me.

We are not immortal. Brian and I will die. We set up our wills and a special needs trust to provide for her financial future. We are exceptionally careful with the money we have. We do not want a situation for Brielle where she outlives our money. We have written instructions for her care and a letter generally outlining our wishes. Yet, we still worry, sometimes even about the small things.

Who will cut up Brielle's donuts in the morning? Who will take her to buy a new DVD once in a while? Who will be her safety net when we are gone?

Could someone who is not a family member make good decisions for Brielle? It is unlikely that our parents will outlive us and still be capable of caring for her needs. Ashley inherited Brian's eyes and my full eyebrows at birth. Through shared experience, she inherited Brian's silliness and my love for reading. One day, she will inherit Brian's great grandfather's diamond ring and my grandmother's silver. Will she inherit Brielle as well? We cannot expect Ashley to drop her life, whatever it might be, and take over our responsibilities. These tough issues about guardianship are important to consider and there must be a plan in place.

The future is like the horizon, a far off line that continues to recede as we approach it. We have plans for Brielle's future, even one without us. Despite all of the planning in the world, we can really only hope for the best. Like a gardener who plants tulip bulbs in the fall, we might not be around in the spring to see Brielle bloom.

Unattainable Perfection

As we move into the unknown future, I continue to strive for perfection in parenting my special needs child. Perfection can never be obtained. I am quite imperfect and always will be. However, I get frustrated and often beat myself up when I fail to live up to my own expectations.

At best, I can achieve a fragmented form of perfection, like the reflection of the shore on the bouncing waters of a lake. I cannot help but to see the imperfect distorted reflection of myself and our family – not what is, what will be, or what I might hope. Instead, it is a distortion of all of those together, as if reflected in a shattered mirror.

Looking in the mirror, I see the face of someone who has lived through a lot of life, good times and difficult times. I tell my reflection that she is all Brielle needs in life, imperfections and all. I am Brielle's world. I am her conduit for communication. I care for nearly her every need. I teach her academics and so much more about the world and life in general.

However, I cannot do it all forever. Frankly, I cannot and do not do it all now. Brian knows best how to make her laugh. Ashley shows her fun teenage things like taking silly selfies with her cell phone. Her Sunday school teacher does crafts with her I would find too messy and never attempt. Even our dog, Cooper, shows her how to continue to love unconditionally. Everyone in her life plays a role. Mine may have top billing, but this is an ensemble cast working together.

Each person or experience in her life is a small thread in a large tapestry. Each thread adds to the person Brielle is by weaving their influence into her life's experience. The pattern in her tapestry will be slowly revealed. No one will see the final masterpiece the tapestry will become until the end. However, from my angle, the tapestry is already precious and beautiful.

Finally, brothers and sisters, whatever is true, whatever is noble, whatever is right, whatever is pure, whatever is lovely, whatever is admirable— if anything is excellent or praiseworthy, think about such things.

— PHILIPPIANS 4: 8 (NIV)

CHAPTER 30

Reflections on Lessons Learned

I am an apprentice in life, still learning and growing as a parent. However, after 17 years of raising a disabled child, I have learned a few things. Some lessons were easier to learn and integrate into my daily life than others.

Recognizing that every family is different, I do not suggest that these lessons apply to all families who have children with disabilities. However, this is what works for us, what I wish someone had shared with me, and, in most cases, what I wish I learned sooner.

Mourn and then move on

One might hover around the same issues of loss for a long time. Just when there is a feeling of hope, one might come back to sadness again. I am still mourning the loss of the child I expected to have. However, I keep my sorrow at bay most of the time. A sappy chick flick can send me into newfound tears. I let the tears flow freely, but then that's that. No good can come from perpetually wallowing in self-pity. For the sake of everyone, including myself, every day I must make a choice to be positive.

Gather information

As we face new challenges, I seek out information from any source I can: books, the internet, social media, family, friends, physicians, therapists, teachers, and even my own child. It is a thorough search, which often results in differing opinions and conflicting data. I take it all in, filter through it, and, in the end, make my own conclusions.

Be organized and well prepared

My grandmother often said, "Life is full of surprises." The surprises tend to be bigger with a disabled child. Being organized is a trait that has served me well. Routine helps me make sense of our chaotic world by making it a bit more predictable. Preparation makes doctor visits, school meetings, and household duties much easier. Being organized and prepared for life's surprises takes time and effort. In my experience, the payoff is worth it.

Empower the child

My primary parenting philosophy has always been "Empower the child." By teaching Brielle life skills (all on her level), I am empowering her to become as independent as possible. I let her do as much as she can for herself and have her try to do what she cannot. It gives her as much freedom as possible as well as confidence and dignity.

Have expectations

Parents typically expect their children to do chores, behave a certain way, demonstrate good manners, and have a sense of right and wrong. Because Brielle is disabled and emotionally much younger than her biological years, it might be easy to lower my expectations and treat as her a perpetual preschooler. Instead, I try to treat her in age appropriate ways and never underestimate her abilities.

Appreciate small victories

There are many things Brielle cannot do and may never do. However, I notice the small accomplishments she makes that other parents might overlook. Without celebrating small steps of progress, I could fall into a pity party over the endless disappointments. I am realistic, but find joy in her abilities and avoid focusing on the negative aspects about her disabilities.

Allow failures

My instinct as a mother is to save my children from any physical or emotional pain. However, children learn and become stronger from their experiences failing. Brielle is no different. If I take failure away by either saving her or keeping her from attempting new things at all, I am taking away her ability to learn from the greatest teacher – experience.

Find the person within

Brielle is not her disability. She is a child who happens to have disabilities that trap her potential. The person she could become calls to me, "I am in here!" It is my responsibility to discover her potential and nurture it.

Be patient

Frustration with a child is natural and can compound when the child does not learn and progress at the expected rate. Patience was never something that came naturally to me. Although I am still not patient all of the time, I have learned to control my frustrations, not let them get to me, and not take them out on those around me. Being graceful under stress is my goal.

Recognize joyful moments

Brielle is happy and excited over the smallest things. A box of donuts or a letter from Grandma can send her into pure glee. She has taught me to find pieces of joy from simple things as well. They are worth stopping for and embracing.

Accept curiosity

People are often curious about things that are out of the norm. Many things about Brielle are not normal. I have learned that others' interest can be an opportunity for them to learn about Brielle and people with disabilities in general. Although I am still not always successful in putting this into daily practice, I keep working at a more positive attitude when our family is the target of someone's inquisitive nature.

Encourage others to interact on their terms

I cannot be everything to my child. There are times when I have been bewildered watching someone interact with Brielle in ways I never would. Instead of coming between her and others, or judging how others are with her, I slowly learned to accept and encourage others to interact with my child in any way they can. I know that the unique interaction they provide can enrich her life.

Nurture friendships

Friendship is precious and for disabled children, it seems to be quite rare. When it has been difficult, even one-sided at times, I try to keep the friends connected. Everyone deserves a good friend. Even me.

Let others help

People not only want to help, they *need* to help. By asking others for help, I show them respect and let them into our world. I was quite stubborn about this lesson, trying to be supermom at all times, never showing weakness. I must still remind myself to accept and ask for help, even from my own family. In the same way others want to help, Brielle wants to help. Even when it makes my job more difficult or slow, giving her even the smallest task gives her a great sense of pride and self-worth. That is priceless.

Take time for self

The flight attendant's instructions for passengers to put on their own air masks first before helping others is contrary to my natural tendencies as a mother. I have a strong pull to give everything of myself to others, especially to my disabled child. For a long time, Brielle's needs were my primary concern, making everything else in life seem peripheral. However, I slowly realized that if I am not at my best, I cannot be my best for Brielle or anyone else. Without guilt or remorse, I now invest in myself, because I am worthy of that care.

Nurture the marriage

Having a disabled child is definitely an added stress on a couple's relationship. Although it is sometimes very difficult, Brian and I put great effort and attention on protecting our marriage by nurturing the very root of our relationship, separate from our children. A healthy marriage is worth fighting for, not just for the children's sake, but for both members of the marriage as well.

Recognize the sibling's value and separate identity

Siblings of a disabled child might feel overlooked and underappreciated. I constantly remind myself to give both my daughters the respect of acknowledging their uniqueness. They each deserve my time and attention. It may not always be equal, but I want them both to know that they are special and loved.

Give back to others

I feel a deep sense of gratitude to the many generations of parents of disabled children who blazed the trails before me. They left a legacy by helping to establish the laws and social culture in which I now live and raise Brielle. My goal is to pay it forward to my peers and others who follow behind me. I am inspired to volunteer my time and talents to causes I believe in. As much as I want to give, I have also painfully learned the value in the word, "No."

Plan for the future

They often need to be somewhat flexible, but once they are in place, having plans can be very reassuring. To the best of our ability and means, we must plan for Brielle's future, including one without us. Financial planning, life insurance, and wills become particularly important to families with special needs children who cannot provide for themselves.

Have faith in something bigger

With all that can go wrong when life is created, I find myself asking, "Why not?" rather than "Why?" With those basic questions behind me, I often now ask myself, "So, what do I do with this?" I believe there is a master plan carefully designed by our Creator. There is a reason for Brielle's disabilities and I know her life has purpose. When she was born, I landed on my purpose. I was something different before. Me in the "after" is better.

*Take my yoke upon you and learn from me, for
I am gentle and humble in heart, and you will
find rest for your souls.*

— MATTHEW 11:29 (NIV)

Epilogue

As 2013 comes to close, our family is thriving. Brielle is a junior in a local public high school. She participates in a work study program. She works two hours two days a week at two local drug stores. She dusts shelves, cleans the glass of the front doors and refrigerator storage units, and vacuums the front rugs. She absolutely loves it and the experience is what we hoped going back to public school would offer her. Ashley decided to change majors and is now attending a college only 90 minutes from our family. Brian is still working at the company he has been with for the last 17 years and golfs most weekends. I am excited to take a short break from writing and focus on my blog (http://brielleandme.net/). However, I have a novel rattling around in my brain and hope to start writing again in a few months.

Appendix A: Timeline

1985

June   Kerith and Brian meet

1986

May   Kerith graduates from high school

1989

May   Brian graduates from college and moves to Bloomington, Illinois for first job

December   Kerith graduates from college

1990

March   Kerith and Brian marry

1993

May   Kerith graduates from graduate school
Kerith and Brian move to Eau Claire, Wisconsin

June   Kerith is pregnant

October   Kerith begins job helping disabled high school students find jobs

1994

March — Ashley is born

1995

January — Kerith begins job in personnel at health care organization

June — Ashley and Kerith get chicken pox
Kerith is pregnant

September — Kerith begins job in marketing at health care organization

October — Kerith has detailed ultrasound and learns baby is a girl

1996

January — Kerith has second detailed ultrasound and amnio; CMV diagnosed

February 13 — Brielle is born

March — Brielle's colic begins
Brielle's cough and congestion begin

April 5 — Kerith takes Good Friday picture

May — Kerith returns to work

June — Brielle's colic subsides
Brielle gets first developmental test
Brielle begins Early Intervention

September — Brielle's cough and congestion subside (after death of family cat)

October — Family moves to Freeport, Illinois
Brielle hospitalized for four days with pneumonia

1997

January — Brielle begins private physical therapy in Rockford

1998

January — Brielle begins crawling

April — Brielle rejected from Christian daycares/preschools

November — Brielle begins using walker

1999

January — Brielle begins water therapy in Rockford

April — Brielle begins walking independently

May — Brielle accepted at preschool in Wisconsin

2000

June — Brielle accepted at school for the deaf

2001

June — Family moves to the Austin, Texas area

October — Brielle begins to read

2002

August — Brielle starts kindergarten at neighborhood school

2003

November — Brielle has salivary gland surgery

2004

April — Brielle is potty trained

August — Brielle begins Resource Room instruction (2nd grade)

Brielle has first round of Botox injections

2005

| January | Brielle begins wearing glasses |
| March | Brielle has second round of Botox injections |

2006

| May | Brielle has third round of Botox injections |

2007

January	Family moves to the Toledo, Ohio area
July	Brielle has first (and only) seizure
October	Brielle has endoscope and swallow study
December	Brielle has heel cord and hamstring release surgery

2008

| June | Family moves to the Atlanta, Georgia area |

2010

| August | Brielle begins homeschooling |

2011

| January | Brielle has eye surgery for cysts |
| April | Brielle has wisdom teeth removed |

2012

| August | Ashley leaves for college |

2013

| August | Brielle returns to public school |

References

[1] http://www.CDC.gov

[2] http://www.vaccineinformation.org

[3] http://www.americanpregnancy.org

[4] King, Peter. "Countdown." Sports Illustrated Oct. 30, 1995: 22-26

[5] http://www.mayoclinic.com

[6] http://www.divorcestatistics.info

[7] http://www.educationnews.org

About the Author

Kerith Stull has been a memoir writer of sorts from her early days of writing in her diary and continuing with regular journaling throughout adulthood. She blogs about life with Brielle and special needs parenting issues. Kerith, her husband, Brian, and daughter, Brielle, live in the Atlanta, Georgia area with their white Miniature Schnauzer, Cooper.

You can follow their on-going journey at: http://brielleandme.net/

CPSIA information can be obtained at www.ICGtesting.com
Printed in the USA
BVOW09s2039270214

346241BV00002B/157/P